STORM
IN A C CUP

STORM
IN A C CUP

Caroline Flack

**SIMON &
SCHUSTER**

London · New York · Sydney · Toronto · New Delhi

A CBS COMPANY

First published in Great Britain by Simon & Schuster UK Ltd, 2015
A CBS COMPANY

1 3 5 7 9 10 8 6 4 2

Simon & Schuster UK Ltd
1st Floor
222 Gray's Inn Road
London WC1X 8HB

www.simonandschuster.co.uk

Simon & Schuster Australia, Sydney
Simon & Schuster India, New Delhi

A CIP catalogue record for this book
is available from the British Library

Hardback ISBN: 978-1-4711-5438-6
Trade paperback ISBN: 978-1-4711-5439-3
eBook ISBN: 978-1-4711-5441-6

Typeset in Dante by M Rules
Printed and bound by CPI Group (UK) Ltd, Croydon, CR0 4YY

For Jo

Contents

1 The Bubble   1

2 Great Hockham   13

3 'The Time Warp'   41

4 *It's a Wonderful Life* in Colour   63

5 Cambridge   85

6 The Highgate end of Archway   103

7 'See you after the break!'   123

8 Camden   145

9 *Gladiators*   169

10 'You mustn't take it personally'   189

11 The Jungle   207

12 Bub-feelings   227

13 Fanta and *Limón*   249

14 *Strictly*   271

15 'Roxie (the Name on Everyone's Lips)'   301

16 Boot camp   315

Acknowledgements   323

1

The Bubble

June 2015

'Three, two, ONE ... Eyes to the camera, Caroline! Beautiful!'

I tilt my head, shake my hair and smile down a lens the size of a church candle. And I laugh.

Click, click, click ... the photographer's knees are bent now, he crouches, sideways on, forearms all muscle, black jeans, grey T-shirt. Everyone else is wearing black, the standard uniform on a shoot, including his assistants who hover like altar boys, holding other cameras, other lenses.

'Perhaps lean forward? Nice. Flick the hair. Love that ...'

Around the monitor are a cluster of *Cosmo* people – the creative director, a couple of others. At each click, versions of me flash up on the screen in rapid succession and it's hard not to turn my head. But I catch glimpses of the scarecrow-haired figure perched on an old wooden stool: boyfriend jeans, white silk shirt, grey jacket – very Left Bank.

The stool is like the one my nan had in her kitchen in Clacton, except this one is 'distressed', shabby chic and spattered with paint, something she would never have understood. Nanny Flo had a very hard life, born in the East End, eight children, widowed at forty-seven, worked till she was seventy-three. But with her everything had to be spick and span and I loved her. 'Carolina Moon, keep shining . . .' That's what she used to sing to me, and it's written under the butterfly tattoo on my back.

'Can you try a bit of a fake laugh?' says the photographer.

'Can't do a fake laugh!' I say, and everyone roars, as the laugh that has got me into so much trouble gurgles up at its most naughty.

'Lovely! Amazing!' *Click, click.* 'Beautiful! Incredible.'

'He's run out of words,' I say, as Gemma dabs at my forehead before the heat undoes all her good work. We are four floors up in an old warehouse in Shoreditch; the sun blasting down on the roof plus the arc lights have turned the place into a loft-style sauna.

All that 'wonderful, lovely' is just to keep you in the bubble, like the music that is blasting out – Kylie telling us she should be so lucky, which still gets me going twenty-five years after my sister Jo and I first pranced around our lounge singing, 'Lucky, Lucky, Lucky!' We should be so lucky.

'Don't mock it. I'd love to have people say, "Gemma,

you're wonderful, you're amazing,'" Gemma says with a practised pout as we head back to the dressing room for the next look and a caffeine hit.

'Gemma, you're wonderful, you're amazing,' I say.

And she is. Gemma Wheatcroft does my hair and make-up but she's also my friend, in fact more than a friend. She's my confidante and fellow conspirator in naughtiness. We met in 2011 when she was doing Dermot O'Leary's make-up on *X Factor* and I was co-hosting *The Xtra Factor* – the backstage spin-off – with Olly Murs. It was September and we were in Mykonos for Judges' Houses, the part in the show where the singers get to work with their mentor, and this was Tulisa's house.

The eighth series (2011), and my first, was the year Little Mix won, Tulisa being their mentor. Gemma and I were both single and both doing a bit of online dating and we had a crazy time. Instead of putting us in a hotel, Gemma and Olly and me and Christian, the guy who was doing my make-up, were given our own villa looking over the Aegean and basically we bonded over wine and olives and didn't go to bed for three days.

'So it's official then . . .'

Enter Rachel, the other member of the gang – my stylist – carrying an armful of denim skirts with a pair of brown suede clogs neatly balanced on top. Even though she's a mum, she looks about twelve, and is never seen without a hat. Today she's wearing a little black butcher's boy number.

'What's that, Rach?' I say, looking up from my phone.

'I heard you on the *Breakfast Show* talking to Grimmy. So what do you think?'

Late-night LA time, Simon Cowell had tweeted that he'd signed Nick Grimshaw and Rita Ora to be the new judges on *X Factor*, replacing Louis Walsh and Mel B. (Me, in the small hours, in confidence to Waffle my cat: 'NO WAY!') The other two were known – Cheryl Cole/Tweedy as was – now Cheryl Fernandez-Versini – would be staying, with Simon himself as the fourth.

So, A/judges, B/format, and C/me-and-Olly rather than Dermot – it's all change on the *X Factor* juggernaut. Hard to imagine it started rolling way back in 2004, the year Nanny Flo died aged ninety-six.

'So did you know?' Rachel continues, switching on a wind machine that someone has kindly brought in to keep us cool.

'No,' I say. Although perhaps I should have done. After all, they're about to be my new family until at least Christmas, maybe beyond.

It's nearly three months since it was announced that Dermot was 'stepping down'. There had been rumours for days, if not weeks, and then came the confirmation, followed by the call from John Noel my agent (Dermot's as well), saying Simon wanted me and Olly to take Dermot's place. It was my dream job, the job I've been working up to all these years, but Dermot is the best, and his wife, Dee, who's Norwegian, helped break my career and I owe her a lot. I know how it felt to be shunted off by Simon, so before I said yes, I needed to find out exactly what

4

happened, but Dermot knew what I'd be thinking and he called me.

'You've got to do it, Flacky,' he said. 'Don't think twice.' But I did.

When it came to the judges, I pretty much knew about Nick although he never breathed a word, even though I'd pushed and pushed, but with Simon you're never safe even if you've got a contract.

'But Rita, no, not a whisper,' I say as I struggle into a faded blue miniskirt and ease up the zip for the next 'look' and Gemma dabs at the mosquito bites on my legs with a concealer, choosing the colour from about a dozen she has to camouflage anything from hangover eyes to a five o'clock shadow. The bites are a souvenir from Mallorca where I've just spent two weeks building up a tan and hosting *Love Island* for ITV2, a revamp of a 2005/6 reality show, where good-looking singles are put together in a villa to fight over each other, and find – if not true love, enough hanky-panky to get their nan hiding behind the sofa on a nightly basis. (It's so full on even the producers are telling their mums not to watch.) The reviews haven't been great but it's early days and reality shows take time to build.

'Look,' I say, holding my bare arm against Gemma's as she sponges gloop onto my legs, 'I'm browner than you are!' It's our standing joke. Her father's from Nigeria and her mother's from Brighton but the only thing she's inherited from her dad is her curly (blonde) hair. Even in the sun her skin stays as pale as my twin sister's, a delicate

English-rose. Our mum has this idea that her dad had French/Algerian ancestry – the only explanation we can find of why I'm so much darker than Jody.

I still can't believe Rita Ora has left *The Voice*. Simon must have walked on water to lure her from the BBC. Or perhaps just offered her loadsa money . . . But then he's a real Svengali – always makes you feel as if you're the only person in the room, and that he can change your life (which of course he can) but for the future of *X Factor* it's a great call. I think it's a really exciting line-up. It makes it really relevant, really young, really fresh, really new, and that's what the show needs to be about. And while Louis was always my favourite (he was the one to have a drink in the bar with afterwards) I think he was ready to go. But I do think having professionals who are involved in the industry at the minute is exactly what it needs.

Rita did a stint as a guest judge on *X Factor* when I was *Xtra-Factor*-ing in 2013 and she came across really well, an edgy mix of sassiness and naivety. As for Nick, it's what Louis would call a no-brainer. Not only is he one of the biggest DJs in the country, he's sharp and funny – a one-man high-wire act with no safety net. I've known him since he was an intern – a runner at the MTV studios in Leicester Square when I was working on kids TV and we were both hanging out with the Camden crowd at the Hawley Arms – and we've been good pals ever since. And if anyone can out-Simon Simon, it's Grimmy.

Rachel steams the creases out of a jumper they want me

to wear for the next look. It was Rachel who first got me into shorts, long before they became 'the next big thing'. They were high-waisted and tailored, and I loved them. At school my spindly legs were just for jokes – at one point I was wearing seven pairs of tights to give them a bit of shape. How times change. Now they're considered my best feature . . . and shorts avoid the risk posed by short skirts in the days of the prying camera.

I met Rachel on the spin-off of *I'm a Celebrity* . . . or the 'Jungle' as it's called in the industry, when we spent an afternoon zipping round Oxford Street – Top Shop, Zara, Miss Selfridge – looking for things that would work in Australia – not easy in November when it's freezing outside and you're not thinking cruise wear. Stylists usually call up what they want from fashion PRs, and you choose from whatever they decide to send. But pre-Christmas that wasn't going to happen, so we did it on the hoof, trying things on, buying what we liked, and generally having a laugh. We've worked together ever since.

But as I watch her now, busying around, reaching up, arms stretching out as delicately as a dancer, I feel sad, in fact more than sad, as I've just heard that she won't be styling me on *X Factor*. Firstly there are two of us – me and Olly – and the schedule is so full on. To have to block out every weekend from September till Christmas is asking a lot for the mother of a little girl, and there's no getting around Saturday nights.

Saturday night has been the great battleground since 1955 when ITV sprang up in competition with the BBC.

The Generation Game, Blind Date, Noel's House Party, Wogan, Parkinson, Game for a Laugh, Kojak, The Dukes of Hazzard, Match of the Day – audiences fought over, lost and won, won and lost, year after year after year after year. And sixty years on, nothing has changed, except it's now boiled down to just two: *The X Factor* (ITV) v. *Strictly Come Dancing* (BBC).

Rachel not coming with me to *X Factor* is the second bit of bad news I've had today. Traditionally the winners of *Strictly* return for a valedictory dance at the start of the new series and I've been so looking forward to it, the whole razzmatazz, Pasha's arm firmly round my waist as we wait for our cue, his certainty, his calm. But the schedules have just been announced, and *X Factor* won't release me and I can hardly bear it.

'Full eyes on the camera, Caroline. Good! Love that! And that. So beautiful! Amazing!'

I'm back on my nan's stool. This time wearing a short denim skirt and a white cashmere jumper – just what I need when it's like the Amazon basin in here. Meanwhile the Jacksons are asking 'Can you feel it?' and even the creative director's feet are tapping.

'Caroline, I need you to laugh,' says the photographer.

'So can somebody please do a funny dance?'

'Can You Feel It' was our first-ever dance, the cha cha cha – Pasha's all-time speciality and we'd spent three weeks practising it. My hair had just been cut off – long locks gone just like that – this would be the new me, no longer a presenter but a performer, complete with

8

swinging gold tassels and attitude. But in rehearsal I could barely hold it together, I was terrified I'd let him down but then, out on the dance floor, something clicked . . .

'OK, break, everyone,' a voice says, and it's back to the dressing room, Gemma and me grabbing a plate of cauliflower cheese on the run, like a couple of thieving foxes; it's like a roast without the gravy. How can we resist?

Then I see a message on my phone to call John Noel – urgent – and my heart skips a beat. John only calls if it's a job or trouble. It can't be a job, so it must be trouble. I'll wait till the shoot is over. I've had enough gloom for today. I just want to be with my gang. That's why I love doing these shoots – it's not being photographed – too many years of thinking that my gums were too big and my teeth too small. (Dad: 'Come on, Carrie, *smile* . . . Just one. It won't hurt!') At the beginning I couldn't bear being looked at and would only allow Gemma and the photographer on set, but now it's just part of the job, and you learn as you go along: what positions to stand in, what faces to do, what angle to tilt the chin, the head.

What I love is being with my friends, with Gemma and Rachel in our little bubble, talking nonsense, laughing, a bit of a gossip. Being proper girls. At 4.30 I'll call Jody, because the kids will be back from school and I'll talk to Willow about her homework, and to Delilah about sports day, and Zuzu will outshout everybody.

Most people don't know what their life would have been like if they'd chosen another path. But I do. A levels, not stage school. Learning to drive at seventeen rather than

twenty-seven. Having three gorgeous children. Being settled rather than putting my life into bin bags every few
months, spending half the time weeping, half the time
head over heels in love.

But first John Noel.

'I've had an email from the wife of someone called
Lestor Simkins,' he says. 'Mean anything?'

'Should it?'

'Think again, Caroline. Lestor Simkins. Wife.'

'Never heard of him. Or her.'

'Well, she seems to think differently. Says that you
arranged to have casual sex with her husband. Says she has
evidence.'

'Is this some kind of wind-up?'

'It seems genuine to me.'

'It's a wind-up, John. It must be. I have never heard of
this Lestor Simpson.'

'Simkins.'

'All right Simkins. I promise you I have never heard of
him. And I have never had anything to do with a married
man. I can't believe you're saying this.'

'Caroline, I have to know the truth.'

'I'm telling you the truth.'

'Perhaps you'd like to think about it. I'm not prepared
to watch you self-destruct. I've seen it happen too many
times before in this business.' And the line goes dead.

I can feel my heart pounding, and tears are brimming
over, my mascara stinging. How can he think that? What's
going on? How can this be happening?

Simkins ... Simkins ... The name does ring a vague bell. Twitter ... so much stuff comes in and I barely skim it. I scroll back, and back, through my Twitter feed ... and there she is – @ClaireAnneSimkins. *You know my husband ... Stay away from my husband.* Dozens of them.

I text Jo.

Can I come over?

Are you OK?

No

Xxxx J

Driver: Stepney is it, Miss?
Me: No. Queens Park.

2

Great Hockham

In most autobiographies there's a point near the beginning where you write, 'I was born on this or that date, in this or that place.' But as I had no sense of being separate from Jo until I was much, much older, I can't do that.

There were always two of us. It's almost as if we were one person who was split down the middle and we each took opposite sides: Jo very placid, very together. Me all the emotions, all the worries. Jo the sensible one, me the wild child.

We were born on 9 November 1979 in Chase Farm Hospital, Enfield. It was a Friday, at half past one in the morning, and out we popped, two peas from the same pod, similar to look at, but not identical. In photos you can tell us apart because I have the square head, Jody the pointy one.

Although Mum knew she was having twins, she had no

idea whether we would be girls or boys or one of each, and she only had one name ready. Caroline. She'd had an Aunt Carrie and had always liked the name. But when the first baby came out she looked like a squashed bird and Mum decided a squashed bird couldn't be called Caroline, which is why Jody is called Jody. Then, six minutes later, I turned up, less squashed because I was on the top, and this time Mum thought that Caroline would do. My second name – Louise – was picked by Paul, our brother, and Jody's – Suzanne – by our big sister Liz. How clever was that? How could they resent these two little cuckoos once they'd given them a name?

Mum falling pregnant long after she imagined her nappy days were over was definitely 'a surprise', though a pleasant one, she maintains. Less so for Liz, who was ten, or Paul who was eight. Mum always says that having Liz to help was 'a godsend' and that she was 'a little angel'. Frankly looking after two screaming babies isn't something I'd put top of my Christmas list, but far worse must have been saying goodbye to Enfield and moving nearly a hundred miles away to nowhere land, where they had no cousins, no aunts, no uncles, no friends and had to change schools and start all over again. But it was hard for Mum too. There she was, eight miles from a doctor, in the middle of winter with newborn twins and no car.

In fact the move to Norfolk had nothing to do with Jody and me. Dad worked for Coca-Cola as a sales rep based in Harlow in Essex. But then came promotion – a job in management – responsible for Norfolk. It was too far to commute, so for a whole year he left the house on a Monday and came back on the Friday. But that was hard on Mum – by then pregnant with us – so moving was the only practical solution.

Mum says now she would have loved to have gone to Norwich, but Dad's an old-style romantic and he liked the idea of living in the country and one day he said, 'Let's try village life!' So they bought a house in Great Hockham just east of Thetford Forest surrounded by fields and woodland.

We lived in a seventies cul-de-sac of about twenty houses – the newest buildings in the village – most of them owned by families with kids like us, except for a few bungalows at the end. Until recently I imagined that my dad's parents – Nanny Ivy and Grandad – had always lived there and that we'd gone to Great Hockham to be near them, but in fact it was the other way round. They didn't arrive till Jo and I were about four. Then when one of the bungalows came up for sale they decided to enjoy their grandchildren on a daily basis.

Perhaps it was because Mum and Dad were Londoners and not used to the country that they never let us out of their sight. Dad now claims that many more children went missing in those days and that's what made him fearful. But, whatever the reason, as far as they were concerned, danger lurked round every corner, and it was the bane of our lives from the moment we could walk until the day we left home.

I have to admit that there was something a bit strange

about that part of Norfolk. There was talk among us kids of witches (probably untrue) and abandoned villages (true) filled with ghosts (not sure . . .). Opposite the old Victorian school on the village green where Jody and I went to playschool, and where Mum worked for years, there was a house that was said to be haunted. My friend Victoria lived next door, and everyone said her mum and nan did black magic. In the middle of the village green was a huge stone, probably weighing half a ton, and every year there was a ceremony called the Turning of the Stone, where six men of the village would come together and using sticks as levers heave it over. Why? Nobody knew . . .

At night there were no lights anywhere beyond the village, and no sound except owls and neighbours' televisions. Our house backed onto fields and, unless there was a moon, you could see nothing beyond the back fence. Great Hockham itself was like a lit-up island in the middle of a flat black sea and I am still scared of the dark and always sleep with the landing light on.

There was a film I wasn't supposed to watch but I crept down when Dad wasn't looking. It was about this froggy gremlin, and once I was in bed and the lights were out I thought he'd creep into the bedroom and put his fingers into my nose and a hand over my mouth.

Every night my dad used to say: 'Carrie, why tonight of all nights, would someone come in the room and get you?'

'I don't know.'

'Why tonight, why not last night?'

I was also scared of lions. There was a lion ornament in our lounge, and I dreamt that it came to life. In our next house I was convinced I saw a ghost on the landing. I thought it was my brother. He walked out of the bathroom and into my bedroom and I thought nothing of it. But then I went downstairs and my brother was in the kitchen . . .

The countryside wasn't always so empty. During the war in 1942 it became a D-Day training ground and six villages were evacuated. The people who lived there were never allowed back, although a few times a year you can visit the churches and put flowers on the graves. Then there were the airbases (the American air force is still there today). Some were swallowed up in the military training zone – all 30,000 acres of it – but, when Jo and I were six, one of these became HM Prison Wayland, and in fact the girl I sat next to in my first year at high school works there as a guard and actually banged up one of the boys who'd been there with us.

From any normal standpoint, Scotgate Close was about as safe as it gets. Although everyone had cars, the only time they left their garages was when the dads went to work, and even then they drove at five miles an hour. But for Mum and Dad, it could have been the M25. Instead of crossing the road to play with Carly and Emma – identical twins a year younger than me and Jody who lived directly opposite and who had wild corkscrew hair that I was so jealous of – we'd have to go all the way round the bottom and then up the other side. It was the same if we went to see Nanny and Grandad. We had to hold hands and WALK slowly along the pavement until we reached their bungalow. And while all our friends – Emma, Gemma, Carly, Megan and Robert – were allowed to go to school on their own, we were taken by our mum, even though there were no roads to cross and it took all of four minutes to get there. And then, after tea, there they'd be, playing just the other side of the close, or going off to feed carrots to Pepsi the donkey in the field, and we'd be shouting 'Wait for us!' and have to walk all the way round. This went on until we were seven and we moved house . . .

Apart from that it was a lovely place to grow up.

Nan and Grandad's garden backed onto the school field, and every playtime there they'd be, waving to us over their garden fence and we'd run across and tell them what we'd been doing. More often than not our friends would rush over too and we'd all cluster around, gabbling over each other, our voices getting higher and higher and Nan and Grandad loved it. They hadn't been around when Liz and Paul were growing up, but they could be for us.

Jody and I were the first children on both sides of the family not to be brought up in London. Mum was born Christine Callis, the youngest of eight. Her parents, Florence and Bill, met at the Old Bull and Bush, the legendary pub near Hampstead Heath. Bill was two years older than Flo and working as a pastry chef for the famous Jewish bakers in Stamford Hill called Grodzinski's – it's still there today. Florence was a 'nippy', a waitress at one of the big Lyons Corner Houses in the West End. They married in 1926 when she was eighteen and he was twenty. She wasn't going to make the mistake her own mother did: Florence was illegitimate, born out of wedlock, and spent the first two years of her life in a 'home' waiting to be adopted. But when she was two, her grandmother couldn't stand it any more, so she scooped her up and took her home and brought her up as her own. It was years before she discovered that her real mum was in fact her 'older sister' Alice who had gone on to have another baby, Jimmy, although that one she kept.

Contraception didn't exist in the twenties, and Florence and Bill's first five children came along as regular as clockwork, one every two years until war broke out when Bill joined the Royal Navy as a ship's cook. The next three arrived once he got back from sea, again one every two years, the last one being my mum. Sadly she hardly remembers her dad as he died of a pulmonary embolism when he was only forty-nine on 30 June 1955. The date is stamped on her memory because it was the day she turned five, and when her brothers and sisters and their children all started gathering at the house she thought they had come for her birthday.

Once the second batch of children had started coming after the war, Bill Callis bought a house in Enfield, in Carterhatch Road, and took a job at the local baker's called Humphreys. When he started getting dermatitis from the flour, he had to stop, but Nanny Flo still bought her bread there so she stayed in touch. A few years later, Mrs Humphreys died of cancer, and her husband took to the bottle. The business was saved by their delivery man, who over the next few years turned his hand to everything, from baking the bread, to working in the office, 'head cook and bottle washer', as he later described it. The Humphreys had no children of their own, so when Mr Humphreys eventually died of cirrhosis of the liver, he left everything to this Good Samaritan who had kept things going. His name was Arthur Flack. He and his wife were ordinary working-class people with no expectations and one of the first things he did when he took over the bakery was to drive over to Carterhatch Road and offer Nanny Flo a job.

Later, my mum, aged around fourteen, would go to the baker's to meet her mum after work and sometimes she would bump into the Flacks' son, who'd be there helping out. Ian was two years older than my mum, with twinkly eyes, springy hair and a wicked smile, while she was just 'a knock-out', a bit like Twiggy but not as tall and absolutely beautiful. In fact it was Ian's mum (Nanny Ivy) who asked Mum's mum (Nanny Flo) if she had any objections to Ian asking Christine out.

Dad says he thoroughly enjoyed his courtship with Mum. He suddenly found himself part of this huge boisterous family, all seven of Mum's older brothers and sisters, all their various husbands and wives, boyfriends and girlfriends, all of them great fun, and they would spend their evenings at Carterhatch Road, playing cards, with people popping in and out, always with stories to tell, always having a laugh. It was wonderful, he says. He and my mum married in February 1967.

The great thing about having a twin is that you always have someone to play with. During the whole of my child-hood, from the moment I woke up until the moment I went to sleep, I never knew what it was like to be alone. People sometimes ask if we ever got jealous. Would you be jealous of your left leg, or your right arm? You can't be jealous of something that's part of you. And that's how it was with us.

It helped that our parents were always 'fair'. We'd get identical presents at Christmas and on our birthday. For the first few years Mum even put us in matching outfits, but as soon as we learnt to get dressed by ourselves, we wore what we liked, even though Mum still bought us the same things so there'd be no bickering. But bicker we did. We bickered over everything all the time. We went out of our way to annoy each other, saying the worst things, but then ten minutes later it was over. We'd constantly tell on each other – Jo did this, Carrie did that. If ever a ball went into the road or over the fence we'd make sure the other one got the blame. And if anything happened when we were playing – a grazed knee, a cut hand, or your bike had a dent in it – it was never your own fault, it was always the other one. When a frisbee cut the heads off Dad's flowers, or hit next door's cat, we'd both be completely innocent, our voices shouting in unison, 'It was her!' We were like junior gladiators, fighting to the death not to be the one who got told off.

In the village post office there was a charity box for the blind and we were always asking Mum to give us her change, though she rarely did, so we decided we'd open a shop and make some money ourselves. We called it The Blind Club. We knew about running a stall from Brownies (we were both expelled for being 'a bad influence' – probably my fault), so we brought out the folding card table and set it up by the willow tree in the front garden. We sewed little bags which we stuffed with lavender from Nan and Grandad's garden and made perfume from rose petals and scoured the house for things to sell, mainly ornaments from the lounge, little things we didn't think they'd miss.

'Do your parents know that you're doing this?' a neighbour asked, as she handed over fifty pence for a pretty little china box. 'Oh yes,' we chorused happily. 'It's for blind babies!'

When everything had been sold, we got Paul to come with us to the post office, and asked Anne, the postmistress, to pass down the charity box.

'Goodness, you have been industrious,' she said as she watched us slip the coins into the slot one by one.

A few days later a neighbour dropped by to see our mum. She had something she wished to hand back, she said. Her son had given it to her as a birthday present but when she saw it was hallmarked she'd had her doubts ... Gradually word got out and things that the Flack twins had 'sold' began coming back. Whether these people asked for a refund, whether everything was eventually returned I have no idea. But, apart from a strict telling-off – a lecture from Dad about the morals of not taking things that don't belong to you – there was no real retribution. In fact just the opposite. A few weeks later, Anne, the postmistress, knocked on the door and asked if she could speak to the twins.

'I thought you'd like to know that I wrote to the National Blind Children's Society about how much money you raised,' she said, 'and they sent you this.' She handed over an official-looking certificate made out in both our names, thanking us for our most generous donation . . . And we were like 'Wow!' and up it went on our bedroom wall.

When we were about seven we moved. Although Dad had built an extension above the garage, he felt that we needed more space. He had this dream of breeding chickens so he'd need room for a proper hen house and a good-sized run where they could grub up the earth and not ruin the rest of the garden.

The new house was about two-and-a-half miles away, the other side of Thetford Forest. A builder had bought a plot of land by some old garages and built three houses, and ours was the first to be finished, the other two took years. The village was East Wretham and Dad called the house Lane End because it was at the end of a little drive and completely hidden by hedges. We had a pond and a climbing frame, as well as the chickens and a rabbit called Boris, because our big sister was in love with Boris Becker.

We continued to go to school in Great Hockham but at least now we went by bus and we still saw Nanny and Grandad every day at playtime when they stood by their garden fence.

Until we got rooms of our own – which wasn't until Liz left home – my messiness was a point of constant friction between Jody and me. Jo was naturally neat and tidy. Every morning she'd fold up her pyjamas and put them under her pillow, and at night she'd lay the next day's clothes on her bedside chair ready for the morning. I was the opposite. I would spend ten minutes before bedtime just looking for my pyjamas which were hidden some-where under the jumble of clothes I'd thrown off earlier in the week ... And in the morning I'd be scrabbling around just trying to find something clean. At bedtime, once we'd had our bath, Mum would put our hair in plaits and we'd go to sleep looking identical. Twelve hours later Jo would be still the same – like Sleeping Beauty, unruffled and not a hair out of place. But my pyjamas would be inside out and back to front. As for my hair, it looked like a bird's nest and would take a good ten minutes of careful teasing the knots out to make it respectable enough to go to school.

Jody always looked beautiful and her hair was long and golden like a princess. And when Mum used to say 'These are the twins', people would look at Jo and go 'Oh look at her lovely hair'. Then they'd look at me and go 'Ah'.

One real difference that still sets us apart is our skin. I suffered from eczema from a really young age, with flaky-dry patches everywhere – from the usual elbows and wrists, to all the way round my mouth. On some days I'd go to school looking like a clown, covered in cream. Mum cut my hair like a pudding basin to stop it going on my neck.

Eczema was the reason we didn't have pets, and I still can't eat fruit like apples or nectarines or cherries, all of which can bring on an attack. I can eat bananas and oranges, but that's about it. The worst thing by far was the itching, which was sometimes so bad that Mum would take me to hospital. Even this was fair game for ridicule. Jo would point out just how stupid I looked, covered in gunk. But when we were teenagers I got my own back when she got acne and I didn't.

Everyone in our family was passionate about music, just not the same sort. Mum knew the whole of the Dusty Springfield songbook by heart. She also loved Doris Day and you'd hear her in the kitchen mashing potatoes for a shepherd's pie, or doing the ironing while singing 'The Deadwood Stage', or 'The Black Hills of Dakota'.

Dad saw himself more as 'a child of the sixties', and for him it was the Beatles and other sixties pop. But equally it could be Ray Charles or Frank Sinatra or Little Feat. The one thing they both loved was musicals and in October 1986 there was great excitement as Dad had managed to get tickets to the premiere of the brand-new Andrew Lloyd Webber musical *The Phantom of the Opera*. I watched

Mum get ready, standing beside the dressing table, handing her the things she needed as she 'did her face', carefully building up layers of mascara and choosing the right lipstick to go with her outfit. She and I shared a passion for make-up, which Jo didn't understand at all. And then Dad came into the bedroom in a smart suit and new tie and smelling of aftershave. And then I remember running after the car and waving them off. Only when they arrived at the theatre did they discover it was the wrong day ... Luckily it was a day early rather than a day late ... So the next evening they went through the whole business again.

The worst thing about this was having Liz as a babysitter two nights in a row. Whenever Mum and Dad went out she would ask her boyfriend round and we'd be sent upstairs even though it was only seven o'clock! Jo and I called her Chucky Poppins because one moment she'd be sweet as pie, the next moment she'd turn into a monster. The way she looked didn't help because she was like something out of the Addams Family, a typical Goth, white-blonde hair, white face, kohled eyes and into Tears for Fears, The Jam and Paul Weller. (But I would still creep into bed with her at night when I was scared.) We'd much rather have our brother in charge. Paul was a lot more chilled and would let us do anything, though when he was riled he was ruthless. One night he put me in a sleeping bag, tied it up and carried me around the house like a sack of potatoes. He'd only allow me out, he said, if I could guess where I was, like in the bathroom or the kitchen. He was completely mental. He was always going off to illegal raves and spent his life listening to dance music. And Jody and me? We weren't into any of that. We loved Kylie.

Kylie was my absolute idol and I just wanted to be her, even if it meant training to be a car mechanic, the part she played in *Neighbours*, which we watched religiously until Charlene and Scott (Kylie and Jason Donovan) got married and Kylie left the cast. Sometimes when my eczema was too bad to go to school, I'd get to watch *Neighbours* twice in one day and Jo would be so jealous!

East Wretham was even more remote than Great Hockham, so we spent much more time on our own, most of it singing, after we'd written down the words of the songs we liked from the radio, which always took hours. One of our favourites was 'Especially for You', a duet Kylie did with Jason for his first album. Like Kylie's hit single, 'I Should Be So Lucky', it was produced by the phenomenal songwriting team Stock, Aitken and Waterman. We'd spent so long perfecting it, we decided to do it for Mum and Dad – Jo doing Jason's part, as obviously I had to be Kylie. Once Mum and Dad were sitting comfortably on the couch in the lounge, we would emerge from behind the pink velvet curtains pulled across the French windows that led on to the garden, and the show would begin. From then on these 'curtain shows' became a regular feature of life in Lane End. At first we did mainly Kylie songs, interspersed with sketches we wrote involving Kylie and Jason. When that became a bit limiting, we invented two characters called George and Alfred, where I was George and Jo was Alfred. They were hairdressers, and for props we had polystyrene heads, the kind of things you see in shop windows to display hats. Mum bought cheap wigs from the market in Snetterton where we would some-times go on Sundays (and where I also built up my collection of rip-off cassettes), and while doing the dia-logue we'd pretend to brush this fake hair or put rollers in. We wrote everything ourselves – proper scripts that we rehearsed for hours, but the last word always led up to a song, which we also wrote.

'Did you see that Mabel? What a sight.'

'Funny, I used to think she was quite pretty . . .'

That would be a cue for a song called 'Pretty, Pretty, Pretty'. The only one I can remember in full now was 'Bad Manners'.

> Never pick your nose and don't pick your toes
> Bad, bad, bad, bad manners.
> You must always brush your hair,
> You must brush it everywhere
> Good, good, good, good manners.
> Manners, manners,
> Good, good, good, good manners.

To this day I have no idea where it all came from. But we were brought up on Dad's videos of *Monty Python*, *Fawlty Towers* and *Blackadder* where logic barely comes into it. I knew the words of *Fawlty Towers* off by heart because I had the scripts – I'd asked for them for my birthday – and Jo and I would sit on the sofa doing the dialogue while we were watching, so perhaps subconsciously it was that. We were always learning. We knew all the words to *Dirty Dancing*, even though it was years before we were allowed to watch it.

By this time Jo and I were already seasoned performers, members of the East Wretham drama society. All it really meant was that we did the pantomime every year in the village hall. We had barely arrived at Lane End before the woman who ran it turned up on the doorstep asking if we'd like to join. Of course we said yes! For the first couple of years we just played village children, dancing about and joining in the chorus. Our first proper role was as the pantomime horse. I can't remember now which pantomime it was because, from this distance, they all tend to merge into one, but it might have been *Jack and the Beanstalk* when Jo and I took it in turns to be the front end and the back end.

Singing was what I really loved, and the first time I sang on my own was in our school nativity play – a modern dress version in order to show us 'the true meaning of Christmas', our teacher explained. Jody played some ruffian kid who wanted all the presents given to the Baby Jesus for himself. I played Mary. And while everyone else was wearing ordinary clothes, I got to wear the traditional blue dress with a white scarf draped over my head that you see in every religious painting ever done. My song – when the Angel Gabriel comes down and tells Mary she's going to have a baby – started off: 'Why me? Why have I been chosen?' And as I sang these words, I was thinking along much the same lines. 'Why me? Why have I been chosen (to play Mary)?' It was a big moment in my life. Before it started I felt sick with nerves but once I began to sing, all that fell away.

The best thing about doing the pantomimes was learning the scripts – not ours, we never said anything – but all the other parts, because we'd hear them so often they just seeped into our heads, then we would act them out in our 'curtain shows', which gave us much more scope for our sketches and songs. In fact we would burst into song at every opportunity – though always well rehearsed and word perfect – such as when Dad came home. The moment we heard the car crunching up the drive, we'd position ourselves on the staircase and as the key turned in the lock we'd start singing, 'Daddy, father, pop, pa, dad, darling, da!'

Saturdays were always full on. If we got up early we'd go with Dad to the poultry auction at Swaffham as now he'd started his chicken-breeding project in earnest – we'd eat the eggs ourselves and if there was a glut he'd give them to friends. This was proper old Norfolk, a shed with a curved corrugated-iron roof that looked as if it had been left over from the war and probably was. Inside rows of cages were piled up on top of each other filled with chickens and cockerels and ducks and geese (and presumably turkeys, this being Norfolk). Once he'd got what he came for, and enjoyed the 'craic', we'd turn around and drive back home. Then it was on to Bury St Edmunds – totally the other direction – for Rollerbury, where we learned to skate on roller boots in the club for the under-thirteens. We did this for two years, until we were about eleven, and we absolutely loved it.

Saturday afternoons was when we'd go for walks, mainly just with Dad. These were usually in Thetford Forest. It wasn't an ancient forest, like Wayland Wood. It had been planted at the end of the First World War to help the unemployment situation and then continued during the Depression. Although the forest is new, the seeds came from trees already in the area, with local people collecting pine cones. Now it's the largest Scots pine forest in England and if we weren't too noisy we'd see hares and rabbits and masses of pheasants. Because everywhere looked much the same, the tracks were numbered. Our favourite was 'No. 83' mainly because it had a pond at the end where you could catch tadpoles, and at the right time of year we'd bring them back in jam jars and transfer them to our own pond.

One Saturday when Jo wasn't feeling well, Dad took me skating by myself and as we left the house I spotted a baby bird lying on the path by the hedge.

'Poor thing,' I said. 'It must have fallen from its nest.'

'Whatever you do, don't touch it,' Dad warned when he saw me bend down.

'But I want to look after it!'

'You can't pick it up, because its mother might come and rescue it,' he explained. 'She's probably up there some- where watching even now . . .'

'Please, Dad . . .'

'No, Carrie.'

'Please . . .'

'I said no.'

'Please . . .'

'Well, if it's still there when we come back from skating, then that's different.'

By now we were already in the car on our way to Rollerbury. It was the early days of car phones when they were the size of bricks, and Dad had one for work, so I picked it up, dialled home and told Mum I needed to speak to Jo urgently.

'Jo, there's a baby bird on the path by the hedge that's fallen from its nest and Dad says if it's still there by the time we get home, we can keep it!' Because of eczema I had never had any kind of pet. I longed to have a dog or a cat but if I couldn't have one of them, I'd settle for anything. Like this baby bird for example. Usually I wanted our roller-skating to go on for ever, but that day I couldn't wait for the session to end.

When we got back, Jo was waiting outside, standing guard over the bird. Dad rolled his eyes and sighed, while Jo and I went off to the garage to look for something to put it in. Basically that garage was Dad's warehouse. Open the doors and all you could see was Coco-Cola. It was almost as if he was a soft-drinks gangster, because crates were everywhere. And not only cans and bottles of Coke, but towels, mirrors, umbrellas. All the towels in the house were marked Coca-Cola. All our mirrors were Coca-Cola. Whenever we were asked to give something for a tombola or a raffle, or a prize for a flower show, it was always something to do with Coca-Cola. 'But doesn't it belong to Coca-Cola?' we'd say, as Dad handed over whatever it was for us to take to school, or Brownies, or the village hall, remembering his lecture about what belongs to you and what doesn't. 'This is different,' he said. 'This is publicity.'

Finally we found an empty shoebox in Mum's utility room and used that. We filled it with grass and cotton wool and jammed in the top of a Marmite jar which we filled with water. As our bird obviously needed a name, we called him Chirpy – not that he was, he stayed completely silent – but we were optimistic. As we didn't know what type of bird he was, we didn't know what to feed him. Worms? Seeds? Insects? We argued about it for about half an hour. In the end we gave him milk from an eye-dropper with a rubber bulb which we found in the bathroom cabinet.

We put the shoebox in the kitchen near the stove, which was the warmest place. And it wasn't long before he began to perk up, and even to chirp! And oh, how I loved him! Like any newborn creature we knew that he had to be fed all the time, so first thing every morning I'd rush downstairs and check he was all right. He had little beady orange eyes and when I showed him the dropper he opened his beak so wide that his whole head was an open mouth! We'd had him for about a week before we decided that he must be a blackbird and that worms were the next thing on the menu so then we argued about how we would collect them. That night Dad was taking us out for a curry at our local Indian; as Paul was revising for his exams he wasn't included.

'Can you look after Chirpy please, Paul,' I yelled upstairs before we left. 'Just give him some milk.'

I looked in on Chirpy when we got back, and said, 'See you in the morning!'

Next day when I came down I did see him. But he didn't see me, because he was dead. He was flat on his back, his legs sticking up like two cocktail sticks and his bright beady eyes were now totally opaque. It was the most horrible thing and I was distraught. My first ever pet! One whole week we'd kept him alive, and now this. That evening, when Paul got back from school, I asked if anything had happened when we were out at the restaurant.

'Nothing,' he said.

'Did you feed him?'

'Yes. I'd used up all the milk for my cereal so I gave him some yogurt.'

'YOGURT!'

'Yes, yogurt. It's the same as milk. Or nearly.'

I didn't talk to him for over a week. I could not believe anybody could be so stupid. Our yogurt was the kind that had bits in it, really thick and gloopy . . . poor Chirpy probably choked on a piece of apricot.

The one good thing to come out of this was that the following Saturday after Dad came back from Swaffham market he told us he had a surprise.

'In the garden,' he said. 'Behind the garage.'

And there, in a special little enclosure, were these two ducklings waddling around, and they were so cute, and they were ours! Dad went on to get more ducks, but these two were always the special ones, and we were perpetually terrified they'd get eaten by foxes. Because that was always the risk if you didn't keep them locked up, which Dad didn't. He liked to let them roam about the garden during the day and they would only go back in their cage at night when it was time to roost.

Animals were an obsession for Jody and me, particularly me. You are never very far away from a pig farm in Norfolk and there was one just behind our house. The pigs were mostly huge, the size of Shetland ponies, and wandered about turning the field into a quagmire whatever the time of year and so they always looked as if they could do with a good wash. But there was one pen, near the farm, where they put pigs that had something wrong with them, like the blind ones. So that's where we would go. As they never got near any mud, they were perfectly clean. Not only did we feel sorry for them, but it was the only opportunity we had to be up close to animals, so we'd climb over the fence and get in with them and stroke their ears and generally give them as much love and affection as we could.

In our last year at the village school, Liz left home and moved in with her boyfriend, Leigh Gracie, who she'd met at sixth form college and from then on she lived with him in Norwich. I don't blame her for leaving. Mum used to say she'd turned from a little angel into a strop after we left London, and once we'd moved to East Wretham it was worse because it was so isolated. Poor Liz hadn't had it easy. When we were tiny, she'd be holding one while Mum was feeding the other and it was the same if ever Mum and Dad went out. The babysitter often couldn't cope so Liz would have to take over. To be honest I barely thought of her as my older sister, she was more like a second mother. But by the time Liz was a teenager, the atmosphere was never great because she was always arguing and, when Mum or Dad took her to school, she made them drop her off way past the entrance so she wouldn't be seen with them. Even though she had now passed her driving test and had a job, Dad was still very strict. One evening she came down wearing white stiletto boots because she was going out with Leigh. And Dad said they were too high, so she gave him one of her looks.

'They're too high, Lizzy, take them off.'

But she didn't. The next day, Dad fetched a saw from his shed, went into her bedroom and sawed off the heels. When she came back and realised what he had done, she went mental . . . It wasn't long after that that she left.

For Jody and me Liz leaving home was fantastic. We'd never had that much to do with her because she was so much older than us – ten years is a lot when you're still at junior school – and basically we were beneath her notice. Now it meant that we could have our own rooms so there would be no more arguments about (my) mess. Instead we argued about who should go where, and in the end it was Mum who made the decision. Jo would have Liz's old room and I would keep the one that used to be ours. At first I was really angry, because it meant Jo got Liz's double bed, whilst I was stuck with my single one. To make up for it, Mum said I could have my room redecorated while Jo's stayed as it was, a version of Goth-meets-Punk and there wasn't even a proper carpet down. I chose a flowery duvet and matching wallpaper which Mum and I put up by ourselves. For a while it looked like a proper girl's room, but then I started cutting photos of Kylie and Jason from *Smash Hits* and sticking them on the wall with Sellotape. Mum wasn't pleased, but by then it was too late as, if I'd taken them down, there'd have been marks left by the Sellotape. I know because I tried, and then I had to add even more photos to cover them up. Later on, when I went to Wayland High School, these came down and were replaced by photos of my friends, dozens of them – again carefully positioned to cover up the holes in my wallpaper. But pride of place, beside my bed, went to a huge poster of Lenny Kravitz who was just A God.

The summer of 1990 was when my childhood ended. It was our last term at primary school, but things were very tense at home because Grandad was ill. I loved Grandad. He was so funny, and – although he was my grandad – he didn't look like a grandad. He had a big fat belly, big black glasses, a comb-over and a really loud laugh.

He'd been poorly for about a year. Jo and I had been round at their bungalow having dinner and he kept coughing, and we'd felt very uncomfortable so we called Mum and asked to go home.

'Grandad's not going to die you know,' Mum said that night when she put us to bed. So that gave me peace of mind though a bit of me wasn't sure. Of course I knew notionally that people died, but only when they were really old, and Grandad wasn't. His face wasn't wrinkled like other people's grandads, certainly not as wrinkled as Nanny Flo's who was much older and never got ill.

Then one night they shipped Jo and me off to stay at Liz's. She turned up in her car, picked us up, then drove us back to Norwich. We didn't connect it with Grandad – why should we? For us it was like an adventure. Liz hadn't been the easiest of sisters, and now here she was being extra nice to us. Stopping at a garage on the way up and buying us chocolate and magazines, and then letting us camp out on her lounge floor – it was all quite exciting.

It was when the phone started ringing in the middle of the night that I realised something might be wrong. But it was only when I heard Liz crying that I twigged. She really loved Grandad and was very close to him – she'd known him ten years longer than we had after all.

In the morning I didn't say anything, and neither did Jody. Liz drove us back to East Wretham and still nothing was said, by her or by us. Only when we were all sitting in the lounge did it come out, when Mum and Dad started talking about the funeral.

'Why did nobody tell us?' I kept asking. 'Why did nobody tell us he was going to die?'

'Because we wanted to protect you,' Dad said. I felt myself completely cut off, like I was sitting in a huge jam jar and nobody could hear me through it, and I couldn't hear anybody. About a week before I'd had a dream that Grandad had died and I'd been so frightened that I'd run into Mum and Dad's bedroom and clambered in with them, still shaking from the memory. Because in my dream I'd seen my nan standing outside their bungalow on her own, and I'd run to her and said, 'I'm sorry Nan,' and buried my face in her arms.

'Does this mean Grandad's going to die?' I'd asked Mum.

'Of course not,' she said. And it was a lie. A big fat lie. And I remember feeling so, so angry with her. I remember thinking: I'm much more aware of things than you think.

They didn't even tell us when the funeral was. We came home from school on the bus as usual and found everyone was dressed in black and having cups of tea and sandwiches, so of course we knew what had happened. We weren't stupid. But that morning, when we'd gone off to get the bus, nobody had said a word. And as for being asked if we wanted to go – I don't think it even occurred to them. I regret that I didn't say goodbye to Grandad when he was still alive, and I regret that I couldn't even say goodbye when he was in his coffin. I regret it to this day.

And it was about to get worse. A few days later Mum's brother Reggie died, also of cancer. Reggie was the fourth oldest of Nanny Flo's children, the one Mum was closest to and she absolutely adored him.

I had never experienced death before, and now it was like an epidemic, two people dead in one week, and there was no one who wasn't affected, no one who could comfort us. Mum was distraught. Dad was distraught. Nanny Ivy was distraught. Liz was distraught. I'm sure Nanny Flo was distraught too, although she wasn't there. But Jo and I weren't really included and were treated as if we couldn't possibly understand. We only got through it thanks to the football World Cup in Italy. It had started on 7 June and Grandad died on 21 June, when it was at the halfway point ... We loved watching football as a family, and later everyone agreed that it was the World Cup that got us through.

There were only a few weeks left till the end of term, but I couldn't talk about it to anyone. Not even Jo. At playtime friends from school would see my nan standing at the fence at the far end of the field, and say, 'So where's your grandad then?' And I'd say, 'I don't know.'

3

'The Time Warp'

Although Nanny Ivy only lived across the road, I didn't feel I knew her that well until Grandad passed away, because they were always together. Only after he'd died, did I see just how strong she really was. She was proud and found it difficult to accept help from anyone. Her great line was she didn't want to be 'a burden'. But she was always very kind to Jo and me. Every week without fail on a Friday, she'd give us our pocket money. One whole pound! (Though it never went up.) Whenever we went for dinner, she'd do carrots 'especially for Carrie'. One slight problem: I didn't like carrots and to this day I've never told her! If she ever telephoned – which was not often – she'd talk for a minute, say what she had to say (she would never just call for a chat) and then it would be 'Well, I'll let you get on now' and put the phone down.

She'd learnt to drive shortly before Grandad passed

away and then only because he'd insisted. He knew he was dying and knew that she'd be completely stranded when she was on her own. Once she'd passed her test and bought a little Nissan he felt free to let go.

My other grandmother, Nanny Flo, couldn't have been more different. She was full of energy and vitality and it was infectious. She used to say that me and Jo coming along so unexpectedly at the end of her life was like the most wonderful gift and she absolutely adored us. She'd had all these children but I don't think she'd ever had time to enjoy them. There'd been a break during the war, but then there were other things to worry about, and of course she could never be sure that her husband would ever be coming home.

Although the Carterhatch Road house was bought, Nanny Flo still had the mortgage to pay because they couldn't afford the life insurance, which was why she'd ended up working at the bakery – and I've already told that story.

Sometime in the seventies Humphreys the baker's was compulsory purchased by the council to build a health centre. Grandad and Nanny Ivy had no choice but to leave and they decided to buy a pub, the Blue Boar in Abridge – which funnily enough has often been featured in *TOWIE*. Later they sold up and moved to another pub in Epping called the Spotted Dog. Then, in their final move, they came to Great Hockham.

Anyway, the bakery closing had left Nanny Flo without a job. As she still had the mortgage to pay, she had to get something else. For someone of her age – she was well into her sixties by then – the options were limited, and she went to work for J. W. Spear's, the board game company, who had their headquarters in Enfield.

When Jo and I were born, Nanny Flo was seventy-two and still working at Spear's on the assembly line. She only stopped the following year when her real mum – Alice, the one she'd thought was her older sister – passed away. Alice had retired to a little house in Clacton-on-Sea on the Essex coast some years before and she left it to Nanny Flo in her will. This finally allowed Nan to sell Carterhatch Road, give up work and move to Clacton, and some of my happiest memories are of going to stay with her there.

Nanny Flo was a proper picture-book grandmother with curly grey hair and little crinkly laughing eyes. She was tiny, smaller than Jo and me, so probably not even five feet tall. Everything about her was round and cosy; she had a chubby face and permanently rosy cheeks because she put lipstick on them, which is how she taught me to do my blusher. She always wore the same thing, trousers with a blouse and then a cardigan on top. I don't think I ever saw her wear a skirt.

We were the youngest of her grandchildren and she adored us, giving us all the love that she had never had time to give to her own. And it seemed to me, she loved us most of all when we were naughty and then she would laugh and laugh till tears streamed down her rosy face.

Her house was a little Edwardian terraced cottage with

two bedrooms. The best part was the cupboard under the stairs which was full of old toys, teddy bears and bricks, but mostly board games which she'd got from Spear's: Snakes and Ladders, Ludo, Chinese Chequers and Scrabble and others I can't remember now. But Nanny Flo's special love was cards and she taught us to play every card game she knew. We started with snap and beat your neighbour out of doors and old maid, and then later there was pontoon, and various kinds of whist, like hearts. But when we graduated to gin rummy we were hooked. Mum would drive us down to Clacton – it took about an hour and a half across country via Ipswich – and the moment we walked in we'd get out the cards and play gin rummy for hours.

Nanny Flo's house was about ten minutes' walk from the front and if the weather was nice we'd go down to the beach and she would roll up her trousers and paddle at the edge, whilst Jo and I sat in the water. And then she'd take us onto the pier and we'd have candyfloss, or she'd buy us each a bag of chips.

One of the reasons I loved watching telly was that Nanny Flo loved watching telly and I associated it with her. I loved it when I'd get home from school and found she'd come to stay. Dad would separate out the L-shaped living area into two rooms and in the evenings he and Mum would sit in the lounge part, while Nanny Flo, Jo and I would curl up in what we called the little room and watch telly.

We'd always get to stay up later if Nan was there, and

we always seemed to have nicer food, but perhaps it was just that she made everything seem like a treat. The 'little room' became almost like her room. Dad stopped moving everything back when she'd gone and me and Jo would sit on the sofa and watch videos.

Although we gave up on *Neighbours* once Kylie had left, I always loved telly, especially in the winter when there was nothing else to do except write, sing and rehearse our curtain shows. These days people who work in telly are always saying, 'I don't really watch TV.'

WHAT?

I loved telly. I still love telly. And in my view you've got to love telly if you're in telly.

There was *The Littlest Hobo* about a Canadian dog without an owner, but my favourite was probably *Woof!* about a boy who turned into a dog. Then there was *Byker Grove* and *Saved by the Bell*. Best of all was *Going Live!*, which opened up a whole new world once we'd stopped going to Rollerbury on Saturdays.

Going Live! was just brilliant TV, so creative, and I couldn't imagine how grown-ups could think it all up. Then one Saturday Mum's sister Carol got us tickets to watch it being done at the BBC in Shepherd's Bush. We were *sooo* excited! Philip Schofield, the usual presenter, was doing *Joseph and the Amazing Technicolor Dreamcoat* in the West End, so Ricky and Bianca – characters from *EastEnders* – were on as guest presenters and I met Andi Peters who did the 'The Broom Cupboard'. And it was just so amazing to actually be there and watch how it was all pieced together. I was like WOW! It was all so interesting. I wanted to know how it was done, how it was made. I wanted to be a part of it.

The big problem about East Wretham was that we didn't have a social life. It was the opposite of Great Hockham where everybody lived round the corner. Nobody lived round the corner, except a girl called Hannah Denty whose father built racing cars. But she lived across the main road, so we couldn't just pop over and see her.

At least we had Ceefax. In many ways Ceefax was like an early version of online networking. The screen was black and the lettering was white – it looked like it had been written on a typewriter in negative – only the name Ceefax itself was coloured with yellow lettering on a blue background. There were hundreds of 'pages' so you could look up things, like what was on telly, or the football scores, or the latest news, and this was in the days when you had to wait for the *Six O'Clock News*, or *News at Ten*. Not if you had Ceefax. The pages would change whenever something happened in the world even if it was in the middle of the night. Most importantly, for Jo and me, it had this section called Pen Pals. There were hundreds if not thousands of people 'advertising' there. It was like a dating site, except it was just for friends – pen pals – and there were no photographs. If there was someone you liked the sound of, then you could write to them, a normal letter, buy a stamp from the post office in Great Hockham and post it, and if they wrote back then you carried on. The main problem was the waiting – sometimes I'd have to wait two weeks to get a reply. But because I'd be writing to loads of kids at the same time, there'd usually be at least one letter on the doormat in the morning though it might not be for me, because Jo and I were both doing it. So then we'd go, 'I got a letter, you didn't.' But we'd never let the other one see our letters. They were ours and strictly private.

For years we'd both longed for a diary with a lock. We kept seeing them on TV and in the shops and the first Christmas after we left junior school, Dad bought us one each. But as they were both exactly the same, same colour, same key, it was really stupid. We would go into each other's rooms, unlock each other's diary and read it. But there the similarity ended. The entries couldn't have been more different even though we were leading the same lives, living in the same house, doing the same things, seeing the same people. Jo would put, 'Dear Diary, Today was a very sunny day and we went to Tesco and did some shopping with Mum. Nan came to visit and we made a pie. It was lovely and we had a great day, love Jo.' Mine would be, 'I HATE MUM.' That would be it. Nothing more. Jo would write about the weirdest things, like 'Carrie had bacon for tea, I wish I had bacon but I had something else.' What was all that about?

We started at Wayland High School in Watton in September 1990, just a few months after Grandad died. Watton was eight miles away so we still took the bus, but an earlier one which was all right in the summer but in the winter it was horrible, as East Wretham was one of the first stops and going round all the other villages to pick up kids took well over an hour.

Around this time we began to develop our own individual styles. We both had really long hair (except for when my eczema was really bad) until one day Jo cut mine off to about chin level. Mum was furious and Jo got grounded. But Jo hadn't forced me to have it done, quite the opposite. Then a couple of weeks later I read her diary which said, 'Dear Diary, ever since Carrie had her hair cut she thinks she's it. She's walking around school like she owns the place.' We found out everything about each other in the diaries. We never let on until years later that we'd been snooping, but we both guessed that the other one would try. Not because we were telepathic or anything twin-related, just that we'd spend all of our lives together and could read each other like a book.

Until Grandad passed away, we'd usually go to Spain on holiday, to Roquetas de Mar near Almería down in the south, where he and Nanny Ivy had an apartment which they'd bought when the bakery was sold. One day Mum was sitting out on the balcony – the apartment was on the third floor of this L-shaped block – while the rest of us were down in the pool. In fact there were two pools, a shallow one for children and a deep proper one which was huge. Jo and I must have been about five or six and, as neither of us could swim, we were wearing rubber rings. I was playing on my own in the little pool when I decided to join the others in the big one, so I got out, ran across and jumped into what was the deep end. And I flipped over. Mum had been watching from the balcony and suddenly all she could see were these two legs sticking up from the surface of the water. And Dad says he just heard her scream.

'Ian! Carrie's drowning!'

I can remember nothing of what happened, except the terror. What is certainly true is that Dad saved my life. The moment he saw my legs in the air he'd swum over at breakneck speed. Because once the ring had flipped over, it was never going to flip back again of its own accord. It is also true that the experience scarred me for life. Eventually I did learn to swim, though it took a very long time – I mean years – to persuade me back into the water. Even now the idea frightens me stiff and it has to be about forty degrees in the shade before I will even consider going swimming and I would never, ever go out of my depth.

Once Liz and Paul had left home, or didn't come on holiday with us any more, we began to go to caravan parks in England. Jo and I weren't that interested in getting a tan which was all Liz and Paul seemed to think about. And while they loved just lying in the sun, we didn't see the point. Why would you want to get so hot?

The first time we stayed in England was the summer before Grandad died. It was a Hoseasons caravan site, I think, south of Plymouth just into Cornwall. We'd been camping in France previously with Paul and Liz because they liked being abroad, but for Jo and me this was much more fun because they had kids' clubs where you did competitions: dancing competitions, singing competitions, every sort of competition. But that first year we were too scared to enter, so we just watched and enjoyed every minute of it. One thing we could join in was something called Tussle with the Teamsters when we would all troop into the bar and dance 'The Time Warp' from *The Rocky Horror Show*. It was every night at nine o'clock and we were so desperate not to miss it we made Mum and Dad come back early from visiting Mum's sister Ivy in St Ives, which was about as far away as you can go in Cornwall. And then the fog came down and Dad had to drive across Bodmin Moor for about four hours, with his nose six inches from the windscreen, while me and Jody were telling him to hurry up, or we'd be too late! When we finally got back he must have been exhausted, but I don't think we even said thank you. We just flung open the doors, jumped out of the car, and raced to the club house. No way could we miss doing 'The Time Warp'!

Best of all we were making new friends for the first time in years, meeting other kids who enjoyed doing what we enjoyed doing, and Jo and I just loved it. It didn't matter that you wouldn't see them again. As long as you remembered to get their address you could write. The only bad part was the long journeys because Jo would get horribly car sick and basically she'd make every trip twice as long because Dad would have to keep stopping so she could throw up. It was better if we went at night because then we would sleep for at least the first part of the journey. Dad had a Volvo estate at the time and we would set off at four in the morning with me and Jo tucked up in sleeping bags lying full length in the back. Once it got light we'd wake up and ask 'Are we there yet?' but we never were. So the rest of the way we'd play games. It was non-stop entertainment. We'd have to sing 'Summer Holiday' starting with every consonant in the alphabet, so it would be 'Bere ball boing bon a bummer boliday' and we'd be in stitches, because obviously 'bummer' was so naughty it always made us laugh. Each letter would throw up some really stupid words which would have us cackling like hens. Alphabet games were always good value because they lasted twenty-six rounds. 'I packed my shopping and I put in an apple . . .'; then the next person would say, 'I packed my shopping and I put in an apple and a bun.' Then the next person would say, 'I packed my shopping and I put in an apple and a bun and a cauliflower . . .' Then there was the bridge game. Dad would shout out, 'Right, bridge ahead. Close your eyes.' So we'd all close our eyes and you'd have to yell 'Waah!' when you thought you'd got to the bridge. This was more difficult than you'd imagine as Dad would sometimes specd up or slow down just to catch us out. If we ran out of games we could always play I-Spy. And I remember once Mum said she'd give us a pound for every Eddie Stobart lorry that we saw. We never got paid because she didn't realise how many there actually were on the road, and she'd have been cleaned out, she said.

The next year we went to a campsite at Holywell in Cornwall, just south of Newquay. This was very small, just some caravans in a farmer's field with a clubhouse. We arrived just too late to enter the competitions which were always held on Saturday nights. But we now realised that everywhere had them and that to have a chance of winning we had to be properly prepared.

So the next year Jo and I rehearsed for months beforehand. This time we went to a Hoseasons at Perranporth. We arrived on Saturday afternoon, having left Norfolk when it was still dark, and signed up the moment we arrived. I borrowed my mum's make-up and used her lipstick to put on my cheeks, like Granny Flo taught me. We sang 'Like a Prayer' by Madonna. It wasn't the idea that we might win the prize – I can't even remember what it was – probably a bottle of Coca-Cola – but I loved being up there on the little stage. Forget our curtain shows with two people in the audience. There must have been a hundred people out there, and they all clapped! Even better, we came second!

The winner was a boy who had really come prepared. He was like a mini professional, dressed up as the Artful Dodger in *Oliver Twist*, and his outfit was the opposite of home-made and looked like it came from a theatrical costumiers. It was no surprise when he sang 'Consider Yourself' and it was no surprise when he won. To be honest I don't think it would have mattered how well Jo and I had sung, against that sort of competition – nostalgia central like the Hovis ad – we didn't stand a chance. But we had come second, and gave ourselves high fives when we came off. But really all we wanted was to make friends.

*

Although Jody and I were always known as 'the twins', we looked different. I had olive skin and dark hair whereas Jo had pale skin, and was blonde. She'd started using a spray called Sun In that gave it blonde streaks and the more she used it the blonder it got.

Jo was really, really beautiful from very early on. She never wore make-up, she had a natural look which needed no help at all, unlike me who plastered myself with foundation. At school when she walked past the boys, she'd just flick her hair, so they used to call her Jody Flick, not Jody Flack. And I'd go, 'Ugh, Jo, you're such a flirt.'

Once we started at Wayland we became interested in boys. Until then we'd thought they were completely useless. Just before we left the village school we'd been to a disco in Watton. I have no idea now how we were even allowed to go. And everyone there seemed so much more grown up, not only the way they looked, but the way they behaved. This was a completely different world. I saw people kissing. I mean, KISSING!! I had never seen people kiss, or not like this anyway – they didn't even keep their mouths shut! And I remember thinking, So this is real life. Mum and Dad have hidden it from us quite well.

That was when I first spotted Lee Charlton. In our village you never saw gorgeous-looking boys, but there he was, with blonde curtains, *shaved* at the sides and wearing a baggy T-shirt and I thought he looked like a pop star. He was the double of Zack from *Saved by the Bell*. I had never seen a boy who was that pretty in real life. All I could think of from then on was Lee Charlton, so I thought I'd ring him up.

I was so used to contacting kids I didn't know through Pen Pals, that ringing up a boy didn't seem like such a big deal. Why write when I had the telephone number? Because it hadn't been difficult to track him down using the phone book.

A woman's voice answered.

'Can I speak to Lee please?'

Then there was a silence. Then came Lee's voice and only when I heard him speak did I start to feel a bit nervous.

'Who's that?' he said.

'I met you at the Youth Club disco.'

'So which one were you then?'

'I was the girl with the red hairband.'

'Ohhh. I remember you . . .'

But as neither of us had anything to say, I just said 'Goodbye' and hung up.

From then on Jo and I used to phone everyone. It became our new thing. We put a tent up in the garden and 'borrowed' Dad's mobile which never had any reception and crackled.

'Is Robert/Darren/Mark/Craig/Damon there?' But mostly all you'd hear would be 'crackle, crackle'. In those days everyone's number was in the book, including our teachers'. So that was another of our pastimes. We'd just call them up, wait for them to answer and put the phone down.

We would call in to Norwich Radio – Broadland FM –
Late Night Love. Jo and me and all our school friends used
to listen when we went to bed because that's the only way
we could communicate. And it would be, 'Mum, Mum,
can I call *Late Night Love?*'

We had this little portable with an aerial that you pulled
out and we'd put it by the window to get reception. So we'd
be lying there, and the DJ would go, 'I've got a request here
from Caroline; she's asked for Mariah Carey for Sue, Jackie,
Heidi, Sarah, Carla and Jody, singing "Without You".' And
our friends would do the same for us. We'd dedicate them
to each other and say: 'You're the best friends ever.'

That was the full extent of our social life.

As for Lee Charlton I still had this terrible crush, but I
had no idea how you were supposed to behave and at
Wayland I spent my days just following him around and
staring at him. He was going out with a girl called Kerry
Pegg, and one day he stopped, turned, looked at me and
said, 'You should take a photograph, it'll last longer.'

Gradually I learnt that this wasn't the way to do it. You
had to be a bit breezy. But how?

Going to Wayland had been a shock. We had really led
a very sheltered life up until then, sheltered from
everything. At our junior school we'd had 'discos' where
boys danced with girls. The boys learned to say 'Will you
dance with me?' and the girls would say 'Yes'. Then you'd
both hold hands, your arms outstretched and swing them,
swaying back and forth. It might have been *The Sound of
Music.*

So at our first school disco we weren't really prepared. We were just standing around when a boy in our class called James Tanner came up to me and said he wanted to dance with my sister and could I go and ask her. I assumed that this was normal. So I passed the message on saying, 'James Tanner wants to dance with you, Jo.' The music was Elton John singing 'Sacrifice' and I remember feeling so jealous because no one was asking me to dance, when suddenly, without warning, James Tanner lunged at Jody, and I went cold with the shock of it. I had never seen anything like this in my life. I don't know if he was trying to kiss her or attack her. But the weird thing was that Jo and I both pretended that this was completely normal and didn't say anything about it either to anyone else or each other.

Jody had definitely outgrown me by this time – not so much in height, but in womanliness – we didn't even look like twins any more. I might have been thirteen but I looked about nine. One problem was that I didn't eat enough. I didn't have an eating disorder, as far as I know, I just didn't like most of what was on offer and I was never really hungry. It had started when we were still at the village school. We'd both been in the netball team, and I think the PE teacher must have said something, and I ended up going to the doctor. His verdict was that, although I was naturally small – I only take size-two shoes even now – I was also very underweight so I was given some pretty disgusting medicine to take. But while medicine might give you the vitamins, it doesn't compensate for lack of proper food and apart from Fridays when I had school dinners (fish and chips!) I lived on biscuits.

In those days Mum worked from home, typing manuscripts from tapes, and once she had her headphones on she heard nothing and wouldn't even know when we got back from school. So the first thing I'd do after turning on the telly, was to put the kettle on, make a cup of tea and open the biscuit tin. Digestives, Rich Tea, Chocolate Digestives, Jaffa Cakes, I just loved biscuits – any biscuits . . . Jody would eat biscuits too but she'd top them up with fruit, which I couldn't have because of the eczema . . . There was nothing Jo wouldn't eat, and at home I would shovel everything onto her plate, so Mum and Dad weren't really aware of how little was actually going in. The main problem was that I didn't like sandwiches, which was what Mum made for our packed lunches. I wouldn't eat them, so I'd keep them in my school bag and chuck them away when I passed a bin. But I didn't always remember, and one day, when Mum was looking for a gym shirt that needed washing, she found them, a whole load that had turned green with mould, and that was the turning point. Finally I was allowed to take pot noodles to school and gradually things began to change, but even toast was hard at first. By then I was desperate to put weight on mainly because I wanted to wear older clothes, things that older girls would wear. And Dad would say, 'Not until you start eating your dinners.'

By this time Jody had a boyfriend called Bub, and when he went off with somebody else, she kissed Mathew

Webb. Bub was so incensed that the next thing she knew he was back, but by that time she'd gone off him! And that feeling – that what you first felt about a boy would completely disappear – became known by us as 'Bub-feelings'. Then 'Bub-feelings' gradually evolved to mean negative feelings of any kind, but usually to do with boys.

'So what do you think about X then, Jo?'

'Bub-feelings.'

It eventually got shortened to 'Bubs'.

'So what do you think of Dad's new Hawaiian shirt then?'

'Bubs.'

When Jody and I went to parties, or the school disco, we were always the first to leave. As we got older we'd try to negotiate to stay out till midnight, but it never worked. No matter how hard we wheedled or cajoled, Dad's last words when he dropped us off were always 'Ten to eleven'. And we'd begin to sing under our breath one of Grandad's favourite songs, 'Roll Out the Barrel', but we improved the words.

> Ten. To. Eleven. We'll have a barrel of fun
> Ten. To. Eleven. We've got the blues on the run
> Ten. To. Eleven. Ring out a song of good cheer
> It'll soon be ten to eleven, but the gang's all here!

Because, wouldn't you know it, at ten to eleven all the cool people would turn up – the ones who'd just saunter in after having spent the last few hours in the pub – and Dad would be there waiting in the car park. And we always had to make sure we were out there at 'ten to eleven' otherwise he'd come charging in saying 'Seen the twins?' which was so embarrassing.

It was even the same on New Year's Eve. Imagine it: 'Bye everyone! Have a great New Year!' So we got home and Mum and Dad said, 'Don't worry. We can all sit down and watch a film together.' They made us watch *Pal Joey*, and to this day, every time Jo and I see *Pal Joey*, or hear any mention of *Pal Joey* we go 'Happy New Year!'

All the cool kids used to hang out after school on 'the Green' which was in the middle of a fifties' council estate just off Watton High Street, and hardly a day went by without us hearing somebody say, 'Oh yeah, well last night on the Green . . .' And Jo and I would be like 'Grrrrr, why weren't we on the Green . . .' The Green was where everything happened, where they'd all be smoking and drinking. In other words nirvana. It couldn't have been more than a hundred yards from the school but it could have been a hundred miles as far as we were concerned because we had to get the school bus, and if we missed that there would 'be trouble'.

We decided we needed to practise before we tried smoking in public. The only cigarettes we could get our hands on were actually mini cigars. They were the same size as cigarettes, just a different colour, so we didn't think it would make much difference. There was a box of them in the drinks cabinet in the lounge and as long as we left the top layer looking the same, Dad wouldn't notice. So we'd carefully remove one then go into the garden and light up. I'd take a couple of puffs, then pass it on to Jody, and she'd take a couple of puffs. Then we'd consider that was enough to begin with, and stub it out and bury the remains behind the chicken run. A few days later we'd try again. Eventually, after several goes of 'practising' we gave up.

'I don't like it,' I finally admitted when my throat felt like sandpaper.

'Neither do I,' Jo said. And that was it. We never smoked again.

Alcohol was different. We'd get an empty Coke bottle (plenty of those around), go to the drinks cabinet and using an egg-cup as a measure pour a bit out of everything that was in there: rum, gin, Advocaat, ginger wine, cherry brandy, whisky, Cointreau, sherry, vodka . . . Most of these bottles never saw the light of day except at Christmas, so we knew they would never notice that the levels had gone down. Then we'd add up all the percentages on the labels and tell each other 'This is 297 per cent alcohol!' or whatever it was. (Clearly maths wasn't our strongest subject.) Then we'd take it to the school disco, and drink it outside, but as it was always shared out between about twenty other people, the effect wasn't so bad that it would put you off for life.

That fate is reserved for cider, which I cannot even smell now without wanting to throw up. Watton had an inexhaustible supply of no-hopers who hung around the sweet shop we called Chockies. For £2 they'd go into Gateway and buy us a bottle of cider. They didn't care if we were underage, they'd just do it because everyone in Watton was in the same boat.

However you looked at it, Watton was a dump because there was just nothing to do. There had once been a railway but it had been closed in the sixties, and now there was no way to get out unless you had a car, and then it took for ever because it was single carriageway all the way through Thetford Forest. Until the early eighties there had been an Odeon in Watton. Even in my memory there was a skateboard ramp until it was vandalised. The youth club – a concrete building that looked like a bunker – was open only once a week on a Tuesday. And that was it. There weren't even any late buses to go to the cinema in Norwich, which was twenty-five miles away. In fact there were only two buses a week, one on Wednesdays and one on Saturdays.

Anyway, one evening we were staying the night with a friend whose mother let her do anything and someone bought us a bottle and four of us set off to the Loch – Loch Neaton, a Victorian lake with lily pads, the kind of place fishermen set up their rods at weekends, and people take their dogs for walks early in the morning and mums would push buggies around, and warn their toddlers to keep away from the edge. But after seven o'clock, the loch was where everyone came to smoke dope, to have sex, and anything else they could think of to stop the boredom. So the four of us flopped down by the side of the water and shared this one bottle of cider. We didn't have a glass, or even a plastic cup. We just passed this bottle around as if we were derelicts.

Swig, swig, swig, swig.

Until we were rat-arsed.

And then we were sick.

4

It's a Wonderful Life in Colour

Christmas was always a big thing in our family. It was the best time of the year and this was all down to Dad – he could have had a job as a Christmas-kids-exciter. I think he genuinely liked it himself, but he was just good at making Christmas really fun. Take Father Christmas – he would even make fake footprints on the stairs!

Jody's and my presents would be stacked in two piles, perfectly symmetrical, one each side of the fireplace in the lounge, but once we started opening them, there the symmetry stopped. Jo unwrapped her presents one at a time. I ripped mine apart at 100 mph, and they'd all be done in five minutes, whereas Jody would still be opening hers half an hour later, savouring every single moment. Because we got exactly the same things, she would have to try not to look, otherwise it would all have been spoiled.

I don't know how long we continued to believe in

Father Christmas, but it got to the point where I knew but saw no reason to stop pretending. It was Mum who ended it one year by saying, 'You don't believe in him, surely?' And that was that.

The one thing that never changed at Christmas was watching *It's a Wonderful Life*, the Frank Capra film with James Stewart. The original was made in black and white in 1946 but a 'colorized' version came out in 1989, when Jody and I were ten. So from then on every Christmas Eve, Dad would say, 'And now it's time for *It's a Wonderful Life* in colour.' And for years and years, that's what we thought it was called: *It's a Wonderful Life in Colour*! At the end of the film George Bailey – James Stewart – isn't sure if he's dreaming or not, and he looks in his pocket for two petals his six-year-old daughter Zuzu had given him. And there they are . . .! The little girl playing Zuzu looked just like Jo when she was that age, and every time I see it – and I still watch it every year – it gets me crying for all the right reasons: family, Christmases and the power of love to change things for the better. That film played such an important role in our lives that when Jody's third daughter was born, that's what they called her: Zuzu.

But Christmas 1992 was different to any other. Johanna Young, a girl a year above us at school, was murdered. She went missing on 23 December and they found her dead on Boxing Day. She was fourteen.

We knew of her, but she wasn't a friend. She lived directly opposite the school, just before the turning to the Green. She was last seen walking off towards the High

Street at about half past seven but it was really cold so nobody saw her after that, so nobody knows for sure where she went or what she did. She had just split up with her boyfriend, or rather her boyfriend had just split up with her, and her parents thought she had been going to see him because she hadn't told them that it was over. They didn't realise she was missing until the next morning, Christmas Eve, when her alarm went off for her paper round. Her bed hadn't been slept in and the bag she carried the newspapers in was still hanging on the back of her bedroom door. They phoned all her friends just to make sure, but eventually they had to call the police. Her body wasn't found until three days later, half-naked, in a flooded clay pit down a track not even a mile away.

Once the news got out the press descended. There were plenty of kids around who were happy to talk, the kids who lived by the Green, and hung around Chockies, Dens Cafe and Gateway. Dad kept us away as much as he could, but he couldn't protect us completely. I started not going out after dusk, convinced I was going to be murdered, convinced that the murderer was somewhere around . . . just waiting.

Every day the school bus turned into the school gates just past her house, and every day we would all fall silent. You could see her Christmas presents piled up in the window and it was so, so sad. Nobody said anything but none of us would ever forget.

There was never a trial. No one was ever arrested. Everyone in school said they knew who had done it. I never knew the name, or – if I did – I have forgotten, but it was someone she knew, who lots of people knew. This wasn't a murder in the Sherlock Holmes or Agatha Christie sense. No one set out to do it. No one stood to gain anything by Johanna's death. She wasn't raped. She wasn't attacked. That's why it was never solved, because there was no motive and without a motive, where do you start? It was about bored kids with nowhere to go and nothing to do and things going tragically wrong.

Since that dreadful week in 1990 when Grandad died Mum had felt increasingly unhappy in East Wretham. 'Everything bad happened when we were at that house,' she used to say. 'We lost Grandad, we lost Reggie.' And in fact a few months later Mum's oldest sister, Ivy, also died. But it wasn't only that Lane End had so many sad memories, it was also very isolated and, with Dad away so much, Mum would get very lonely. We did have some neighbours by then, an older couple who'd moved into one of the other new houses, Mr and Mrs Roeder, parents of Glenn Roeder who played football for Newcastle. Glenn Roeder was a great friend of Gazza's and we were always asking Mr and Mrs Roeder to ask Glenn to get us Gazza's autograph. They did better than that. They got us a pair of signed tracksuit bottoms! We tried to wear them but they were so big we'd trip up and fall over.

Great Hockham had been the kind of place where neighbours knocked on your door just to have a chat. Mum had worked at the playschool for years and so she knew all the young mums who brought their kids in. She was naturally friendly and outgoing, so being cut off from all that didn't help. In terms of isolation, it wasn't much better for Jody and me. In Great Hockham there were loads of kids our age. In East Wretham there were two boys, who occasionally used to come and stay with their grandad who lived in the house behind ours and sometimes I would clamber through the hedges and ask them to play, but not once we went to secondary school. Then there was Hannah Denty who got on the bus at the same stop. As she lived the other side of the main road, which we weren't allowed to cross on our own, we'd end up just talking on the phone, even though her house was probably no more than two hundred yards away. We phoned so often I can still remember her number: Thetford 8808.

It wasn't so bad for Paul. He had his bike, and in the evenings after work he'd play football. But the older we got the more difficult it was to live so far away from our friends, and doing things after school always involved Mum coming to pick us up. Even so, Jo and I were never lonely in the way Mum was lonely because we always had each other.

By 1993, when we were around fourteen, Mum and Dad made the decision to move back to Great Hockham. But the chances of finding what they wanted seemed nearly impossible. Dad wanted to build his own house. He wanted a decent-sized garden. In Great Hockham. He put the word out and within days the impossible happened. A friend told him about a building plot for sale right on the village green. It had been the kitchen garden of a big house and was owned by an old boy called Townie Warren, who was mostly famous for ill-treating his dog.

Within two weeks they'd bought it. Dad's plan was to build a house that was modern inside but looked like a traditional cottage outside. Inevitably the whole process took for ever. First it had to be designed – Dad and Mum did it themselves and got a guy to draw it up for planning. Then they had to sell Lane End. Everything seemed to be on course when the buyer pulled out at the last minute. Luckily Nanny Ivy came to the rescue and lent Dad enough so he could make a start right away.

The place had always been a bit of a mystery to us because there was no gate or entrance from the road and it was surrounded by an old brick-and-flint wall about five foot high – too high to see over. One Sunday Dad asked us if we wanted to help him break in – he owned it by then – so we literally took part of this wall down, being very careful to save all the bricks and stones because everything was going to be reused, Dad said. And it was amazing to see inside after all these years of just walking past and never imagining that one day it would be ours. Dad called it 'a little paradise'.

'More like a wilderness,' I muttered to Jo, as we waded through the undergrowth in our wellingtons. It was totally overgrown, all trees and bluebells, and the vegetable patch was knee-high with weeds. Over the next year we watched the house grow, layer by layer. First the foundations, then working out what room was what. The builder was an old man called Mr Thetford who worked with his son, and Mum and Dad did a lot of it themselves. Suddenly everything in the garden looked rosy.

As that part of Norfolk was so sparsely populated, Wayland had a huge catchment area and took kids from all kinds of backgrounds. There were the cool ones who hung around the Green and mostly lived on the council estate, but there were also some who came from well-off families like Chris Gulliver and his brother James. They lived halfway between Watton and Great Hockham in a house that was so big it even had an indoor swimming pool.

Chris Gulliver was one of the naughtiest boys in the school. One particular teacher – I'll call him Mr Atkinson – couldn't keep order so we regularly got away with murder. Once you got him talking, he didn't know how to stop. So somebody would say, 'Please, Mr Atkinson, tell us about your home life / your dog / your thoughts about Aristotle . . .' and off he'd go like a wind-up train, on and on until he ran out of steam, and then we'd simply ask another question and he'd be off again.

One day Chris Gulliver and James Tanner hid in the book cupboard. Everyone in the class knew they were there, but poor Mr Atkinson didn't have a clue. He was a really nice man and I don't know why we made his life such a misery. Anyway, when he noticed that these two boys were missing he asked where they were.

'In the sickroom, Mr Atkinson,' a voice piped up.

'What, both of them?'

And then of course we started giggling. Then somebody's hand quickly went up: 'Please, Mr Atkinson, could you tell us about . . .' Just to get the ball rolling. It was only right at the end of the lesson, after about an hour, that there was a sudden crash and the door of the book cupboard flew open . . . Mr Atkinson was more shocked than angry, and he just stood there scratching his head as if he were mulling over some deep philosophical problem.

'Well, I can't believe you were in there the whole time.'

They both got a detention obviously. But so did I. First it was just a giggle, which turned into a laugh, until I was laughing so hard I fell off my chair. I just couldn't stop, and the whole place was in uproar. It wasn't the first time it'd happened. Something would set me off and then I'd be finished, and I'd just laugh and laugh and laugh. So it would be, 'OUT! DETENTION!' and I'd stagger from the classroom, my hand clapped over my mouth, tears streaming down my face, collapse in the corridor and the noise would echo around the entire school like some demented demon.

Around this point in my less-than-brilliant school career I started dancing. There were six of us and we called ourselves Funkin' Up. Like most other little girls, Jo and I had done funny junior ballet classes with a woman called Miss Fiona – I don't even know if she was a proper ballet teacher. Then, when we got to Wayland, we'd gone to a proper dancing academy once a week after school. Jo was much better than me, and we were about to do our first exam when Mum pulled me into the kitchen and said, 'Don't be upset if Jo gets higher grades than you.' And she did. But it only made me work harder. Then after about two years, Jo got bored and gave up. But I carried on. Although I was much older than the other girls in the class, who'd started when they were about eight, I loved it.

So we got this little club together, like a proper dance troupe, and we'd make up routines. We'd rehearse in our lunch hour or after school when we could, and then once they were perfect we'd perform them in assembly to the rest of the school. Finally here was something I really enjoyed and was good at. Even better, other kids would come up and say: 'You're very good!' Including boys! Suddenly I wasn't this annoying girl with stick-thin legs who everybody laughed at.

That's when I started going out with Paul Outlaw. We didn't 'go out' in any real sense of the word, but he was now 'my boyfriend', which meant that we'd go off and kiss at the end of the school field. Paul was one of the cool kids who used to hang out on the Green. And then, guess what, after three years of totally ignoring me Lee Charlton – the blond boy with the curtain hair I'd had a crush on since I first clapped eyes on him – started hovering around saying things like 'I really like you.'

'Well, I have a boyfriend now . . .'

It took me two days to decide what to do, and then I dumped Paul and started going out with Lee. Paul wasn't that bothered. He was good-looking and he was funny and all the girls fancied him. And then something really strange happened. After only a few days of going out with Lee it was 'OH NO!' It had taken me three years of misery, three years of being laughed at, three years of driving myself crazy with thoughts of him, imagining him and me together, imagining that it would be amazing and that we'd be together for the rest of our lives. And now ... Bub-feelings!

It was surprisingly easy to tell him I wasn't interested and not long after he started going out with Jo. It wasn't the first time Jo and I had dated the same boy. We must have been about six when Darren Green said he wanted to marry us – both of us. So that afternoon, after we'd had our tea, we met him under the oak tree in the field where Pepsi the donkey lived and we got married. The ceremony was very simple from what I can remember, and certainly solemn. But when it came to putting the rings on – obviously the most important part of the proceedings – they turned out to be too big, so we put them on our thumbs. One was a gold band, and the other had a sparkly green stone, which was the one I got. It was an emerald Darren said, and we were suitably impressed, because naturally we'd seen *The Wizard of Oz*.

Later that evening we were up in our bedroom when the doorbell rang and Mum called out: 'Jody! Caroline!' She never called us by our full names except when she was cross. So down we went. Standing on the doormat was Mrs Green, Darren's mum ...

'Did Darren give you any rings?' Mum asked. One look at our faces told her Yes. Mrs Green's expression changed from worry, to relief, to extremely cross at which point we ran upstairs to fetch them. I hate to think what punishment was meted out to poor Darren when his mother got home . . .

Until I met Mark Balaam I didn't know what love was. Forget Lee Charlton . . . Mark was seventeen, two years older than me and he'd already left school. I knew him by sight because he used to hang around outside the school gates and talk to the cool kids and show off his blue Escort while me and Jo would get on the bus . . . He was absolutely beautiful – curly dark hair and a bit of a beard going on. I mean, how grown up is that!

He worked on the waltzers when the fair came into town and I thought he was a hundred per cent the greatest thing on Planet Earth. The fair was a big bone of contention between us and our parents because we were never allowed to go, but we kept hoping that at some point they would relent. And finally one year – about 1994 – they did. So we got all dressed up and were really excited to finally have some social life. And it was everything we hoped it would be. We wandered around mesmerised by the colours, the music, everyone milling around, all the rides, the stalls with the gaudy prizes, like over-sized Day-Glo teddy bears and goldfish. It was just magical. We were just standing beside the swing chairs that went round and round on chains, waiting for our turn, when Clifford Jones, a boy in our class, threw up, high in the air and his sick came hurtling down and landed all over me.

At least it gave me something to talk about, and the next thing I knew Mark Balaam was asking me out! When I told Mum she went mad. It was, 'No, NO, NO!' How unfair was that, given I'd confided in her?

'You're too young.'

'But, Mum, I'm fifteen!'

'You're too young!'

I didn't care what she thought. This was L.O.V.E. and I would secretly see him at lunchtimes, and on afternoons when Jo and I were rehearsing for Funkin' Up (which meant we didn't have to get the bus, which gave us a whole half an hour of social life before we went back to Wretham) we would wander along to Dens Cafe (pronounced caff) where Mark and his friends would hang out. The first time we ventured in, there was this really strong smell and Jo said, 'Is that tea?' Neither of us had any idea what it was, while Watton's local hoods hissed: 'Shut Up, Shut Up!'

I took to forging doctors' notes in my mum's name, because her signature was easy to copy, which was so naughty but I was in love and what else was I to do? Then one lunchtime Mark said, 'Come round and see me at my mum's tonight.' I knew where he lived, down an alley off the High Street. I asked Mum if I could see some friends after school, then went to Mark's house instead. We were just settling down when the doorbell rang. He looked out of the window, opened the door, said something I didn't hear, then came back in, picked up my things and handed them to me. 'Sorry,' he said. 'I don't want to go out with you any more.' Then he led me out, got in this car and drove away.

It all happened so quickly. One moment we were in his lounge having a smooch, the next minute I was on the pavement having my first break-up. I was devastated. All I could think of was finding my brother. He had recently moved to Watton, sharing with a friend, so I walked to his flat, my face streaming with tears, knocked on his door and the friend answered. Paul wasn't there. But the friend called him. And then Paul called my mum and she came to pick me up and I told her everything. She wasn't angry, which I thought she would be, she was just lovely and took me home and I lay on my front on the green sofa in the little room and sobbed until Saturday.

'Just remember, Carrie,' she said. 'That you're never going to feel this bad again. The first one is always the hardest.'

What a lie that was.

But for our big sister Liz the forever-after dream had come true. Liz and Leigh were now getting married! And guess who she was having as bridesmaids!

Our dresses were made by Leigh's cousin Ingrid, and they were royal blue, the nearest she could get to the Tottenham colours. One of Liz's great tragedies caused by moving from Enfield to Great Hockham was not going to White Hart Lane any more. The whole family on both sides had always been Spurs fans, and she had no shortage of people to take her, Dad, Grandad, uncles, aunts – in fact the whole family was football mad except me. I never did understand the attraction.

Although I had been to a few weddings before, they were Greek weddings because Mum's best friend was Greek (half the people she knew in Enfield seemed to be Greek). This was my first traditional English wedding and it was lovely. It was held at Wretham church, at the end of the little road opposite Lane End. It was a celebration but it was also goodbye to the house because by now it had been sold, and on 4 May, the day of the wedding, we only had two days left before we had to move out. Most of the furniture had already been put in store, just leaving the beds and the fridge. It had been a late spring that year so we filled the house with daffodils – boxes and boxes of them – which we picked ourselves, one of Jo's and my holiday jobs. There was a marquee in the garden, but in fact the weather was beautiful and we didn't really need it. There must have been two hundred people – us, Mum's family, including Nanny Flo – and Leigh's family as well as all Liz and Leigh's friends. Leigh was a brilliant guitar player and he had his own band, and so the band played and it was brilliant. Poor Jo missed most of it because she got drunk on champagne. We were still only sixteen so officially underage but a friend of ours was running the bar . . . My main memory of the day is seeing her sprawled out on a bed upstairs, dead to the world. Even by then I had a much better 'head' for drinking than Jo. She once got so drunk with her friend Sue Freeman that we had to pretend that she had food poisoning. How Mum didn't smell the Bacardi on her breath, I'll never know.

I think Mum was a complete innocent, probably because she got married so young. But although we were naughty – I mean I obviously shouldn't have forged her signature – we never got into serious trouble. Jo and I were naughty only so that we could have fun; we'd never have done anything to be nasty. Dad would say to us: 'If you're going to do anything bad, think about how me and your mother would feel about it before you do it.' And we did.

Drugs for example. While they were hardly unknown at our school we never got involved, though I did once have a drag on somebody else's spliff, and all it did was make me cough. I was staying at my friend Helen's house, not long before Liz's wedding, and the next day I was back in my bedroom going through my CDs because we were packing everything up, when Mum walked in and peered at me and said, 'You've got bloodshot eyes.'

Two days after Liz's wedding Jo and I were in ecstasy. We were moving to Watton! As the new house wouldn't be ready until September, Mum and Dad had rented a flat just off the High Street, right in the centre of town. Near all our friends! And there were even pubs! Even though we weren't old enough to drink, we could still play pool and just hang out with the cool kids and do all the things we had never been allowed to do.

Our euphoria didn't last long. We'd lived so long with this idea of bumping into friends spontaneously and saying

'Let's do this!' or 'Let's do that!' – because we knew that's what everyone else did. All that freedom and just mooching around! But the place was dead. It was such an anticlimax. Where were the visitors to give it a bit of life? Nowhere. Because why would anyone want to go there? The coast was miles away. The Broads were miles away. As for local culinary specialities, you had a choice between the Wayland Sausage or the Wayland Bap. Watton's main claim to fame is that Wayland Wood is said to be where the Babes in the Wood fairy tale actually happened, where the wicked aunt and uncle paid some villain to murder their niece and nephew. The two little orphans escaped by hiding themselves under some leaves, but they died anyway, presumably from exposure, so not exactly a crowd-puller.

We made the best of it. At least we could go out at night. Not officially, of course. Officially we always had to be in by ten to eleven, and we were. Our rule was always Be Good and Keep the Parents Happy. So we would wait till they were asleep and one of us would sneak back out again while the other one would stay awake so she could open the door to let them back in. And we'd go round to boys' houses, or go back to the caff. We were very fair and took it in turns: one night Jo would go out, one night me. But whenever I went out I was terrified. By this time it would be really late at night and there was always the chance that I'd be murdered . . .

That summer, after we finished school, six of us went off on our first holiday without our parents. That was the idea, anyway, but in fact Mum and Dad wouldn't let Jody and me go on our own, so then all the mums decided to come and they ended up renting somewhere just two miles away 'in case anything goes wrong'. There were six of us, Sarah, Donna, Naomi, Heidi, Jo and me and we had an apartment by the sea just south of Newquay not far from Holywell and the caravan park where we'd missed out on the competitions. It was summer 1996 at the height of Britpop, when Oasis and Blur were fighting it out for control of the charts. But we were into Ocean Colour Scene because they were far more cool. The weather was hot and we wore crop tops, hipster shorts and we'd go down to the beach carrying a ghetto blaster and play it full volume. In fact we'd take it everywhere, even in the streets. We played the same song over and over again, 'The Day We Caught The Train'. We weren't planning to win the popularity contest. I remember it was the first time Jo and I ever argued over a boy. We had been to a nightclub called Berties and met some proper lads.

All through that last term, the big question had loomed. What next? Wayland didn't run to a sixth form. The previous summer we had done work experience and Jo had spent two weeks in an old people's home just off the Green. I'd worked in a photography studio, which I absolutely loved, learning all about printing and developing. But just as Jo knew she wasn't going to spend her life being a carer, I knew I wasn't going to be a photographer. I wanted to be a performer, to do musical theatre, like *Grease* or *Phantom of the Opera* or *Cats*. But how?

I knew about stage schools, but what chance did

someone like me have of getting into one of those? Places like Italia Conti and Sylvia Young, you went there when you were about ten. Then there was Anna Scher, where half the cast of *EastEnders* started – and that was mainly for people who lived in Islington. And what experience could I claim to have? Back legs of a donkey? Coming second in a caravan-park talent competition when I was thirteen? Funkin' Up? As for showbiz connections, well that was easy. My mum had an uncle who had been a doorman at the London Palladium . . .

And even if by some miracle I did get in, stage schools were private. Mum had looked into it and when Dad saw how much money was involved he put his foot down. After all, he said, I was only sixteen and there was no way I was going to live in London on my own. Then two girls in my class told me about a place called Bodywork Dance Studio in Cambridge. It focused on dance and musical theatre. Perfect! And Cambridge wasn't that far – about forty-five minutes by train from Thetford. It wasn't London but it wasn't Watton either.

Mum applied and got me an audition. The instructions were very specific: I had to wear a black leotard and pink tights. Pink tights? In Watton? We found a pair of white tights, put some Ribena in the washing machine and hey presto!

On the day I was so nervous. All the other girls – and I can only remember seeing girls – looked so professional, with their hair up in ballerina buns and netting, and there was I in blackcurrant tights . . .

For the audition I had to choreograph my own dance, sing something and read a monologue. I sang 'Love Letters', by Ketty Lester, one of Mum's favourites that she was always singing about the house. I can't have done too badly because I got in. When we got the letter Mum and I both burst into tears. She then called them up and asked about grants. They were sorry, they said, but they only had one scholarship and that had already gone.

So I went from this enormous high to the depths of despair. Dad said he'd heard about a BTech Arts course at Bury St Edmunds Technical College. He was adamant. I had to try that first. 'You never know, Carrie, you might love it.'

I hated it. I stuck it for two whole days but I absolutely hated it and they all hated me. And when I got home I just wept and wept and wept.

We had now moved into the new house on the Green, called Hazelgrove. I should have been happy to be back in Great Hockham, with Nanny Ivy down the road and friends to catch up with. But it couldn't have been worse. From Carly and Emma, the twins with the corkscrew hair who'd lived opposite and who'd gone to Thetford Grammar, to Anne at the post office and various of Mum's friends, everyone saying: 'So what are you going to do now then, Caroline?'

And for the first time in my life I didn't have Jo. She had opted to do A levels in Norwich, at the City College – media studies and history. Term had already started. Dad would drive her up to Norwich most days when he went to work but if he was travelling around she'd stay at Liz's.

Meanwhile Mum was going on to Dad about Bodywork, and how it was a really nice family atmosphere run by a husband-and-wife team called Patrick Kerr and Theresa Confrey, and when Dad heard their names he stopped in his tracks and said, 'I know them!'

'What, you mean you actually know them, Dad?'

'No. I mean I know who they are. They used to do those dances on *Ready Steady Go!*'

Ready Steady Go! was *the* TV music show in the sixties and Dad had always said how much better it was than *Top of the Pops*. Every so often, he explained, new dances would come along – like the Hully Gully, or the Locomotion or the Watusi ... (don't ask) and the girls and boys in the studio would learn them live on air, and Patrick Kerr and Theresa Confrey were brilliant teachers, Dad said. 'Back in the day, they were as famous as Pan's People.'

'If only it wasn't quite so much,' Mum said. 'I mean, at a stretch we could probably manage half.'

Mum called Bodywork again, and this time spoke to Patrick and asked if there was anything they could do to help. Could we pay in instalments for example? I will forever be in his debt because out of the blue he told Mum that they could probably manage half a bursary ...

The weekend I left home for good, Jo was there and Dad put on a CD of Cat Stevens's *Tea for the Tillerman* and played us one of the tracks. It was his message to us, he said, and he asked us to listen carefully to the words. The song was called 'Wild World'. I'd heard it before – it had a very catchy chorus that we would sing along to – but until now I'd never understood what it meant. And if you listen, it's all there – about how Dad knew we had to go and start new lives without him, that he didn't want us to be sad or bad, but that we should know it was dangerous out there – the 'wild world' of the title – but that we should never forget we would always be his little girls.

5

Cambridge

The Bodywork Dance Studio was based in a former furniture warehouse in Glisson Road, about five minutes' walk from Cambridge railway station. For the first few days Mum drove me, but after that I went on my own. Mum would take me to Thetford, then I'd get the train to Ely, then from Ely to Cambridge. It took for ever; by the time I'd walked to the station and waited for the connection it was about an hour and a half each way.

I was by far the youngest in the college – everyone else had done A levels – and it wasn't only academically that I lagged behind; most of the girls were at performance standard the minute they started whereas I'd had no proper training at all. So I was put with a few other near-beginners in a foundation group to learn the basics, and from then on it was a matter of sheer hard work. Ballet all morning, a bit of jazz in the afternoons as well as drama and singing – it was gruelling, but I absolutely loved it – I would work and work and work and work. I was determined not to let Patrick down. I knew that he had really pushed for me. I knew that without him giving me that bursary I wouldn't be there.

One group of girls were really protective from the start, took me under their wing and really looked after me. They treated me like their little sister probably because – although I was sixteen – I looked about ten and they were much older than me anyway. Then, in the second or third week, one of them came up and said that she and three others had found a house and there was a box room going spare and would I like it?

The other girls were Debbie Jennings, Claire Winsborough, Anna Marcel and Bernadette Woodford and together they'd rented this five-bedroomed house just inside the ring road. With Cambridge being a university town, student accommodation was in short supply so they were lucky to get it, they said, and although it was a long way out, there were regular buses going down Histon Road into the centre.

Seven Pelham Court was a modern, eighties Lego-house masquerading as a Tudor cottage and when they said the last room was a box room they weren't joking. There was a single mattress on the floor and that was it. We all moved in on the same day, Mum and Dad brought me and my stuff down from Hazelgrove where I'd only lived for a few weeks. When we got there they were horrified at what £50 a week rent would get you in Cambridge and felt really sorry for me because everyone else's rooms were lovely.

'Look, we don't think Caroline should pay the same rent as the other girls,' said Mum when all the parents were downstairs discussing the practicalities of bills etc. 'It's just not fair.' So they all trooped upstairs to have a look and agreed. For a few minutes I wished the floor would open up and I could disappear, but thanks to Mum, I got a big discount which I would never have had the nerve to ask for myself.

Meeting up with these girls was just the most incredible stroke of luck because they were amazing fun and completely got my sense of humour. Not everyone at college was like that – there were girls who could be quite bitchy and competitive – but this was like the gang you always wanted to join, and never thought you would. And now I was one of them! To be honest I was just happy to be there, doing what I wanted to do, and to have these girls as my friends was a huge bonus. I would go on and on about them to Jo when we talked on the phone. 'You have to meet them,' I said. 'They are just so great. They don't take the mick, they don't laugh at anyone, they're just fun girls with no strings, no underlying motives, no agenda. Jo, you'll love them.'

So Jo got the train and came down, and the one thing I was determined to do was to go to a pub and have fun, just because we had never really done that in Watton, at least not to drink because everyone there knew we were underage. Here it was different. The girls were all much older and could get us in without any questions being asked.

The Blue Boar was in the centre of Cambridge, near the river and the colleges, but it wasn't a touristy place, and we started drinking Blue Lagoons, which I'd just discovered, a mixture of vodka, curaçao and lemonade. It tasted just like lemonade so it was easy to get really drunk, really quickly. And we did.

It was late when we toddled out, and the street was pretty much empty when I spotted a builder's van that had a ladder leading up to the top. A ladder? Ladders are for climbing, aren't they? So up I went and once on the roof, I started tap dancing. I wasn't really a big fan of tap but the noise reverberated rather spectacularly on the metal roof and it was like 'Look at me! I'm a dancer! I'm a performer! I'm at stage school! Look what I can do!' By the time I clambered down there was just me, Jo, Debbie and another friend from college called Bianca. Then we said goodbye to Bianca and the three of us set off to walk to Pelham Court, winding rather woozily up Histon Road in the hope that a bus might show up or we might be able to hitch a ride because it was a really long way. I mean miles. So when we saw a van coming Jo jokingly flagged it down – we didn't think for a moment that it would stop. To our amazement it did! We told the driver where we were headed and he was like 'OK. In the back.' And then we were off.

There were no proper seats, so as the van lurched this way and that, we were being thrown about and laughing like mad until finally it came to a standstill and the driver opened the doors and we tumbled out. But where were we? Where was the little front garden? Where was the horrible front door? This wasn't Pelham Court ... It turned out we'd flagged down a police van and they'd taken us to the local nick. Although I hadn't done any serious damage with my aerial tap dance the owner had seen us wandering off, called the police and given them our description. They probably couldn't believe their luck when Jo flagged them down ...

Just like in films we were allowed one phone call, so we called Bianca to tell her we'd been arrested and to have a good laugh because we were still really drunk.

When they led us to the cells, it was like 'What?' We still didn't realise what had happened because we were so drunk on Blue Lagoons. I was wearing a catsuit and Buffalo boots, chunky Spice Girl-type trainers, and they made me take them off in case I tried to tie the laces together and strangle myself...

I remember opening the little shutter in the door and Debbie was in the cell opposite.

'Debbie, what are we doing in here?'

Silence.

The 'bed' – more like a bench you might get in a doctor's surgery – was hard and the only thing to keep you warm was a thin blanket with holes in it and I remember being so cold.

I had no idea where I was. I only knew I had to be sick, and there was just this toilet in the corner ...

It didn't feel real until we woke up in the morning – 'Oh God.'

Dad was not pleased, he said, to get a call from the police saying, 'Excuse me, sir, but we've got your daughters in custody . . .'

Two weeks later we appeared in court. Mum cried and the judge said, 'They are obviously very young and they made a big mistake.'

'That's it,' Mum said afterwards. 'You've had your chance, Caroline. It's time to come back home.'

'Please, Mum, it was just one mistake, you heard the judge. I'll never do it again.' And she knew really. She knew we weren't bad girls. We were just stupid. In fact the whole thing was pretty stupid. Dad was much more sanguine. His attitude was, 'If that's the worst that happens to them, they'll be all right.'

I think we went a bit wild that night because we'd been cooped up all our lives, and so the first time we were out together, the two of us, like normal kids, just having fun, we went a bit mental . . .

It was an awful experience. But I learnt three lessons: 1) don't mix your drinks – or even better, don't drink. 2) look after yourself. 3) the urine/vomit combo is not great if you can't flush it away.

I don't think there was anyone at Bodywork who didn't have a job. Cambridge had massive numbers of tourists, who all needed feeding, but undergraduates at the university weren't allowed to work during term time, which meant less competition for us. All those cheap eateries were always looking for staff which was how I ended up at Pizzaland.

It was my first proper job and I loved the people there and because I'd just left home they became my family and when it closed I cried because I didn't want to go anywhere else. But by that time the other girls were all working at Pizza Hut so when somebody left they persuaded me to join them. It was in the centre of town, about five minutes' walk from college so it was really easy. But dancing most of the day then being on your feet all evening was hard.

Shortly after New Year the Pelham Court landlord gave us notice to quit. I still don't know how or why it happened, but in fact he did us a huge favour. Only a couple of weeks later a friend of Patrick and Theresa's who'd renovated a big Victorian house in Rock Road just the other side of the station, asked whether it might be of interest to any of their students and we couldn't believe our luck.

Although it was expensive, it was huge and ramshackle, just like *Fawlty Towers*, with enough space for twelve. Best of all it was much closer than Pelham Court – you could walk to the Bodywork studio in about fifteen minutes. Basically it was a house full of bedsits with each room having its own shower with a hob next to it. We had one payphone in the lobby but we soon worked out that if we just plugged a normal phone into the socket, we could make calls for free. You just had to make sure that whenever the landlord came round the payphone was plugged in and there was no sign of the other one.

On the ground floor there was me, Theresa, Debbie, Nikki and Bryony. On the first floor were Claire, Bianca, Debbie (another Debbie), Sasha and Joe. On the floor above that were Karen and Paul.

One of the new girls – Nikki – was incredibly glamorous. She had a footballer boyfriend and was never short of money and we were totally in awe of her because she had a car and even a Gucci watch!

Question: how many people can you get into a Peugeot 206? Answer: eight: Me, Debbie, Bianca, Theresa, Bryony, Nikki, Paul, Sasha. How we were never stopped by the police I don't know. But Nikki used to drive us everywhere whenever we went out.

Everything was a squash in those days. It was never just the twelve of us in Rock Road, there'd always be people staying over. As for our clothes, all we needed for college was our dance gear and leg warmers, everything else we shared – Nikki's clothes, of course, being the most sought after.

Nikki always looked incredible whatever she was wearing and, while we were really struggling – juggling classes with working at Pizza Hut – she got away with one shift at PizzaExpress. We'd see her sashaying through the house looking amazing in all her finery pushing Monza, the bike we all shared, on her way to work.

We were the naughtiest bunch, always getting up to mischief, but at the same time we all worked really hard.

We never had days off. But I remember once we were all on the same shift one night and none of us wanted to go and work. So we hired a punt, capsized it on purpose, then all fell in, just so we could all call in sick to Pizza Hut. We even made it to the local radio because Bianca looked like Marilyn Monroe. So it was 'Marilyn Monroe lookalike falls in river'.

Looking back I don't know where we found all that energy, because we would stay awake for days without really going to bed, just napping in between classes or during lunch breaks on the sofas, or we'd run home and nap between college and going to work. And yet, at the same time, I had never felt so fit in my life. At school I'd never really done sport, so all that training was doing what it was supposed to do, and building up stamina. Most of us had no money so we'd just fill up with beans or grab something from the canteen. The fallback was pizza, because at some point, you'd always get a pizza because of where you worked. So when Nikki said the pizzas at PizzaExpress were nicer, we all moved over there.

Those years were the best years of my life, and we all felt the same. We never had any money or sleep but we managed to go out and get drunk every night.

But it was really hard work. In the morning I was always tired and, as the classes started with ballet, you had to be ready and warmed up by nine o'clock. I wasn't a ballerina and I had had no real training and the teacher was really strict. Although some teachers would come up from London, the core was Theresa, Patrick and their daughters

Jane and Emma. Lucy, their other daughter, did all the admin. So it felt like you were part of a family and that brings responsibilities, or that's what I felt anyway.

Leaving home had been hard, but leaving Jo was harder. We would talk on the phone and sometimes she would come down – and occasionally I would go up to see her in Norwich (there were more boys in Norwich, there were only four at Bodywork) but it wasn't the same. She was much more in touch with the family than I was. Before she passed her driving test she would often stay the night at Liz's who was glad of the company because by now she was pregnant with her first baby which was expected in April.

On the first day of March I was doing a ballet class, really pushing myself and dripping with sweat when I was called out. A personal phone call, Lucy said. It was Jo. Liz had gone into labour early, the baby – a little boy called Max – had been born that morning but it wasn't looking good.

I had the quickest shower I have ever had in my life, and just ran to the station and took the first train up to Norwich. I met Jo at the hospital in the mother and baby unit and we just hugged. Liz was OK, she said, but the baby was in an incubator and probably wouldn't make it through the night.

I remember Jo and me looking at each other and then saying, 'Nothing matters.' We'd never had this feeling before. We used to moan about so much, but actually nothing matters.

It was the first time in my life that I'd ever experienced

genuine worry. Life-and-death worry. As I had a cold, I didn't want to go too close to the incubator. But I was allowed to look at him and he was so, so tiny. It was just heartbreaking. How could something so small hope to survive? Obviously I knew about premature babies but I had never seen one before, never properly realised just how tiny they were, with huge great tubes coming out making him look even smaller . . . he looked so vulnerable and you knew you could do nothing.

Liz says that that night she didn't sleep. They had put her in a room on her own, and she just lay there watching the minute hand move around the clock. Then, she says, she felt this overwhelming feeling of peace come over her. She had always been very close to Grandad, and she sensed him with her, and that everything was going to be all right. And she phoned Nanny Ivy first thing in the morning and told her.

Max was so, so tiny. Even when he was allowed out of the incubator, he fitted in the palm of one of Dad's hands. So yes, Liz was right, and he was fine. Is fine. Although he's still very pale – when he was little and running about the beach I used to call him Caspar the Ghost – and he's a lovely, lovely lad just about to start university.

By now I had a boyfriend. He was much older than me – thirty-two, while I was seventeen – and his name was Stuart Banks. He was a DJ and promoter and he used to run the clubs that the girls took me to. I think that his family was Portuguese and he had the loveliest skin and he made me laugh and I fell head over heels in love. It was because of Stuart that I got the only double room in Rock Road, on the ground floor overlooking the garden, which was ironic really as, in all the time we went out together, I don't think he ever came back. The bad news was that the rent was higher . . .

I'd only been at PizzaExpress for about a month when someone told me about an opening at Browns. Not as a waitress, this time, but as a seater.

Browns at that time was the best restaurant in Cambridge. It was directly opposite the Fitzwilliam Museum, the big art gallery with exhibitions that people would come up from London to see. And whenever something was happening at the university, and the parents came up, it would be full to bursting.

It was so much nicer being a seater than being a waitress. You didn't have to do any food or remember who ordered what, you just had to sit people down and hand them a menu. So, 'Table for four? This way . . .'

The end-of-year show was always the big one, always so emotional. It's the culmination of so much hard work – not just the show itself, the hours of rehearsals for that, but the entire year – and in the case of a third of students, the work of three years.

The college didn't have a theatre of its own but we mainly used the Mumford Theatre, which was part of the Anglia Polytechnic University (now Anglia Ruskin University), Cambridge's other university. It was just round the corner from the studio, behind Parker's Piece, a kind of common where, when it was sunny, we would go and sit on the grass. The show was basically to demonstrate what you could do, and it was often quite long but I'd make Mum and Dad and even Jo sit through them anyway. Dad had decided I must be doing quite well because I'd get put in the front. He didn't realise I was only there because I was good at smiling, and behind me I'd hear the girls say, 'But she's not even doing it right!' The truth was I was never as good as the others.

That first year, the summer of 1997, I had never done an end-of-year show before, so I didn't know what to expect. But suddenly, when the applause had died down and we were just standing there on the stage, Patrick held up his arms for hush. He was pleased to announce, he said, that the Sally Crowther Memorial Scholarship had been awarded to Caroline Flack. My ears began to buzz and I couldn't hear, as the girls around me were smiling and some came over and kissed me. I knew I had tears in my eyes.

Sally Crowther had had no direct connection with Bodywork, but her friend Chris Bond was a friend of Theresa and Patrick's and a huge supporter of what they were trying to do. Sally had been big fan of dance and the arts generally and when she passed away her friend had decided to put a scholarship in her name and I will be eternally grateful to both of them.

Once term ended that first summer, most people drifted home, but I stayed on at Rock Road as I still had the rent to pay. However, with no early morning classes to force myself out of bed for, it felt like a holiday anyway. By then Nikki had left PizzaExpress and had come to work on the door at Browns as well, and once term started again all the girls came, one by one, until it was pretty nearly just us. So if it wasn't busy, we'd just gossip and once they were closed we'd sit in the bar. At £50 a week my rent was higher than the other girls so I had to work hard and while the hourly rate was more as a seater, you didn't get tips. At least now I didn't have to wear a uniform. As long as it was all black and smart I could dress how I liked. So I used to wear really tight flared trousers and a black vest. To add a bit of height I wore Buffalo boots but they were completely covered by the flares which practically reached the floor.

I was still only seventeen but my circle of friends was growing wider and wider. I got to know some because they worked in the restaurant, such as Elly, who started as a seater but then decided to be a waitress because you got tips. I still keep up with her. She became a chef and now runs her own cafe in Bath and is about to publish her own cookbook.

Most students from Bodywork wanted to work in musical theatre, musicals was the dream and the ultimate goal was the West End. And that's what I thought I'd end up doing. That's what I wanted to do. I had grown up with musicals, from *Calamity Jane* (good ol' Doris Day) onwards. In 1995 we'd seen two shows in one weekend. Dad had come home and said, 'I've got the biggest surprise ever!'

And I was thinking, Oh my God, it's a karaoke machine! Then he said, 'We're going to the West End!' and Jo and I weren't that impressed because we didn't know what 'West End' was. But once he explained he'd got tickets to *Miss Saigon* and *Five Guys Named Moe* we jumped in the air! It was so exciting! We even got to stay in a hotel! That was the first time we'd ever properly been to London. Until then I'd thought London was Enfield.

From the moment we came back we had the *Miss Saigon* soundtrack on constantly. I knew every word of every song. I went to see it again recently and belatedly realised that it was about prostitutes! Bloody hell, Mum! You couldn't have been that innocent! When I listen now to what I was singing about . . . We went to see it again with the college and I just wished I'd been Asian and been able to play Kim. It's like *The Phantom of the Opera*. I'd love to play Christine, the only trouble is I can't do opera. I haven't got a high enough register.

When Jo passed her driving test Mum let her have her old Nissan Sunny. It was so rusty it looked like someone had shot it with a machine gun – we called them bullet holes and they went all the way round the car – but it did mean she could drive down to see me more easily. Apart from the nights she stayed with Liz, Jo was still living with Mum and Dad at Hazelgrove and thought she was leading quite a sheltered existence compared with the rest of us. She wasn't really, but Anna, Debbie and Bianca decided to play up to it and told her she needed to get in touch with her wild side. That evening our local pub The Rock had a theme night – strippers basically. We stayed till there was no one left but us, and we ended up taking these boys home where they did a personal strip. They were fully dressed when we walked the two hundred yards from the pub back to the house, and then we put on some music and they did the whole thing, though only down to their thongs. When I think about it now, those girls were so, so naughty!

The next time Jo came down, a hairdresser cousin of Nikki's was cutting everyone's hair. So when this guy said he'd do Jo's and mine as well, we thought, Why not? Jo's was quite short, but mine was comparatively long. And the guy cut it all off! It wasn't just short, it was a crop! So although the girls were all saying 'Oh it looks so cool' I just burst into tears.

Meanwhile life at Browns continued. And the longer I stayed the more I enjoyed it. In the end I was there for two years. And yes, it was sometimes complicated because you had to work your college schedule around it. But in all that time I never felt 'Oh God, I've got to go to work.' It was like being paid for doing what I would have done for nothing. Browns was now my social life. It was just one of those places where there was always something happening. I stood out at the front and I'd talk to people as they came in and as they went out. I remember Stephen Hawking coming in. Then there was the time when a consultant who I'd seen a few weeks before arrived with his wife. He recognised me and as I showed him to a table he said:

'So how are they feeling?'

'Oh fine, thank you.'

'Not too sore?'

'No, thank you.'

He was talking about my breasts!

Browns had originally been some kind of hospital, with a big heavy revolving door and one of the seater's duties was to make sure children didn't get their fingers caught. There was an outside terrace so you could watch people approaching, and you'd have to try to get there before they did. One day I had just seated a couple towards the back of the restaurant when I spotted this toddler running towards the door, a little girl with long hair, and the door was still moving from the people who'd just left. I didn't even have time to think, I ran as fast as I could and scooped her up. The first shock was when she felt really heavy, and then the second shock was when she turned round and I saw these eyes blazing with anger. It was a woman of about fifty who just happened to be very, very small . . .

During my last year at college the pace speeded up. There were no more visits from Jo because she had finished her A levels and was now doing a degree in editing and post-production at Ravensbourne in Kent.

I had broken up with Stuart by this time and was dating a guy called Pete Edwards. He ran events at the Cambridge Corn Exchange – a big music venue – so he had almost the same kind of job as Stuart though he was a bit younger. We'd been going out about six months when I went to live with him in a village north of Cambridge called Cottenham. College had ended and everyone from Rock Road had gone their separate ways. I should probably have gone to London like the other girls, but I was in love, and I was still only eighteen. I thought I could find work just as well from Cambridge. I gave up Browns because Tottenham was too far to get back at night, so I got a job at Gap.

Although officially I had left Bodywork, Patrick continued to send me for auditions. He had always had such faith in me and he wasn't going to give up on me now, he said. In the end we had become really close. I had thought it was going to happen really easily, because I had done quite well, but you don't realise that once you get out there and go to auditions you see these girls that are just incredible.

I went up for *Cats* and I went up for *Starlight Express*. And the girls I was up against were so beautiful, their bodies, their talent, I felt I didn't stand a chance.

The ridiculous thing about *Starlight Express* was that thanks to Rollerbury I could roller-skate already, but because so few people could, it didn't form part of the audition. They said they'd teach you once you'd been cast . . . And of course I didn't make it that far. I got down to the last three. I got down to the last three for *Cats*. It seemed like I would always get down to the last three but I never quite got the part.

6

The Highgate end of Archway

I realised that I had to go to London. I didn't want to break up with Pete, but I knew I couldn't stay in Cambridge and he wasn't prepared to move. And I understand that. His life was up there. He chose. We both chose.

I was still in touch with the girls from college and I heard that another girl called Charlotte – not one of the Rock Road gang, but not one of the bitchy ones either – had a room going in Leytonstone. I had no idea where Leytonstone was, but it was London and only £30 a week, though the downside was that I'd be sleeping on a couch in the lounge as there were three of them already. In addition to Charlotte there was a ballerina dancing in *Phantom*, and another dancer called Fern.

My first priority was to earn some money, so I spoke to PizzaExpress in Cambridge who put me in touch with the Farringdon branch, near Blackfriars, which they said was the nearest one to Leytonstone. Nearest? Getting a train from Cambridge would have been just as quick and considerably easier. It took over an hour to get there.

So much in life depends not so much on the job itself, but on the people you work with, and the manager at the Cowcross Street PizzaExpress was horrible. For the first time in my life, going to work was a misery. Every morning, when I arrived I'd say, 'Hello!' and she'd say, 'Yes.' When I left I'd say, 'Goodbye!' and she'd say, 'Yes.' She was just nasty, pure and simple.

Cowcross Street catered largely for workers in the City so it closed early. As I knew no one and had no money, once I'd finished I'd take the train straight back to the flat which was seriously depressing, really damp and there were mice. As for having a social life, Charlotte had a boyfriend and the other two girls were working.

I had thought it would be like Rock Road. I had thought we'd be doing things together and having fun. But it was the opposite. I was really, really lonely. There was nowhere to eat – it was all kebab shops – so I lived on bread, biscuits, pesto and pasta. My entire weekly shop came to £5. Plus, of course, a pizza a day at PizzaExpress.

As for finding a job in showbiz, the first thing was to get an agent. The way it worked, you sent in your CV and if they liked the sound of you, you went in to audition, and if they liked the look of you, they'd take you on, and if a job came in, they might put you up for it. You didn't just sign with one agent – whoever got you the work, they got the commission. So the more agents you had the more chances you had. Charlotte had more agents than I had fingers to count on, but then she was pretty.

I remember watching her on *Top of the Pops* and thinking, Why don't I get things like that? After all, it wasn't that difficult. The truth is that in that corner of the dancing world you had to have 'The Look' and she had 'The Look'. She had the sharpest, blondest bob you've ever seen. She had the perfect little nose and she looked like a beautiful mouse.

Looks were very important. In some way you were supposed to look different, and above all to have an edgy haircut. Mine was about as edgy as a Bourbon biscuit. I had brown hair, and was skinny and everyone used to say, 'You need to pump iron to make yourself look a bit stronger.'

I was like 'Pump iron? I don't want to pump iron ...'

And even if I had wanted to, I couldn't afford to join a gym. What little money I had went on rent and food. As a dancer it was far more important to do class. And class was expensive.

So I trawled the various agencies. The Pineapple Agency: no thank you. The Tommy Tucker agency: no thank you. Then I went to Dancers, in Charlotte Street, and a really nice woman called Debs took me on. In fact it couldn't have been better because the agency didn't only handle dancers. It operated in two halves, the other half was called Features which did the non-dancing stuff. I didn't mind what I did, I just wanted to work.

Top of everyone's list were commercials because they paid so well: you got more, the agency got more. The first audition Debs sent me to was a mop commercial. 'Look, Caroline,' she said, 'he's a very well-known director and it'd do you good to get in with him, so go along and do your best.'

So, OK.

With commercials they don't tell you what's going to happen. Or they didn't then. You found out when you got there and they handed you the script. So I walked in for this mop ad, smiling like it would break my jaw.

'Nice to meet you.'

'Nice to meet you.'

'Right,' said the well-known director, 'take this mop. Now make me laugh.'

That was it.

I have no idea now what I did. Perhaps I just pranced around holding the mop like it was a dancing partner, or perhaps I rode it like a hobby horse. Then the director raised his hands and stopped me in mid prance.

'That was the most un-entertaining audition I've seen all day. Next!'

On 9 November 2000, Jody and I turned twenty-one. To celebrate we went to the Hard Rock Cafe in Piccadilly with Mum and Dad. Celebrate? Jody might have something to celebrate: living with her boyfriend in a nice flat in Finchley, about to get her degree. And me? I was sleeping on a couch in a horrible flat in Leytonstone with a rodent problem, sharing with three girls, all of whom had jobs in show business, while I was serving pizzas in Farringdon with a Gestapo-style overseer. Oh, and no boyfriend.

Perhaps you have to go right to the bottom before you can start to rise; in that case my feet were touching the ground, but then I pushed and up I went . . .

My first success was a TV commercial for champagne. In fact not even champagne, it was fizzy Spanish wine called Rondel. There were to be two girls, one representing a green bottle of Rondel (dry), the other a gold bottle of Rondel (sweet). I was the gold bottle.

This wasn't a dancing advert, it was a singing advert. And because it was Spanish, for a Spanish audience, we had to sing in Spanish . . . Or rather mime, because neither I nor the other girl understood a word of Spanish, let alone spoke it.

I remember turning up at the audition and thinking that I was absolutely not the right person for the part. I was still feeling down (not helped by one of the girls in the flat having landed some once-in-a-lifetime job) so I had gone along wearing trainers with my hair pulled back in a ponytail because, as usual, I'd been given no brief, no hint of the scenario.

And as the director described what it was he was looking for, I was thinking, What you're really saying is that I don't look like the gold bottle of champagne. So I sang my thing and said goodbye.

That weekend I went back to Great Hockham and Mum was with me when the email arrived saying I'd got it!

'And they're paying me £2,000!'

'Quit your job!'

I quit my job.

(Me: I'm leaving! Overseer: Yes.)

Two thousand pounds was a *huge* amount of money in those days, enough to cover my rent for well over a year. Not only that, they flew me and the other girl out to Barcelona. I had always wanted to go to Barcelona, ever since Dad and Jody went there in 1992, the summer of the Olympics, a few weeks before the whole razzmatazz began. We were staying in France, just over the border from Spain, and Mum and I didn't think a long hot train journey was worth the effort so we just stayed by the pool. Then Dad and Jo had gone on and on about how brilliant it was for about five years.

What a difference a costume makes! It really was like being transformed from an insect into a butterfly – all wind machine, floaty dress and glitter, to the point where I actually believed I was champagne, bubbly and full of fizz. Whether it actually translated into anything convincing on the screen I have no idea, because I never saw the ad.

It was my first-ever job in the entertainment industry that I was paid for. It would be nice to think that from then on things started to snowball, but they didn't. In fact I began to think there was something wrong with my voice, because I'd get all these foreign jobs where I'd be dubbed. In particular I remember a German one for a clothing brand. This wasn't either singing or dancing. It was 'acting'. Me and this male model (English) were flown out to Düsseldorf or somewhere. I was supposed to take the mickey out of him because he had terrible taste in clothes, so I had to look at him with an ironic expression, raise an eyebrow and say 'Chic'. One word – and even that was dubbed!

The Leytonstone chapter of my life was now closed. Jody had split up with her boyfriend and had found a flat in Kenworthy Road, just north of Victoria Park in Hackney with three others: Emily who Jo had been to college with, Lisa – our brother's girlfriend's sister, and a guy called Paul who would move in later. He had also been at Ravensbourne but Jo had only really got to know him when they'd worked together in a bar. There was also a little room for me if I wanted it, Jo said.

Kenworthy Road was the loveliest house, and my room was at the top. It was small but it had a nice double bed and wardrobes. Best of all I was reunited with my sister.

I was still living off my £2,000 but it was shrinking fast and it was Jo who finally said, 'Carrie, you've got to get a proper job,' not least because of the rent which she had to pay. I had been putting it off and putting it off because somehow it felt like it would be giving up, that I was a failure. I was still trying to get bits and bobs when I could. I did a Lionel Richie music video, I remember, just dancing in the background.

But where to start? I didn't know London at all. Farringdon had turned out to be a complete disaster.

'Islington,' Jo said. Islington was buzzy and only a bus ride from where we were living. But I should forget pizza places and get bar work, like she had done. It was much more fun and I'd meet people, she said. So, having primed me on what to say, we wandered along Upper Street, stopping at the places we liked the look of and asking if they had anything going. And finally we found the Medicine Bar.

Looking back it was the best thing I could possibly have done because for the first time I started to get to know people in London, to meet people who were interested in the same things that I was. Until then I'd just been hanging out with my sister and her friends, which was fine, but I needed to have my own social life, I needed to move forward. And it was great. The Medicine Bar was a proper little neighbourhood local – Alex James was a regular. I began to make friends and even date guys I met there. There was one evening I will never forget because it was just so awful. I was dating three different men and one evening they all came in at the same time. I was only dating them, but even so . . . So there I was chatting with the first one at one end of the bar when the second one walked in and went to the other end. That was bad enough, and then the third one arrived . . . Luckily it was quite busy that night and I told each of them that I couldn't really talk and, 'I've got an audition in the morning, so I need to get an early night.' It was often true, though not on that occasion.

At least with ads the money was always good. The one that got away was Nutella. The fee was £15,000. I mean

£15,000!!! It was like a rerun of *Cats* and *Starlight Express*. I got down to the last two . . .

That whole world was totally surreal. One day you could be working at PizzaExpress, living on little more than £5 a week over and above your rent, the next you could have £15,000 in the bank. As there was so much money at stake the whole process turned you into a nervous wreck. If you got through the first audition you'd get a call from your agent along the lines of 'Hey, Caroline. Yes, you've got a recall for the Nutella ad. Friday at 3 p.m. Make sure you look nice.' Sometimes the brief would be more specific. 'Look ladylike, hair down, natural make-up, don't over-pluck your eyebrows, good luck, darling. Bye.'

And then I'd think, 'Tomorrow, I could buy a car!'

And when the telephone didn't ring, and eventually I'd get the 'Sorry-you're-not-quite-what-they're-looking-for' I'd be so upset. Of course it was far worse losing a job worth several thousand pounds than losing one worth £150.

I would do anything that came up. You just needed to be out there because you never knew who you might meet and what it might lead to. I was a dancer in a magic show – an illusionist. It was a one-off because they were filming it for a video. There were seven of us, three boys and four girls, and all we had to do was dance in the background.

I have no idea where it was shot but it took about three hours to get there in a minibus, and in the end none of us dancers got paid – so that was the £150 I didn't get even though I got the job. But I did meet a nice girl called

Fiona – a commercial dancer who did all the big tours like Take That and Steps, the kind of thing I never even got a sniff at – and we became friends, so it wasn't entirely wasted.

Then one day Debs called and said, 'I've got you an audition for a film. It's in Ibiza and it's the lead . . .'

IBIZA! THE LEAD!!

So I went to this audition and read for the lead girl and waited. And then Debs called.

'Look, they don't think you're right for the lead girl, but they want you to go back and read for another character. OK?'

OK.

So I go back and read for another character.

Debs: 'Look, they really like you but they don't think you're right for that role, but they're going to offer you the part of another girl – Blonde.'

Me: 'What, not even a name?'

Debs: 'No. Just Blonde.'

Me: 'But I'm not blonde.'

Debs: 'And you're going to have to go topless.'

The film was called *Is Harry on the Boat?* It had been a cult book in the nineties and is all about 18–30-style holidays in Ibiza, and now Sky Pictures were turning it into a film. If you know your cockney rhyming slang, the title tells you what to expect. *Harry on the Boat* translates as Spunk on the Face . . . No, I didn't either. (FYI Harry Monk, Boat Race.)

The film is about holiday reps, male and female, getting

their ends off and it's (obviously) a lads' film. The lead character is played by Danny Dyer, who's now Mick Carter in *EastEnders*, but in 2000 he was known mainly for playing gangsters, and I have to admit he was very attractive.

My scene – I only had one – was a dream sequence. Danny Dyer's character falls asleep and Blonde comes into his hotel room. Blonde is obviously drunk and Danny Dyer says, 'What are you doing in my hotel room?' And Blonde, sounding aggrieved/surprised, says, 'But this is my room, 123!' And he says, 'This is room 124.' And then he goes, 'Well, why don't you come over here anyway?'

At which point Blonde totters over towards him. (Luckily, because the scene takes place at night, the fact that I was topless is barely noticeable though they did put a bit of discreet tape across my nipples ...) And then Blonde whispers in his ear, 'Do you mind if my friend joins us?' Danny Dyer looks at Blonde and goes, 'Huh?' Then in walks Blonde's friend who turns out to be Danny Dyer's ex. She's wielding a pair of shears, all set to cut off his intimate friend, at which point he wakes up ...

So that was my debut on the silver screen. But they flew me to Ibiza for a week and I got to stay in a lovely hotel and the cast were all there and it felt like the real thing.

The premiere was in July 2001 and I took Jody along. She had just graduated from Ravensbourne. Short as my part had been on the page, it was now even shorter and I was visible (though only just thank God) for about a minute. But it was a fun experience, it was a really fun experience. However, the best part was when Jo took my hand in the dark and whispered, 'I'm so proud.'

The 'loveliest little house' in Kenworthy Road turned out to be not so lovely at all. 'Lovely', like beauty, it seemed, was only skin deep, or in this case skim-plaster deep. The landlord had done a quick paint job and it was beginning to show. It was time to move on.

We found just what we wanted in *Loot*, a weekly magazine that was entirely made up of classified listings, mostly of places to rent. And there it was: a five-bedroomed house in Highgate. Officially it was Archway, but it was the Highgate end of Archway. It was in Harberton Road and had real character. The house itself was much prettier than Kenworthy Road, with much more generous room dimensions and we loved everything about it. All five of us had gone to see it together and when we walked up Highgate Hill into the village we looked at each other and knew that this was it. None of us had ever been to Highgate before and we fell in love with the place.

As I'd had the worst room in Kenworthy Road, it was agreed I could have first choice here, so I chose the room at the top with its own en suite; in fact I had the entire floor to myself. In the mornings it would be flooded with light and I remember looking down from my window across Holloway to the City, and I could even see as far as Canary Wharf. And for the first time I remember thinking, Now I live in London!

In hot weather we would climb out from my window

onto the flat roof, put down our towels and sunbathe. It wasn't allowed, of course, but who was going to stop us?

Although I considered mine the best room, it wasn't the biggest; that went to Paul, Jo's friend from Ravensbourne, because he needed somewhere with space enough for a drawing board, he said. Not that he ever got one.

Paul was incredibly handsome. When he'd first moved in my reaction was 'Why didn't anyone tell me he was so gorgeous!' And I thought, This is it, I'm obviously going to end up sleeping with him. But somehow we didn't. Instead we became really good buddies. He was completely eccentric and really silly – nearly as silly as I was. He had a very good eye and we'd go shopping together and there was no one who could put things together like Paul could. He designed shoes and bags for Jo and me and brought them home.

As well as working in the Medicine Bar in the evenings, I'd also started working as a dance teacher for a company called Future Faces who put dance teachers into different schools. By this time I had no real idea where I was headed in terms of a career. It felt like nowhere. But I had been trained to dance, so I wanted to use what I had gone to college for in some sort of form. In terms of pay it was no worse than you earned in most dancing jobs and I only did it on Saturdays – I taught three classes in the mornings – so it didn't affect my availability for auditions. In the end I thought I would do it independently, rather than work for somebody else.

The first school I went to was in Benfleet, beyond

Basildon in Essex. It was the weirdest place to get to, but I hadn't realised that at the time I agreed to do it. The train took about an hour from Fenchurch Street in the City, and first I had to get to Fenchurch Street from Archway. So it took two hours to get there and two hours to get back, and my first class started at 9.00 . . . But I had to do something. I couldn't just wait for life to come to me.

Then out of the blue my lovely brother-in-law Leigh, Liz's husband, threw me a lifeline. He'd put a band together called Speedometer – old-style jazz-funk – and they had regular gigs at the Jazz Café in Camden. Would I like to sing with them? I was so amazed! Leigh had always been a brilliant guitar player, and I couldn't believe he'd risk his reputation if he thought I'd let him down. I wouldn't let him down.

They are all amazing musicians – several of them have day jobs in the army, so you'd usually see them doing march-pasts in front of Buckingham Palace. It wasn't much – I'd do about one evening every couple of months – and like the majority of jazz bands, most of what Speedometer plays is instrumental with vocals playing only a small part – but I sang Ann Sexton's 'I'm Losing You' and for me, it was a total dream. There I was, singing in the Jazz Café, and getting paid £50 a night!

Then one day, a couple of days after one of these evenings I got a phone call.

'Hi, my name's Troy,' this guy said and his voice sent shivers down my spine. He'd been at the gig, he said, and

he'd heard me sing, and he had a job for me. He was putting on a night at the Albert Hall to 'empower women'
and he needed loads of singers to come on and sing at the
beginning. And he wondered if I might be interested.

At least I could meet him, I thought. And when I did, it
was like 'Oh my God, this man is so attractive.' It wasn't
just the voice, it was everything about him, every single
thing. We immediately started flirting, and I remember
telling Jody, 'I think he's The One.'

I hadn't had a proper boyfriend since leaving Cambridge.
I'd had a few dates – mainly guys I'd met through the
Medicine Bar – but nothing that lasted more than a few
weeks, if that. And now this gorgeous man had come into
my life.

I don't know what his motive was in calling me. But the
Albert Hall thing was genuine. We were all in black and
we came out from the back and made our way along this
long catwalk. I was wearing leather trousers and a backless
black jumper and we sang 'Respect', the feminist anthem
that Aretha Franklin made famous. The whole experience
was incredible. And then we started dating.

Troy was much older than me – about thirty-six while I
was in my early twenties. He'd just come out of a very long
relationship, he explained, so things were a little strained
sometimes; for example, I never went to his house, which
struck me as being really odd. He said that it was where he
had lived with this woman so it felt awkward. Then one
evening, after we'd been going out for about three months,
he said, 'Look, this is really silly. Come and stay the night at

my house.' So I did. We hadn't gone to bed long when he suddenly said, 'I feel really weird.'

'Because of your ex?'

'No. Because I miss my cat.'

'Your cat?'

'Yes. My cat, Medea. I think I can smell her.'

I couldn't smell anything.

'I really miss her,' he went on.

'Where is she? What happened to her.'

'She died,' he said.

I nodded.

'And then I buried her in the garden.'

I nodded again, thoughtfully, I hoped.

'And when I buried her I put a splint on her leg and tied a string to it. So, even though she's buried really deeply, if I miss her I can go and touch the string.'

'Do you want to go and touch the string?'

'Yes.'

'Well, let's go and touch the string.' And we went out into the garden and touched the string. After that, nothing was quite the same . . .

One day we went to PizzaExpress in Highgate. And we ordered dough balls. I must have eaten five and he must have eaten three, because there were eight in total. Then, when it came to splitting the bill, he said, 'You should pay more because you had more dough balls.'

What?

And then we went on holiday to Mallorca for New Year. And we were in the middle of dinner – nothing special, just a meal out in a restaurant – when he suddenly said, 'Take your hair down.'

What?

'Take your hair down. Look I'm in the business. I know about these things. You look so much better with it down.'

Before coming out, I had it pulled away from my face, in a kind of ponytail. OK, it might not have been ultra chic, but this wasn't exactly the Ritz. But I still thought, Well, he might be right.

But then we were in a street market near where we were staying when he said, 'Go back to the car and put some fucking moisturiser on your face.'

I walked back to the car, my eyes pricking with tears and I knew that the moment I got back to England that would be it. Control freak? Weirdo? Psychopath? Take your pick. Perhaps all three, but whatever name you want to give it, I'd had enough.

In the summer of 2001, as soon as she left Ravensbourne, Jo got a job as an assistant editor in a small post-production company called Martyr Television in Swallow Street in Soho and she loved it. They were very laid-back and I would drop in whenever I was in the area and we'd have lunch or coffee. One day she told me she was working for a man who was looking for presenters for a gaming show.

'A game show?'

'No a gaming show, about computer games.'

'But on TV?'

'Yes. But not proper TV. A gaming channel.'

And I was like, 'I could do that. I could be a TV presenter!'

'Get me an audition, Jo. Go on. You can do it. Get me an audition!'

So she did. She got me an audition through this man. She got hold of a script and I just went in and did it. But I had no real idea what to do so it was hardly surprising I didn't get the job.

But afterwards I thought, Why not? Why not be a TV presenter? And I thought back to the time Mum had taken us to Television Centre to see *Going Live!*, and how much fun it had all looked. Plus I was getting desperate. I clearly wasn't going to make it in musical theatre. I needed to find something I was good at. Perhaps it was this ... So I decided to make a show reel.

'And you can edit it for me!'

Of course Jo did far more than edit it. She was the cameraman, the director, the producer, the lot. We went up to Great Hockham, borrowed Dad's video camera and wandered around the village, with me saying, 'My name's Caroline Flack and this is the village where I grew up ... This is where I used to live ... This is where my nan and grandad used to live, this is my school ... This is Pepsi the donkey ...' And Jo cut it together, and for the soundtrack we had Dean Martin singing 'Memories Are Made of This'.

It must have been the most boring show reel anybody has ever seen, but I put the VHS cassette in a Jiffy bag and posted it to a big TV agent called James Grant, the agency that handles Ant and Dec. They sent it back with a letter saying, 'Thank you for your show reel blah, blah. Unfortunately we don't think you're right for us, but you could try sending it to John Noel Management who you might be more suited to.'

I had no idea who John Noel was, but nothing ventured, nothing gained, I found the address and posted it off.

Not long after I got a phone call.

'My name's Petra,' the voice said, 'I'm from John Noel Management and John would like to set up a meeting with you in a couple of weeks' time. Would you be available?'

7

'See you after the break!'

John Noel Management was in Camden on the third floor of an old factory and there was an ancient industrial lift that clanked up slower than you could have walked it. It all struck me as very ramshackle, not exactly cutting edge, but as I stood at the desk waiting for the receptionist to put down the phone, I looked back at the wall behind me, and there were these huge blow-ups of Davina McCall and Dermot O'Leary and John Leslie, who was really big then, and I was like 'This is the real thing . . .'

'You Caroline?' this man said in a Northern accent.

'Yeah.'

'Your show reel's shit but I think you're quite good. Come in.'

Bloody hell . . .

'I like the way you talk to camera. I like the way you

interact. I feel like you're talking to me, so I want to take you on.'

And then I told a great big fat lie.

'Well,' I said. 'I've an appointment to see another agent called James Grant. So you understand that I can't make a decision right now. I'll have to think about it.'

'OK. Well, when you've thought about it, let me know.'

So I went home, left it one day, phoned him and said Yes.

'Good. Well, you'd better come in and meet a guy called Nik, because he's going to be looking after you.'

Nik was John Noel's son, incredibly handsome and incredibly nice. And I thought, Oh no. That's all I need. How can I resist those eyes? I'm going to fall in love with my agent ... But I didn't. Thank goodness. Instead we developed a lovely friendship. He introduced me to Camden, to the horse stables market by the lock with its vintage clothes and thirties and fifties stuff. We used to go out drinking and to gigs. Only a few yards from the office were some of the most amazing pubs, where bands played every night in back rooms. Camden had this fantastic, vibrant street life – a side of London I hadn't seen before. This was where Britpop had started in the early nineties, and ten years on there was a revival of guitar-based, indie rock giving two fingers up to the manufactured pop that was dominating the playlists in the wake of the Spice Girls. So you could hear bands like the Libertines, the Strokes and the Vines, and guerrilla sessions where musicians would combine with musicians from other bands.

The first thing on the agenda, Nik said, was a new show

reel. The idea was to find out what I was good at, what I was interested in and then showcase my range. I was quickly discovering that John Noel's agency was not conventional. It was very much a family affair – John's sons Nik and Alex and his daughter Hannah were also agents, but the whole team were brilliant. They would bring other clients in so I could do practice interviews, video them, and we'd play them back to pinpoint what I was doing right/wrong or could do better. Most of John's clients have been with him for years and they'll do anything for him, including in this instance being guinea pigs for me.

It was important to get the show reel right, John said, and it shouldn't be rushed. I did a piece to camera (Jody again) on football and how my family had always been passionate Spurs supporters, shot outside the White Hart Lane ground. I did an interview with Ade Adepitan, who used to be a wheelchair basketball player and now presents Paralympic sport. We played basketball together and I interviewed him about his life (he is completely amazing). Another of John's clients, the comedian Leigh Francis, also let me interview him. Finally, John thought that to open the reel there should be a bit of me dancing, so I did the choreography, we shot it in a studio John had hired though I was never really happy with it – so unbelievably cheesy . . . Now all they had to do then was send it out to potential employers, like production companies and producers and wait for requests for screen tests to come rolling in.

*

Apart from *Blind Date* with Cilla Black, I don't remember any reality programmes when I was growing up, but by 2002 they were everywhere. *Castaway 2000* and *Big Brother* started in 2000, *Survivor*, *Popstars* and *Pop Idol* in 2001; *Popstars: the Rivals*, *Fame Academy*, *I'm a Celebrity . . . Get Me Out of Here!* in 2002.

The nineties had seen a revolution in television, initially through cable and satellite, and then digital TV. Soon every kind of niche was being catered for, from classic movies and old sitcom reruns, to porn, not to mention the high-profile and hugely influential MTV (whose studios incidentally overlooked Camden Lock).

It had started with Sky and the Premiership, but soon cricket, rugby, tennis, Formula 1, horse-racing were all available somewhere. Darts? American football? Wrestling? You just had to look for it – hence Jody and the gaming channel she was working for that first got my TV antennae twitching.

The surge in mainstream reality shows was the result of new technology. The formats usually involved some sort of knockout competition with a prize for the eventual winner. Central to their success was viewers' involvement in the whittling-down process. There had been talent shows before – *Opportunity Knocks* being the obvious example – but in those days people had to vote by post! Once mobile phones had become commonplace, viewers could be directly involved in the polling. And these programmes were cheap to make: there were no stars to be paid, just experts and/or judges. As for the contestants,

Andy Warhol's fifteen-minutes-of-fame prediction made in 1968 was coming true and people would do anything to get on telly, and they did it for nothing. Only on celebrity versions would contestants be paid.

The more channels there were, the more shows were being commissioned and most of them needed a presenter, particularly general-entertainment channels such as BBC Choice (later BBC Three) and Bravo and UKTV. According to Nik it was just a question of getting my foot in the door and these were all places, he said, where you could be launched. The more versatile I could show myself to be, the more chance that I'd fit the bill somewhere, which was why we'd included two sports items and the interview with Leigh Francis in the show reel. The three growth areas were sport, reality TV and oddball comedy.

I can't remember now if Channel 4 had already commissioned Leigh to do *Bo'Selecta!* by the time we did the interview for my show reel, but if not, then it was soon after. *Bo'Selecta!* definitely fitted into the oddball category of humour and immediately became a cult comedy show. The title came from a song by the garage band the Artful Dodger and Craig David's 1999 hit 'Re-Rewind (The Crowd Say Bo Selecta)' and Craig David was one of the show's main 'characters'. *Bo'Selecta!* was basically a satire on celebrity culture. The narrator was Leigh himself, in the persona of Avid, an Eastern European sex-obsessed celebrity stalker in a neck brace, who would meet real celebrities. There were also interviews with Leigh as an

oversized 'teddy bear' puppet asking outrageously sala-
cious questions of the unsuspecting guests. But it was his
terrible impersonations of celebrities, with him wearing
ludicrous latex masks, that were the show's trademark.
One of these was 'Michael Jackson', and they decided they
needed a girl to play Bubbles his monkey, not as a monkey
but a blonde girl wearing skimpy clothes. As John was
Leigh's agent, it was easy for him to 'slip me into the mix'
as he put it. So I played this weird bimbette character who
doesn't say or do very much but is just there. And for
doing and saying not-very-much I got £500 a shooting day,
which was obviously great. (For *Bo'Selecta!* fans, Jody was
also in the first episode, in the sketch with 'David Blaine'
having her breasts felt.) It was shot over the summer of
2002 and I was in a few episodes in a later series but as I
was only in the sketches that included 'Michael Jackson' it
wasn't full on. *Bo'Selecta!* was fun, great fun, but it wasn't
the direction I wanted to go.

While you could say that pop music probably peaked in
the sixties and early seventies, it got kicked into the next
century when MTV came on the scene. The weekly Top
40 was still very important in Britain, however, and *CD:UK*
was a countdown chart show that went out live on
Saturday mornings on ITV. There was a studio audience
of kids, with the usual mix of live music, interviews and
competitions. The presenter was Cat Deeley – her first job
on mainstream British TV.

In 2002 Pepsi had stopped sponsoring the Top 40

countdown in Britain, both on TV and radio, but not in the rest of the world. *The International Pepsi Chart Show* was basically just *CD:UK* rebranded for Norway and Tahiti, and Nik was very excited when they came back to him and said they'd like me to front it.

Norway and Tahiti? What kind of a launch was that? No one was going to see it!

'That's exactly why you have to do it,' Nik said. 'Because it means you can learn your trade and make all your mistakes without anyone being any the wiser.'

The International Pepsi Chart Show piggybacked on *CD:UK* using the same studio audience – but the links and interviews were all down to me. So there I'd be, waiting at the side and when Cat said the magic words 'See you after the break!' I'd dash on and present our links, such as: 'And at number two this week, still holding on really strong, it's Blue!' And then we'd pretend to go to Blue playing live – while in fact Blue weren't actually there, they'd simply splice in a previously recorded clip. Then, once the show was over, I'd slip backstage to interview anybody the producers could persuade to talk to me – people like Justin Timberlake, Steps, S Club 7, Ms. Dynamite and Dannii Minogue. They clearly had no idea where I fitted in. I was just a pushy girl with a microphone who said, 'Hi, I'm Caroline!'

With so little time – the commercial break usually lasted less than three minutes – there was no room for mistakes. But I was incredibly prepared. I'd have listened to the music and I'd have read the various bios and, as for the links, I knew them all by heart. Flatmate Paul was my life-saver in this respect, going over the script time after time until I was word perfect – we'd even do it in the pub. Back then I still thought presenting was mainly about memory. Sometimes people would say to me 'Oooh, what a good memory you've got!' as if that was the key that would get me to the top. But gradually you learn that it's not about memory at all. It's about knowing what you're trying to deliver.

It wasn't long before I realised how right Nik had been. I would never have this kind of opportunity again. Week by week, I learnt my craft away from the public gaze and I became a really good student: I'd know my words and I'd be on time. And in fact ever since then I am always on time, scarily on time, annoyingly on time. Actually I am nearly always early.

When I started doing interviews I was so focused on the next question, that I'd forget to listen to the answer to the previous one. You have to listen, because if you listen you don't have to worry about what comes next, it'll happen naturally out of what the other person has just said. If you've done your research, if you know where you want to take the interview, then you'll be fine. But by the time the *Pepsi Chart Show* came to an end, my tendency to 'perform' still needed work. That whole 'Hello-and-welcome-to-the-show!' thing tended towards the manic. But given that for the last two hours these kids had been watching an entirely different programme, and hadn't a clue who I was, I'd find myself looking at a sea of bemused faces, so spontaneity wasn't always that easy . . .

In the summer of 2002, when I had started doing *Bo'Selecta!*, Jo had moved from Martyr Television and was now at The Mill, a huge post-production and special effects company. After her first day at the new job, I heard her come in, and said, 'So how did it go?'

'I love Jason,' she said.

What??!!

This guy was an editor called Jason Watts and she was his runner. She used to make me go to The Mill just to look at him – or as she put it 'show him to me'. It took another year before they actually got it together. Some people are quick workers, others are more of a slow burn, but it obviously worked. I'd long since given up on that approach. My experience with Lee Charlton had set the seal on that. I mean, three years and then Bub-feelings!

By then we had moved out of Harberton Road because Lisa and Emily were moving in with their boyfriends and we didn't want to get two new people. We'd tried it once in the previous house and ended up with a guy who never washed his socks.

So now it was just Jo, Paul and me. We wanted to stay in Highgate so this time tried the local estate agents and found a really cool, three-bedroom flat on the fourth floor of a wonderful art deco block on Hornsey Road. It was unfurnished so we went to Ikea and bought loads of furniture then ripped up the fairly disgusting carpets to find these amazing wooden floors underneath. Pure 1930s.

What we hadn't realised was that the carpets were there for a reason – to stop the noise going straight down to the flat below. When we left we had to pay to replace them.

This time there were no arguments about the rooms. Once we'd decided we loved it, I said, 'So who's going to have the small room?' Jody said she would because she wasn't that bothered about where she slept, she just wanted to be in the flat. So for the second time running I got the best bedroom. Paul chose his because he liked the colour of the walls, which were bright orange.

Nik had promised the *Pepsi Chart Show* would set the ball rolling and it did. I was now a jobbing presenter, picking up odd things here and there when the usual presenter had sprained an ankle or got stuck up the Orinoco or was being helicoptered off a glacier. There were a myriad reasons why you might be called in. The downside was that these jobs were always last-minute so you had no time to prepare, which could be a problem if it was something you knew nothing about.

I remember there was a programme about speedboats and it was for the next day ... What did I know about speedboats? Absolutely nothing. Was I interested in speedboats? No.

'You should take it,' Nik said. 'You should take it because you're a jobbing presenter and that's what jobbing presenters do.' Actually, I ended up really enjoying it, and getting on with everybody and it became a real social event.

It wasn't much but, as Nik said, it all helped the CV, though not necessarily the bank balance. Next came something approaching a proper job. John Fashanu had been a really great footballer in the eighties and early nineties. Then, having retired as the result of injury, he co-hosted the first series of *Gladiators* in the mid-nineties with Ulrika Jonsson. In 2003, Fash, as he was always known, came second in *I'm a Celebrity . . . Get Me Out of Here!* so probably on the back of that came this reality show, *Fash's Football Challenge*. The premise was that he had his own Sunday League football team, and so the programme followed the players and their fortunes on and off the field. Andy Goldstein and Andy Burton were the commentators and I was the pitchside reporter.

Because it was a Sunday league team, we naturally did it on a Sunday. It was based at Hendon Football Club and to get there for 9.00 meant a very early start. Andy Goldstein would pick me up from the Hornsey Road flat early on Sunday morning and we'd set off for Hendon. Andy was a great presenter and I learnt a lot from just watching him. My dad always said knowledge is power, and Andy really knew his stuff, and the way he talked to people always got the best out of them.

It was a combination of knowledge and timing that earned me a few plaudits on one freezing day in January. John Leslie had always been involved with football in one way or another, and he'd agreed to watch the proceedings and be interviewed. Unluckily for him it just happened to be the day after news of the infamous three-in-a-bed footage with him and Abi Titmuss had emerged, and it was too good an opportunity to miss.

Knowing that he'd previously been a goalkeeper, I said, 'So are you very good with your hands?' I asked him about ball control and about whether he enjoyed performing in front of the camera ... I don't know where I got the nerve, but somehow I did, although I could feel my heart pounding. But it earned me a round of drinks in the bar afterwards.

Financially, though, it was a disaster. Six weeks, six episodes at £150 a time – the same as I got paid as a dance teacher.

It was all so depressing. When I had a job, there was always the chance that someone would see it and that it might lead on to something else. The John Leslie interview was a case in point. It got me lots of coverage and it was good because people could see I wasn't cowed by having to interview someone so high-profile. But nothing. There'd be some small job and then a long gap where I had no work at all. Perhaps the reason was staring me in the face. Perhaps I just wasn't good enough. I even considered going to work at John Noel Management as an agent, but I never had the guts to ask. I was just a presenter-in-waiting, thinking, Am I young enough to start a new career? I was twenty-three. What if I never work again? What do I do then? Rob a bank?

It wasn't long before Jo and Jason were an item and I hardly ever saw her. Paul was still around, but he now had a girlfriend, and not long after he decided to move to

Milan. He'd got a great job designing shoes with some big Italian company, so that was that. So then Jo decided that she would move in with Jason. He had a lovely house in Notting Hill, so I can hardly blame her, but it was hard, very hard. I felt totally abandoned.

The day before the move, Jo and I had a huge row. I can't remember now what triggered it, but sometimes there wouldn't be a real reason. If we were angry with each other and we were in that kind of mood, it could be over nothing but we'd argue till the cows came home.

The tension had been building ever since the decision had been made to break up the flat. Jo was busy packing and I could see she was so happy. It was all working out so well. Not for her the Lee Charlton scenario, she had met The One. Of course I wanted my sister to be happy, but at the same time I felt in some way betrayed. What about me? Everyone else was fine and dandy but what about me? Where would I go? I mean, how selfish can you get?

For the first time we had actual furniture to move, not just suitcases and bin bags, so we hired a van and the atmosphere was really tense. We basically did the whole thing in silence. I still didn't drive, so Jo backed this van up in front of the block, opened the doors and we began bringing things down in the lift to the lobby.

The lift doors had just opened, and I was staggering out carrying a chair when CRASH! The lobby suddenly went dark – because something was blocking the light . . . I put down the chair and stared. Jo hadn't put the handbrake on strongly enough and the van had gently rolled back down the slight slope into the glass doors. In fact it had crashed into the brass frames, because if it had hit the doors themselves there would have been glass everywhere. They could never have withstood the impact.

After the initial shock came the realisation of what could have happened. The doors could have been shattered. Someone could so easily have been killed – luckily nobody was around. We had just begun to breathe again when suddenly it dawned on us. The doors opened outwards ... We couldn't get out. We both stood there looking at each other.

'What about that guy?' Jo said.

'What guy?'

'The poet.'

'The poet' was actually a songwriter called Noah who lived on the ground floor. He was always stoned and always happy to see you and would go 'Heeeeey!' whenever I appeared in his doorway. I would go down to listen to his music when I was bored because he was the only young person who lived in the building and by then Jo and Paul were hardly ever around.

So, although it was really early I knocked on his door, and he emerged looking stoned. I was sorry to bother him, I said, '... but we've just got to climb through your window ...'. He came out into the hall, saw the van and went 'Whooaaaa!!'

So Jo crawled out through his bathroom window, then

drove the van away back up the slope and parked it properly. I opened the glass doors and went out to inspect the damage to the van. Nothing! There wasn't a scratch on it. Thank God ... My heart considerably lightened by this, we continued to pack the van till it was all done. I climbed in beside Jo and we set off for Little Venice where I'd arranged to share a flat with a friend of a friend called Tracey. And then SCREECH! because, as Jo turned the corner, she scraped the whole side of the van against a bollard ... And then there was just silence. Because we both knew we'd lost the deposit on the van.

Can there possibly be a silver lining to this story? Yes. Because as we were driving to Tracey's my phone rang. It was Nik.

'How do you feel about going to Tokyo?'

What?

'For three weeks. The money's not great but it's a great opportunity.'

'I'll take it.'

It was a show called *When Games Attack*, which I don't think anyone ever saw. It was *Red Dwarf* meets *Tomorrow's World* and went out on Bravo. My role was to try out different gadgets in Tokyo. These stand-alone segments would eventually be used in each episode when it went out, as WHEN FLACK ATTACKS!

Amongst other things I dated a robot called Asimo. I tried out a dog translator, where the dog would bark and this gizmo would translate it into English:

Dog: woof, woof
Gizmo: I'm hungry

Dog: woof, woof, woof
Gizmo: Take me for a walk
etc.

The whole three weeks was brilliant. We stayed in the smart shopping area, at the Ginza Grand Hotel, the strangest hotel I have ever been in and Tokyo felt like the strangest place. I was completely cut off – my mobile phone didn't work in Japan so, if I ever needed to contact England, I had to go to the business centre in the hotel and use Hotmail.

The production team and I arrived on a night flight so I was feeling pretty weird anyway, and we got in just as they were serving breakfast, and it was soup and sausages . . . Before I'd left home, Mum had given me some advice: 'If you ever get caught in an earthquake, whatever you do, stand in a doorway.'

So, there I was, on my first night in my tiny hotel room, when I woke up. Something was under my bed pushing it up. I went cold. Somebody was in the room. But the shaking just kept going and suddenly I realised what it was: AN EARTHQUAKE! I got up, rushed to the door, opened it and just stood there, absolutely terrified.

Then this man walked past, saw this women standing there in a T-shirt and a pair of pants and said, 'Are you all right? What are you doing?' Apparently it was a really small earthquake and they happen all the time in Tokyo.

Tokyo is the closest I've ever got to landing on another planet. Everything was different but everything was the same. Take going out to a restaurant. First you had to remove your shoes and put them in a little pouch, then they'd give you Chinese-type slippers to wear or you'd go barefoot. The tables were all really low so you'd sit cross-legged. Food was impossible to order because the menus were only in Japanese characters. At least in Spain you can work out what something might be, because you can spell it out and say it phonetically. At the first restaurant, I had to draw a chicken on a bit of paper and an attempt at noodles.

Then there was the whole blowfish thing. Blowfish is a 'delicacy' but lethal if it's not cooked right. Traditionally, if the chef gets it wrong and you're poisoned, he has to kill himself. Why would anyone risk something like that? Because it's a status thing.

And what about sumo wrestlers? They're fed on rice and they die at forty because of their diet and they're treated like gods. As for the sex industry, it's quite open. If you're having a business meeting, you'll take your clients and introduce them to women. It is completely crazy.

The production team were great – seven or eight guys and a local fixer – and we'd go to these gizmo conventions during the day, then off out to dinner. After dinner it would be back to the hotel. But when the rest of them went off to bed, I went to the hotel bar.

It really was like *Lost in Translation*. In the Bill Murray part was this American actor called Sean who lived in LA and after the initial meaningful looks across a crowded bar we got talking and started this little fling. I'd go and meet him in a place called Roppongi, the area of Tokyo where Westerners hang out – completely different to the central area of Ginza. Every district in Tokyo is very distinct, like Harajuku where you go to see crazy Japanese girls. There was a strip where it's nothing but vintage shops and filled with girls with ponytails, big shoes and polka-dot dresses. The fashion there was incredible.

So Sean and I would trawl the bars in Roppongi so there was no chance I'd bump into any of the crew. To go off without telling anybody was really naughty. I mean at the beginning I had no idea who this guy was. But things were so strange in Tokyo, so alien, that you grasped anything normal and he seemed basically harmless and cute and when it was time to leave we exchanged emails, but that was it.

The flat I shared with Tracey would have scored nine out of ten for location – on the Edgware Road, right by Little Venice, meaning I could walk to Selfridges in fifteen minutes. But for liveability it was two out of ten, seriously tiny and my room really was a box room this time, with space for a bed and nothing else.

Tracey was a beauty lecturer and taught in a beauty college in Great Marlborough Street in Soho. She was doing very well, but she had one problem: she didn't have a boyfriend and hadn't had sex in two years, which had become a bit of a joke between us. But one weekend she'd gone to Wales, and bumped into an old friend of hers called Tom and came back cock-a-hoop.

'I'm back in the land of the living!' she whooped. 'I've had sex!'

She didn't think the relationship could work, she said, as he was up there and she was in London, but she was utterly transformed. Then, a month or so later she walked into the flat looking like she needed a stiff drink.

'I'm pregnant.'

'Oh God . . .'

'What am I going to do?'

Gill, the friend who had introduced us, came round, and we all sat there saying, 'What are we going to do?' Tracey was thirty-three, the age when you start thinking about time running out. She didn't believe it. She spoke to her sisters. Everyone said the same thing, 'You can't do this on your own, Tracey.' It was all very well living with me, they said, 'But what about the flat? There's just no room for a baby . . .'

One Sunday Tracey and I were sitting around, talking in circles, not getting anywhere, when I said, 'Come on. Let's go to Camden Market and do some shopping.' The canal at Little Venice is the same canal that runs to Camden, so we walked along the towpath, past some amazing houses in St John's Wood, through Regent's Park and the Zoo, until we reached Camden. It was a lovely day. As we were walking around the horse stables, where most of the things are vintage, we came across a sign for a clairvoyant.

'Go on,' I said. 'Have your fortune told.'

'No,' she said. 'I'm too scared.'

'Just see if she knows. Go on. See what she's going to say.'

'Only if you come in with me.'

So OK.

'Sit down, ladies,' this woman said when we went in. 'My name is Joanne.' She spoke in a soft Northern voice that made you immediately feel comfortable.

Then, without any ado, without putting out any cards, or consulting a crystal ball, she just said, 'You're going to have a little girl!'

I went cold, and Tracey started to get a bit teary.

'What's the matter?' she said.

'I'm pregnant.'

'I know, your little girl's right here.'

What??

'But I don't know what to do.'

In the meantime I was thinking, Why are you telling this woman everything? We're paying her to tell your fortune . . .

Through her sniffs Tracey said, 'But what about Tom?'

'He's your knight,' she said, and turned a card over and said, 'Look.'

And there was a man standing up in a gondola with a baby all swaddled up, and Tracey and I looked at each other. Wow. The clairvoyant was called Joanne Hope and she was well named. Hope was what Tracey now had.

So we paid, left and I took Tracey's elbow and propelled her through the crowds and flagged down a black cab. She burst into tears.

'Look,' I said. 'I'm really sorry for making you go in there ...'

'It's not that. But she's the first person who's ever told me I could do it. Everyone else says I can't ...'

'Tracey, listen. If you want to do it, you can do it.'

'I want to do it.'

'Then we'll do it together. I'll live with you and we'll make it work.' The decision was made. And suddenly she was feeling so positive. But there was one thing she knew she had to do. She had to tell Tom and she had to do it face to face, she said – after all, they were friends – so she drove up to see him in Wales.

Amazingly he didn't go mad. She told me that he just put his arm around her and said, 'It's going to be OK. We'll get through this. I don't know how but we'll find a way.'

And then, little by little, they started texting. And time went on, and they looked at every option, taking it day by day, with Tommy coming to our flat every other weekend. One evening they went for a walk on Hampstead Heath for a talk. By the time they came back it was settled. 'We're going to have the baby,' Tommy had told her, 'and we'll do it together. We don't know each other properly yet, but I want to be involved.'

Now, in 2015, they are married with three kids and live on the Isle of Man. And that baby is ten years old. And, of course, she was a girl and her name is Jessica Summer.

8

Camden

2004 was the year I learnt to play poker, not taught by Nanny Flo – though it certainly helped that I'd had all those years of gin rummy – but by Colin Murray, who combined being a Radio 1 DJ with sports broadcasting. Poker had never had much success on television until the invention of something called the hole cam that allowed viewers to see the cards people had in their hands.

The *European Poker Tour* was brand new and they needed someone to host it along with Colin Murray, he being the knowledgeable half of the partnership. And Colin was a wonderful teacher – he taught me all I needed to know in a couple of days.

The tour is a bit like tennis in that the same star players travel around visiting different cities competing against each other time and time again, but there also other players – often locally based – to provide added interest.

It was recorded for broadcast around Europe by a production company called Sunset and Vine and in England it went out late night on Channel 5. This wasn't jobbing presenting, but a proper six-part series, even if it was stretched out over nine months. The actual tournaments took place over several days, in genuine casinos and we literally toured. It started in September in Barcelona, followed by London, then Dublin. Then, after Christmas and New Year, we went to Copenhagen, Deauville, Vienna, then finally Monte Carlo for the grand finale in May 2005 where the prize pool was nearly $3 million!

Not only was this my only income over this period, I really liked the job. It was an introduction to a whole new world and I met some extraordinary characters. I remember one poker player in particular called Noah who became a friend. Sometimes he'd disappear to play on line and come back after an hour $20,000 the richer!

Once Tracey and Tommy had made their decision, it was time for me to move on. Where to but to Jody . . . I turned up in a taxi at Jason's bachelor pad in Notting Hill with my life in bin bags but as the house was so small I ended up sleeping in his garage and promised that I wouldn't be there long.

Playing gooseberry has never been my thing, but they were soon going on holiday to Thailand and then, after New Year, I was off myself. Even so, it was a very unsettling time. I was unsettled because I had nowhere to live. Unsettled because it was clear that Mum and Dad weren't getting on. Unsettled because this would be the first Christmas Jody and I had not spent together . . .

Instead she and Jason came up to Great Hockham on Christmas Eve, we did a present swap and then they left early on Christmas morning. So Christmas Day and Boxing Day were really tense, with me feeling annoyed and tetchy, just because I hated Jo not being there, and Mum and Dad constantly sniping at each other.

And then news of the tsunami began to filter through . . . Phuket . . .

Wasn't that where Jo and Jason were going? we asked ourselves. We rang Jo's mobile. No response. For two hours we sat there, trying to get whatever news we could . . . I was distraught. I'd been feeling so negative towards Jo, and what if I never saw her again? Then the phone rang and Mum was crying when she picked it up . . . It was Jo. She'd just heard the news, she said. When they'd landed in Bangkok they'd decided to go north first to Chiang Mai. Typical Jo – 1) never having her phone on and 2) changing her mind at the last minute.

After New Year I took off for Goa before the next date on the *European Poker Tour* at the end of January. Everyone I had ever met seemed to have gone to India, but I'd never been and this seemed like the perfect opportunity. To go on holiday when you've got nothing lined up is very difficult in the entertainment industry, not to say impossible. Firstly, you can't get to auditions if you suddenly get called, and secondly, you can't relax because you can't risk spending money. But this year I had the next half of the *Poker Tour* to come back to. Once New Year was over, air fares came right down and staying there wasn't going to cost me anything because a friend of a friend had said, 'Just come out, you can stay at the house.'

This was Adam Baker who was renovating some apartments there. I'd met him through his carer, a Norwegian friend of mine, a singer called Camilla Romestrand. Adam had jumped into a river when he was a teenager and has been paralysed from the waist down ever since.

It was the first time I had ever been to the tropics. My room was on the ground floor of the house and I woke up one morning to see a baby elephant peering in at the window!

Camilla wasn't out there – Adam had another carer called John who was looking after him – but Adam's brother Miles was, so he and I would go down to the beach, John driving us – Dire Straits playing at full volume. When Miles left, I hired a little bike and would pedal up and down feeling really independent.

Shortly after I got back I went to a *Bo'Selecta!* reunion dinner. All sorts of people had been invited – even some celebrities who'd been mocked on the show, including a few who had appeared as themselves as well as being taken off by Leigh. One of these was Jack Osbourne – The Osbournes being obvious targets for Leigh's take-no-prisoners humour. Although Jack had been on the show more than once, we'd never actually met. He immediately struck me as an exceptionally nice guy and really bright. We talked a bit about our lives and he said that if I ever found myself in LA I should give him a call. Then, while we were sitting there chatting, my phone rang. It was Jody. She wanted me to be the first to know, she said. She was pregnant.

Oh.

She had loads of other people to ring, she said, so maybe we'd talk later.

Right.

I flicked my phone off and felt utterly empty. Jo was my twin. No matter what rows we had – there was something you could never break between us. Or so I had always thought. Now that unique link had gone. Now she was attached to someone else, literally . . . Was it jealousy? Betrayal? Sometimes you can't split your emotions up into boxes with neat labels, and this was one of those times. I just remember saying, 'Oh.'

Back on the work front, Nik had a new client called Russell Brand, so Polly Hill was now looking after me. I told her that I would take anything, anything at all. I just needed to work. Between the various poker tournaments, I'd been picking up bits and pieces where I could, including links between music videos on E4: no script, just me, a cameraman and the director in a small airless room for about three hours each time.

I'd also got work on a quiz channel called Nation 217 – three-hour slots where you just talked quizzes. To keep going for that length of time without a script while giving the impression that the whole thing is completely riveting – rather than utterly boring – was exhausting.

Nation 217 was based in Wapping, and in some ways it was like having a regular job. Over the next two years I would do shifts between other things. These shows were always live and, with hindsight, I can see that I learnt much more than I was aware of at the time.

As so often, as much depends on the people you're working with as the job itself, if not more, and at Nation 217 I became friendly with another presenter called Olivia Lee. We were about the same age and we had the same sense of humour, so one day we were chatting in a girly way and she asked if I had a boyfriend.

'Well, I'm kind of seeing this guy who's a musician – never date a musician!'

'Oh yeah, me too. Trouble.'

And we went on like this and her boyfriend and mine had a lot in common, and we were talking about how similar they were.

'So where does this guy live?'

'Belsize Park . . .'

'What street?'

It was only then that it dawned on us that we were sleeping with the same man . . .

'So how do you find the bed?' I said.

'Well, it keeps breaking.'

'Yeah, I broke it.'

So we emailed him a picture of the two of us . . . And he

sent back a photo of his penis. Not even a 'Sorry', just a big ego penis saying: 'Well, look what I've got!'

So that was the end of him, but Olivia and I became friends.

I never lost my optimism that somewhere around some corner was The One. And one day I bumped into Leigh Francis who said, 'Have you met this crazy new client John's taken on called Russell Brand? Because I think he's your perfect man. He's completely crazy but he's amazing. You should go on a date with him.'

So one night we were all out in Camden with Leigh and John Noel and a few others, when in walks this unbelievable character who when he talks to you it's like nothing else exists in the whole world, apart from the two of you. So somehow Leigh engineered it, and me and Russell went to the cinema to see Shane Meadows's *Dead Man's Shoes*. A brilliant film, though perhaps not ideal date material. It turned out not being a date but we became really good friends and Jo and I became regulars at his stand-up nights at The Enterprise, just opposite Chalk Farm tube in Camden. Russell was crazy intelligent and I used to feel I had to take a dictionary with me. Later, when he started doing stand-up with a comedian called Paul Foot, another brilliant guy, Russell asked me to choreograph a dance routine they had at the end of their act and we've stayed friends ever since. And no matter how big he's become, the first thing he ever says when we meet is, 'How's Jo? How's Jason?' He's a really lovely man.

*

Sometime in February I had an email from Sean, the guy I'd had the fling with in Tokyo. We'd been communicating sporadically over the last six months and now he was saying, 'You're not working. I'm not working. Why don't you come to LA?'

So I thought, If you want to go, just go. No building up of expectations, just go, and as I'd never been to LA, what better introduction than to see it with a born-and-bred Angelino?

Few as my expectations were, they were dashed the moment I saw Sean at the airport. He wasn't like I remembered at all. He was like a completely different person. How had I never noticed that he was cross-eyed? I must have had holiday goggles on, I decided. It had happened before – but not on the other side of the world . . .

I lasted two days at his house. But what was I going to do? The only person I knew in LA was Jack Osbourne, who I'd barely spoken to. But he had given me his number and said if ever you're in LA give me a call . . .

So I texted him, and said, *Hi Jack, it's Caroline Flack. You probably don't remember me but I'm stuck in LA and I wondered if you could recommend a hotel.*

Within half an hour he had picked me up and taken me to stay at his parents' house in Beverly Hills. There we were, going down all these iconic roads – Hollywood Boulevard, Sunset Boulevard – both so familiar yet so different and it all felt distinctly weird. And then, when he opened the front door, I could hardly believe it. This was the same house I had seen in *The Osbournes*! The same kitchen, the same lunatic dogs, the same chandeliers everywhere, shabby chic gone mad! Sharon was there and Kelly, and Kelly really looked after me and dosed me up because I had a terrible cold. In fact they were all really nice to me. When the worst of my cold was over, Jack drove me over to their beach house at Malibu. We stayed for a couple of days and it was just bliss. It really was like being in a film with the Pacific Ocean crashing yards away from my bedroom window.

It was never romantic between us – it wasn't like that at all – but we talked a lot, and I soon found out that he is an incredibly wise young man and over the years he's been a lovely friend to me.

A few days later I had a call from Olivia. She was in LA, she said, and had come to rescue me. In fact she was there to interview Will Smith, but we rented an apartment together and had such a great time that I changed my flight and extended my stay.

The Games was a reality show on Channel 4 where celebrities competed against each other in Olympic-style sports. It was presented by Jamie Theakston and had started in the spring of 2003. There was, naturally, a spin-off show called The Games: Live at Trackside on E4, which came on after the main event.

I had had a meeting with them early in 2004, and didn't get it. But the girl who interviewed me, called Anna Reid, told Polly my agent: 'She just wasn't keen enough. She didn't seem like she wanted the job enough.'

Then in 2005 they asked me back again. So Polly reminded me, 'Remember. You need to go in more keen.'

'So fine, I'll go in more keen. "Hello, it's me! I really want this job."' And that was basically what I did. The previous year I'd been blonde. I was now jet-black and the moment I saw Anna, she said, 'Like the hair.' So I immediately felt I was in with a chance. The meeting went really well, and they gave me a little screen test. Then I just had to wait . . . You couldn't get emails on your phone in those days so I'd pop into my local Internet cafe every day, sometimes twice, and log on to my Hotmail account and hold my breath.

And one morning, there it was: 'You've got the job! This is amazing!' Because Polly knew, as we all did, that *The Games* was a really big deal and for a lot of people the spin-off show is the best part. And this wasn't some speciality cable channel. This was mainstream telly.

I was basically a trackside reporter. The fact that I knew practically nothing about sport was irrelevant. For these spin-off shows it's as much about having a laugh as anything else. The main show ends, you change channels and you want it to be different and funny, so I used to take the mickey out of the contestants a bit. Not to push it too far – this wasn't about making me look good or the contestants look small – but it's not supposed to be serious.

It was all done in Sheffield – three weeks starting at the end of March – and yes the show was fun, great fun, and I really enjoyed it. But more important than that, I got to know Anna and Jade her assistant. I had been nearly five years in London but I had never made any real friends of my own – the people I used to hang out with were basically Jo's friends – and, suddenly, it was like we had always known each other. We shared the same sense of humour, liked the same music . . . For the first time since moving to London, I felt like I belonged. It was a complete life change. From then on I just wanted to be like Anna. She was a couple of years older than me but just the most perfect combination – always wise-cracking, clever and funny but at the same time incredibly sensible. She's the friend I'll turn to if I have an irrational thought and she'll go, 'Hmmm. Wellll . . .'

Anna was in a long-term relationship with a guy who managed bands and had the great name of Angus Blue. However Jade, like me, was single and also like me she was between flats. So once the show was over we decided to look for somewhere together, and it was back to Highgate.

Shepherd's Hill was proper Highgate, not Archway-pretending-to-be-Highgate, and Jade and I had the best time. There I was, single, in my twenties, in London, living with a flatmate who was just like me – except that she was incredibly tidy and I was incredibly messy. But it worked. We never had arguments, except one night when we both gave our number to the same boy. We decided to wait to see which one he called and, guess what, he called both of us! Tom McKay is the breaker of many hearts, so I've always been glad that I never fell in love with him, but he's now one of my absolute best friends.

*

I'd hoped that working on *The Games* would lead on to something. It didn't. But at least I had the second series of the *European Poker Tour* to look forward to, starting in September. Not only was it regular money, but I really enjoyed it. I'd been teaching all my friends in a rather second-hand, Chinese-whispers kind of way and one evening a friend of Jade's and mine called Pierre invited us to his apartment to play.

So we rang the bell, and who should open the door but Joshua Jackson from *Dawson's Creek*! I couldn't believe it – I had grown up this with boy! Neither of us said a word until we got out. They were all guys apart from us, and all serious players, but it was Jade who walked out with the pot – about £400! She was a complete beginner – and I never decided whether she was a naturally brilliant player or if it was simply that nobody could read her.

The first season of the *European Poker Tour* finished on a high in Monte Carlo but then I had nothing lined up until the second season started. So in early June, Jade and I went down for a week to Newquay. I hadn't been back since that first holiday with Sarah, Donna, Naomi, Heidi and Jo, irritating everyone with our ghetto blaster.

We made out to our friends that we were going on a surfing holiday, but really we just needed to chill – and it wasn't as if either of us could surf. In fact it turned out to be the hottest week of the year and it was gorgeous. We were both pretty broke so we stayed in a proper hostel complete with bunk beds where we hooked up with an Australian band who were also staying in the hostel. They were playing just down the coast in a bar/shack right on Perranporth beach, and as venues go it was really cool. To get there we'd clamber in the back of their van along with the instruments, amps and cables and the rest of it. Then, once the gig got going, we'd stand at the side of the stage like proper groupies! They were called the Beautiful Girls and I ended up having a fling with the drummer called Mitch. Over the years he and I kept in touch and we met up when I did *I'm a Celebrity* . . . in Australia. He was then in Sydney playing for a band called Angus & Julia Stone, who are now really successful.

It wasn't the first time I'd had a proper two-girls-on-the-loose holiday. That was Jo and me back in 2000 when we were twenty. I had just split up from Pete Edwards and Jo had just finished her first year at Ravensbourne.

From time to time over the years Mum and Dad used to rent a one-bedroom apartment in St Tropez and Jo and I had such good memories of holidays there we decided we'd go on our own. Our budget was definitely shoestring, but we were so excited: Imagine! The south of France! On our own!

The popular image of St Tropez – film stars and millionaires – is certainly true but it isn't all bling and glitz, not in 2000 anyway. The little town itself is very old and absolutely beautiful. The port is a proper port with boats and yachts, and every morning we'd sit and have coffee on the quay and just watch the Beautiful People amble by. And then, about three days in, we met a guy called Ben. He was only young, but he was like 'I've got eight friends on my dad's boat and we want some girls to come over.'

Me: NO WAY!!

Jo: Let's do it!!

It turned out to be a very good call.

They were actually eight really nice guys who had just finished university, and Ben's dad owned a big old yacht moored right by the quay where we had our coffee. Basically the dad had said, 'Look, take my yacht, take your mates out on it and have some fun.' It had everything – from wood-panelled cabins to its own jet skis. There was even a crew, all kitted out in yacht-type trousers and T-shirts printed with the ship's name.

'Listen,' said Ben once we'd idled away the afternoon and most of the evening. 'Me and the guys are planning on sailing down the coast for a few days, so why don't you leave your apartment and stay with us? You'd have your own cabin.'

!!!

So we left our little apartment that we'd fallen in love with in a shoestring kind of way, and spent the next week on this yacht. Blue skies, anchoring in little bays, swimming off the side (not me obviously), snorkelling (ditto), stopping off and going to street markets, lunches on shore, dinners on board, it was absolutely brilliant. But neither Jo nor I had any kind of romance with any of them. They weren't overconfident or arrogant 'lads-on-a-yacht', they were just nice boys.

They dropped us off in Antibes. We had a last meal

together in a cafe in the port, before waving them off. Then Jo and I found a little apartment in Juan-les-Pins, a bus ride away. It was there I met Gary, who worked on the boats, crewing for this person and that. He was from Birmingham and I made Jo go out with his friend Antoine. Antoine was French and worked on mega yachts, but Jo didn't take to him. For me, it was a great holiday romance, if short. Gary and I had two nights together but he never called again. And I started to realise, Oh, so this is what happens, is it? Antoine did keep in touch, and we tried to get information on Gary. But we never found Gary. Gary was long gone.

And now, seven years on from our escapade on the French Riviera, so much had changed. My twin, my fellow accomplice, schemer and conspirator for over quarter of a century was a mum. Willow was born on 7 August 2005.

It was a Sunday. Jason phoned early in the morning to say Jo was in labour and he'd dropped her off at the Chelsea and Westminster Hospital. Things had slowed down, he said, so the baby probably wouldn't be born till the next day, but he'd keep us informed. Much to his amazement, by the time he got back to her room, me, Mum and Dad were already ensconced. Quite reasonably, he'd imagined that it would just be him and Jo at the birth . . . He was visibly shocked, but there wasn't a great deal he could do.

Jo had had an epidural and couldn't feel the contractions, so I was helping with timing, while Mum and Dad were reading the Sunday papers.

In the end Jo was in labour for so long she was given an emergency Caesarean. By then, Mum and Dad had left, but I stayed. They put up a screen so none of us could see what was going on, until all of a sudden out came this little bundle and I remember thinking, My God! As they handed the baby over to Jo, she looked as surprised as I was. James Blunt's song 'You're Beautiful' was No. 1 at the time and it kept running through my head and over the next few days whenever I heard it I thought of Willow. And she is. Beautiful.

That day, 7 August 2005, was the last time I ever saw my mum and my dad in the same room together as a couple. Things had been sticky for some time. They just weren't communicating any more. Mum had been so young when they married and I think she just wanted to do something for herself before it was too late. A few weeks later Dad took early retirement and moved to the apartment they had bought in Sainte-Maxime, not far from St Tropez, while Mum got a job in Norwich working for the local newspaper.

Once Willow was safely back at home, I decided I should go and see Dad. The south of France sounds very glamorous but he was there on his own and I knew he must be feeling very strange. He and Mum had been together for forty years ...

A couple of days into our little holiday, Mum called. She'd seen something in the paper, she said, and thought I ought to know. I was being dropped from the *Poker Tour*. Someone called Natalie Pinkham was doing it instead.

I couldn't believe it. Everyone had been talking about the next series and I knew I'd done a good job. It had only been in a gossip column, so maybe it wasn't true. I called Polly immediately.

'What's going on, Polly?'

'I'm not sure. I'll give them a call.'

A week later she got back to me. The report was true. 'You're going to be replaced by Natalie Pinkham. I'm really sorry, Caroline. This doesn't seem to be happening for you at the minute, does it?'

Dad did his best to be sympathetic, saying he was really worried for me.

'I don't need you to be worried for me, Dad. I need you to say that it'll all be fine and that it'll all work out!' I know he meant well, but Dad's sense of what to say and what not to say wasn't always the best. I remember when I dyed my hair dark and he said, 'I much prefer you blonde.' And he was always saying, 'You look so much bigger on telly.' Thanks Dad.

That was a pretty desperate few weeks. The *European Poker Tour* was my only regular income. Yes, I could go back to Nation 217 but I kept thinking of what Polly had said, 'This doesn't seem to be happening for you . . .' What could I do next?

And then a week before the second series was due to start, Polly phoned and I knew from the sound of her voice that it was good news. John Duffy, the executive producer, had said that it wouldn't be the same without Caroline, 'so we'd like Caroline and Natalie Pinkham to do it together'. This was one of the best phone calls I have ever had in my life. It meant so much to me. I'd got my job back and I had cash!

By then I was back in London and I went out to celebrate with a friend and we agreed that we were in an industry where one day can make all the difference. And it couldn't have worked out better. Natalie had a background in sports telly and she's a really good poker player and I felt like a complete dunce beside her, but she was lovely with a really infectious sense of humour and we ended up becoming really good friends.

Shortly after that Polly called and said the BBC had asked if I wanted to audition for a new Saturday morning kids' show – *TMi*.

It seemed a really weird idea. I was working in adult TV – you couldn't get much more adult than poker. Why would I go back to doing kids' telly? Because generally kids' telly is where you start out. I thought I'd better talk to John Noel.

'Isn't this a backward step? I mean, I'm twenty-seven! Can a twenty-seven-year-old do kids' TV?'

'It's not a backward step, Caroline. Go for the audition and see how you feel about it.'

So I went and did the audition and I absolutely loved it. I came out of the doughnut (as BBC TV centre was then called) feeling several inches taller. Years before I'd auditioned for *Finger Tips*, a painting-and-sticky-back-plastic kids' show which Fearne Cotton ended up doing.

But I hadn't felt confident about that at all. This was totally different. I loved Sam (Nixon) and Mark (Rhodes) the presenters instantly. They had competed on *Pop Idol* in 2003 and came third and second and then they joined forces and were signed by Simon Fuller and released a single which went to No. 1. They'd gone on to do a bit of presenting, doing the *Top of the Pops* spin-off show *Top of the Pops Reloaded* (Fearne Cotton again), and had just finished four months of *Level Up* the daily CBBC breakfast show.

Sam was from Lancashire and Mark was from near Birmingham; Mark was two years younger than me, Sam seven years younger. They were clever and funny and the producers were clever and funny. In fact everyone was clever and funny and the show was silly and I was silly. Kids' telly is all about being silly and so I was a complete natural having spent a lifetime perfecting it. It probably helped that being so little – just over five feet one – I looked younger than I was.

I once dressed up as an angry badger and danced while Sam tried to throw a nut and hit my head. When he did, and I fell to the ground, a kid at home won a prize. I'd dress up as a banana and every time I ran and a kid shouted 'Stop' they won a prize. We had a game called the Human Loot Machine, which was a variation of a fruit machine but using real people. We did the show at the MTV studios in Leicester Square and 'outside broadcast' meant literally popping outside. If they had three of a kind, then of course they won the jackpot! This show wasn't for tiny kids, it was aimed more at teenagers and there was an element of adult humour so that any parents watching wouldn't be driven completely mad. For example, if the three adults I'd persuaded to play the Human Loot Machine in Leicester Square came up with two apples one each side of the banana . . . well . . .

We'd do skits about popular shows – like *The X Factor* – I even got to play Simon Cowell, complete with perma-wave wig and teeth which we made out of polystyrene cups. I was a contestant on *Strictly*, described by 'Bruno Ravioli' as 'dancing like a meatball'. I read the news as Natasha Kaplinsky in a blonde wig. I was a singer in a rock band – Farrah Fawcett meets Brian May. In fact I thought we were rather good – hardly surprising perhaps given that the boys had had a No. 1 record. We were certainly a good deal better than much of the stuff that was out there at the time.

I got to flirt with boy bands – McFly for instance – standing in for all the little girls who at that moment wanted to be me. But much of the time it boiled down to gloop, gunk, slime and gunge, most of it thrown in my face. And while the majority of grown-ups hate all that physical stuff, I just love it. I love playing in the snow. Pillow fight? Bring it on.

But it was the best part of three hours, live. Yes there were bits and bobs that had been pre-recorded but even so. Admittedly there was a script, but as often as not it went out the window. It was like being a child again, we had to be inventive, surreal, non-linear and open to everything.

I'd do a lot of red-carpet interviews and put the questions the kids would have wanted to ask – not necessarily the kind of things top-ranking stars were used to – and not everyone got it. Take Daniel Craig. When I asked him: 'What's your favourite ice-cream flavour?' he looked at his PR as if to say, 'What is this?' And he had reason to, because it was stupid. After the interview I'd always give the celebrity a badge saying 'Friend of Flack', but he wouldn't take his. Nicole Kidman was at the other end of the playing-along spectrum. I asked what her favourite colour of pants was. She was brilliant and funny and she did take her badge. Dustin Hoffman was another good sport. When he'd taken his badge, he said, 'You've got a great laugh,' then turned and shouted to everyone else coming down the red carpet, 'You gotta hear her laugh! She's gotta great laugh!'

Fear? What's that? Embarrassment? It's what makes live (*lyve!*) TV live (*liv!*). We'd rehearse on Thursday and Friday and we'd go live on Saturday. And I learnt so much. For the very first time in my career, for example, I used an earpiece to connect me with the gallery.

Taking *TMi* was the best career decision I ever made, because I loved that job and I still look back on it and think, How come I got so lucky? Yet again, I ended up making loads of friends. Yes, I was exhausted . . . But it was all such FUN. I genuinely felt that I had the best job in the world.

*

STORM IN A C CUP

By now Jade was working as an assistant producer at MTV, overlooking Camden Lock and so we used to hang out at the Lock Tavern just across the road. It's one of the original Camden music pubs, like the Dublin Castle, that always had different bands playing – and still does. The whole of Camden would be posted with flyers advertising this or that band, half of which you had never heard of and never would again. Then quite by coincidence my brother Paul's best friend from school – a guy who I'd always known as D-Day – bought a really rough bikers' pub a hundred yards up the road, called the Hawley Arms. He, along with two friends called Dougie and Ruth, were doing it up, Paul said, and I should go along and say Hi. In the end it became quite a phenomenon, most famous because it was the pub that Amy Winehouse used to frequent.

So the next time I arranged to meet up with Jade when she finished work, instead of going to the Lock Tavern we went along to this place. At that point it was still a bikers' pub and it took a certain amount of imagination to see what it would be like once it was finished. But D-Day was full of enthusiasm, explaining how it was all going to be refurbished, how there would be sofas, and how the emphasis would be on socialising and not heavy drinking and how there was going to be a restaurant and rooms upstairs. So we decided we'd do our bit to help and the Hawley would be our new place to go and drink.

We were soon regulars and it wasn't long before we realised that loads of creative-minded people were going in there, though whether they actually created anything was another matter, but certainly some of them did. It was the same for the bar staff – they were either actors, or out of work musicians, or writers who'd just finished college. It had that atmosphere that gave you the feeling that something was happening. It wasn't long before they opened up the saloon and the public bar and turned it into one long bar. And then they opened up upstairs, and soon it was this bustly, fun place. This was an era when indie music was really big, so there were loads of bands there all the time as well as the hangers-on.

I wouldn't normally go to a pub on my own, but because of D-Day, Ruth and Dougie, the Hawley was different – it felt like family. I would sit up on a high stool at the big horseshoe-shaped bar at the front and chat, and that's how I met Josie.

Josie Naughton was four years younger than me but it was obvious from the moment we met we had at least one thing in common: big boobs. Big boobs come as standard in my family. The Flack boobs are legendary, we all have them and they're a nightmare. All those pretty bras you see in ads? Forget it. Practically the only brand that combines sex appeal with size is Elle Macpherson. Well, Josie was even bigger than I was. Josie's boobs are so big I can get my entire head in one cup.

She was born on a boat in Brazil and is a true free spirit. Her mum used to be a model and is really thin and really tall with red hair, and Josie's sister is just like her mum. Josie is the opposite, small, long dark hair, and these massive boobs. Her dad is Argentinian and she didn't meet him until a couple of years ago and then she walked into this room in Argentina to be greeted by about ten Josie lookalikes! It was like finding the final piece in the jigsaw, she said.

She was really funny and really clever. She'd been to university and had a degree in politics and history (I think) but she still didn't know what to do with her life, which was why she was working in the Hawley.

There's a book called *The Five People You Meet in Heaven*. It's a bit schmaltzy but the idea behind it is true. How you never really know who the key people in your life are, the ones who changed your life. But Josie is one of them. And perhaps I changed hers. Through a friend of mine she got a job working in music-licensing at Endemol, the huge entertainment consortium. Then another friend hooked her up to somebody else. And now she's living in LA where she looks after Coldplay and I miss her horribly. We've had our ups and downs, but – twelve years later – she is still my best friend.

When people say that Camden is a weird old place, I think, Well, perhaps you weren't there when I was. It was like constantly being at Glastonbury: there was never any trouble, never any aggression. There was a whole circle of friends, a big big circle of really creative, down-to-earth people and I was soon lucky enough to be part of it. It was just such a brilliant time to be hanging out in London.

Me and Jody. Two peas from the same pod, similar but not identical. (I'm behind the dummy on the left.)

Even asleep, I was untidy. In the morning my pyjamas would be inside out and back to front and my hair was like a bird's nest.

Me and my mum on holiday in Spain when I was about four. Mum was beautiful, a pocket-sized Twiggy – 'knock-out' as Dad used to say.

Great Hockham village school. The twins with the corkscrew hair are in the front, with Jody and me sitting next to them. I'm the one with white tights. Hannah Denty is top right.

Me and my dad away on our own in Cyprus with his work (hence shirt and tie). Mum didn't like flying – so this was dad-and-daughter time. I was about fifteen.

Jody, Mum and me in St Tropez. I was at college and into scraping my hair back and wearing lip liner.

Charlotte, myself, James, Bianca and Debbie at the front. We never had any money or sleep but we managed to go out and get drunk every night. They were the best years of our lives, and we all felt the same.

Five Go Down to the Sea – less Enid Blyton, more Ocean Colour Scene. Our first holiday without our parents after leaving school – Newquay, August 1996.

Me and my flatmate Paul Edwards in our Archway flat. As well as designing shoes and handbags for Jo and me, he helped me rehearse my lines for the *International Pepsi Chart Show*, my first-ever presenting job.

Me, aged twenty-three, singing at the Jazz Café in Camden, with my brother-in-law Leigh's band, Speedometer. His offer came out of the blue and gave me a much-needed boost.

Leigh Francis as Michael Jackson and me as 'Bubbles' in *Bo' Selecta*, Leigh's satire on celebrity culture, now a cult comedy classic.

Russell Brand, Leigh Francis and me. They are both crazy, I'm just silly.

My first-ever publicity photo taken by Nik, John Noel's son, who looked after me when I first joined the agency.

Nice smile, shame about the flares. An early effort at a publicity photo, taken by Jo.

My beautiful niece Willow, just a few days old – it was love at first sight.

2011: being on *The Xtra Factor* was never like work. It was like being with a bunch of friends. SJ, series producer, is the one in the centre making the peace sign; she's now a close friend, and responsible for getting me back for the winner's dance on *Strictly*.

The Xtra Factor, 2013, with Matt Richardson, who is without doubt the funniest person I know.

Me and Dermot doing the BAFTAs in 2013 – the first and only time I've ever worn a long dress. The corset was so tight, I couldn't breathe so I took it off in the toilet.

When I was doing *The Xtra Factor*, Louis Walsh was my favourite among the judges. He was the one you'd want to have a drink with in the bar afterwards.

The Flackson Five at Latitude, 2012. Stupidly I forgot to take my wig off when I went to bed so ended up keeping it on the whole weekend.

Me and Pasha doing our show dance in the *Strictly* final. Much of the time I was dancing with tears in my eyes.

The X Factor auditions with partner-in-crime, Olly Murs. Wembley, July 2015.

Olly and me freezing at *The X Factor* boot camp. Gemma (behind me) and I are wearing the same dark glasses, which I'd bought at Palma airport following the *Love Island* wrap party hangover.

I adore Olly Murs, a true friend as well as annoyingly good at everything he does.

Summer 2015 in France with Willow, Zuzu and Delilah. We've just had snails . . . I loved them. They didn't.

August 2015, and it's all change on the juggernaut known as *The X Factor* for the start of series 12: Rita, Nick, Cheryl, Simon, me and Olly.

9

Gladiators

*T*Mi (stands for Too Much information) was only on air between September and late spring, then you had a long summer break before starting again the following September. It really was like being back at school and to celebrate my 'end of term', Anna took me to the Isle of Wight. As Angus was a music manager, he and Anna would rent a house every year and they said I could stay in their spare room. We used to call it Rock Villas because every time you opened the door there was another member of a rock band standing there.

Stadium bands are quite different to the little indie gigs I was used to and that summer I finally got to see the Rolling Stones. They weren't on Dad's playlist when I was growing up – he only became a fan a couple of years ago when he finally got to see them playing live – but Liz used to play them a lot.

Isle of Wight 2007 was the first festival they had done in Britain for thirty years and there was a real sense of occasion. They put on such an amazing show and I totally understand why they're called The Greatest Rock Band in the World. Amy Winehouse came on with Mick Jagger for 'Ain't Too Proud to Beg'. She was now at the height of her fame. *Back to Black* was the biggest-selling album of the year, and she had just got married.

Amy was a friend of Josie's and so I knew her, or rather I would see her around at the Hawley which was her local – I can't claim her as a friend. You always knew she was different. As a person she was very welcoming and very lovely, there were no airs and graces or any kind of snobbery, or 'I'm this' or 'I'm that and I wanna be famous'. She didn't want any of that.

There was never any doubt about her talent and I was a big fan. D-Day had got Josie and me tickets to see her at the Astoria in Charing Cross Road that previous February. The Astoria was my favourite music venue of all time – until they demolished it to make way for the Crossrail project. I feel privileged to have seen that concert. Amy Winehouse was without doubt the greatest artist of my generation. And if you've ever been through the agony of heartbreak, you can't fail to be moved. It's not just about listening and hearing, she makes you feel. It's visceral. Everything was so personal. She was singing about her problems, but she was talking directly to you. I was blown away.

I saw her the following year when she was on before Jay

Z at Glastonbury and I could see that she had changed. She looked so vulnerable and even as I was watching I had the feeling that this was the last time I was ever going to see her.

Sometime around Easter 2007 Josie and I went to see Kate Nash. She was just starting out and had come through the Brit school that Amy Winehouse had been to in Croydon. She was very London – Harrow – witty and sharp. It was a really tiny gig, upstairs in the Lock Tavern, and late when we got out and an indie/folk/anti-folk musician called Jay (better known as Beans on Toast) who had dreadlocks and wore a hat and skate shorts – a generally crazy-looking character – suggested we go back to his place for more drinks.

He lived above a music pub called Nambucca in the Holloway Road, halfway between Camden and Highgate. It was a bit run-down and was definitely a pub for young people. By the time we got there it was well past one in the morning. And as we clumped our way upstairs – I thought, Bloody hell, this feels like I'm at college again, because there were all these people living in different rooms. No attempt was made to keep the noise down, and a door opened and a bleary-eyed head peered out and said, 'Hello.' He didn't seem to mind that we had woken him up, and he came and joined us.

I looked at this guy and thought, Hmmm … *Very* handsome.

The ensuing singsong went on until about 4.00 in the

morning and then Josie and I left. She lived in Camden with some other girls and I was headed back to Highgate, but as we parted company I had to ask.

'So who was that then?'

'Dave Danger,' she said, 'he's the drummer with the Holloways.' She added, 'There's this party on Monday, you should come. Everyone'll be there.'

It was in a club called Pop north of Oxford Street. It was somebody's birthday so I'd dressed up, but the moment I walked in I thought, I'm definitely not cool enough for this – everyone else was in ripped jeans and T-shirts. A band called Captain Black was playing, slightly folk-'n'-roll. But everyone was lovely and having crazy fun and me, Josie and Katie Langham, another friend I'd met at the Hawley, were just enjoying the night when I saw Dave heading towards me.

'Hey!' he said. 'Nice to see you again, can I get you a drink?'

I said yes please, and waited. And waited and waited. He didn't come back for two hours. And then, no drink. Then he went away again.

'So where's that drink then?' I said when he finally turned up.

'Oh yeah. I got to the bar, realised I had no cash so had to walk to a cashpoint. But I'll get you one now.' He was so sweet and disarming, and struck me as really kind. So then we exchanged phone numbers.

At some stage we moved on to another bar across the road. By then it was raining and Dave put up an umbrella and held it over me. Hmm, I thought. Definitely making an effort . . .

Then nothing. Not a word for three weeks, but then he phoned and asked me out on a date. He took me for a meal at Fifteen, Jamie Oliver's restaurant run by apprentices.

The next morning I rang Jo.

'I've met this guy and I really like him.'

'Haven't I heard this somewhere before?'

'There's something about this one. Seriously. It's different. I feel weird.'

'Hmmm.'

And then he didn't contact me for four weeks. I mean, FOUR WEEKS! And then when he did I told him I couldn't see him because I was going away. The second series of *TMi* had finished for the summer, and the next day I was heading off to India with Jade.

'Well, text me when you get back.'

I said 'OK' – but in my head I was shouting, Yaaaay!

We were flying to Kerala, then making our way down the coast to a town called Varkala right in the south that people were saying was amazing. We landed at Trivandrum, then got a taxi to Kovalam that had sounded a nice place to begin with. But when the guy let us out, and we'd sorted out our backpacks, we realised it wasn't what we'd expected at all. There wasn't a sign of a palm tree or a beach hut, just dusty streets and manky-looking dogs. Eventually we found a little hotel with a Mexican-bean-shaped swimming pool.

'We can't stay here,' Jade said. 'We need to go straight

to this Varkala place.' It was about two hours away, but taxis were cheap and anything seemed better than staying where we were. But first I went online to check out Tripadvisor comments to see what to expect. One particular comment didn't reassure me . . .

Warning: don't swim in the sea . . . my brother got swept away and we couldn't find him for ages.

'Jade, I don't think we should go,' I said. 'I've got a bad feeling about Varkala.'

'Go to sleep.'

'And whatever we do we mustn't go in the sea . . .'

'Carrie, you panic too much. You're panicking about something that hasn't happened yet.'

'Well, I just think we ought to be careful.'

'Go to sleep.'

The next morning we set off – two hours in a taxi – and then we got there and it looked no different from the last place.

'Are you sure this is Varkala?' I asked our driver.

'This is Varkala.'

So we took our backpacks and started walking in what we imagined must be the right direction for the sea. Suddenly, we go through a palm-tree shack and Wow! The rest of the coast had been flat, but here, high on red sandstone cliffs, is this amazing village looking out over the Indian Ocean. There are palm trees wedged between shacks, and even growing out of the cliff. And we just stood there, looking at each other. It was like coming through a dark tunnel into paradise.

The beach was beautiful – a wide stretch of golden sand – and then the blue, blue sea, which I spent three days not going into.

'Don't go too far out!' I warned Jade every time she went in, while I got hotter and hotter. (This wasn't the kind of place that had swimming pools . . .) Eventually, on day four, I thought, This is ridiculous. I'm just going to have to go in. And when Jade called, 'Come on!' for the fiftieth time, I decided OK.

Sinking into the water was the most wonderful feeling and just to feel cool again was amazing, but within less than two minutes one of the world's biggest waves reared up in front of me. I was still saying to myself, 'I'm gonna be fine, I'm gonna be fine,' when I was swept off my feet, up and under, tumbling over and over, foam, water, dark, gurgling in my ears, shafts of sunlight, all rolled in together. When the wave retreated I was left spluttering lying face down in the sand like a piece of wreckage. My bikini bottoms had come off. My sunglasses were missing.

Was it a freak giant wave? Probably not. The terror from all those years back in Spain has never really left me, and I had panicked and turned into this human jellyfish who just flailed around. Nearly as bad was being the centre of attention because by now the whole beach were rushing over to help while Jade was just sitting there saying, 'Well, no one else fell over.'

*

Dave was just so nice that I had real butterflies when I got back, and was much too nervous to text. What if he'd met somebody else? In the end I called Josie and asked as casually as I could if she'd seen him around. No. He was on tour . . .

So I send him a text. *I'm back, it would be nice to come and see one of your gigs if you're in London.*

Within seconds he replied. *How weird, we're in Brighton tonight if you wanted to get a train.*

So that was the next dilemma. If I go I look too keen. If I don't go I'm missing out. What do I do?

I called Josie again. 'If I go, will you come with me?'

'Of course.'

Josie and I met at Victoria station and I can remember exactly what I was wearing: ripped jeans and a black T-shirt. I never wear T-shirts.

The gig started at 9.00 so we caught up with them all in a PizzaExpress beforehand. And as I sat down Dave went, 'You're so brown!' And I know that I blushed, even though it was totally invisible under my tan. They gave us some passes and we stood at the front. I'd never heard them before and they were great – witty, jaunty, happy – two guitar players plus a guy on the violin with Dave cranking up the pace on the drums. We had a few drinks afterwards, then they went back on the tour bus.

Later that night Dave sent me a message. *I love it.*

Love what? My tan? My hair? My indie look? I could hardly ask that so I just wrote *Thanks for a great night.*

And I didn't hear from him for a month.

A MONTH!

I followed where they were playing obsessively. In mid-June they were set to play at the Camden Crawl, a mini festival where bands play at all the music pubs in Camden: Dublin Castle, Lock Tavern, Good Mixer, Oxford Arms, Elephant's Head, Proud Gallery, The Enterprise. Surely he would contact me then? We got on really well and I'd had all the signs . . . or so I thought. Then someone said they'd seen him . . . and I felt sick. He was here, in Camden. I stared at my phone willing it to ping, but nothing. There was nothing I could do.

All of a sudden, we're in the Hawley and I get a text. *I guess that's a no then.*

What? I realise he must have texted me and got no reply. So I did that old-fashioned, un-cool thing, I went outside and I phoned.

'What's a no?' I said.

'I asked if you wanted to come to the Camden Crawl with me and you never replied.'

'I didn't get the text.'

'Where are you now?' he said.

'I'm in the Hawley.'

'I'm in the Lock Tavern.'

Less than two hundred yards away . . .

'Shall we meet in the middle?' I said.

And so we met in the middle and we had a little kiss and then I took him home.

And that was it. Wherever we were we spoke – or tried to – every single day for the next however-many years.

I was so happy. I got to know the band, and the band's girlfriends; there was Bonnie who was going out with Alfie, George (Georgina) who was going out with Rob Skipper (the one who played the fiddle), and Lois who was going out with Bryn.

We didn't move in together for ages, because he lived above Nambucca and I never wanted to stay there, because it was just so smelly. I used to say, 'You live like a student!' And he was like 'We're a band! We don't have any money!'

All happy days, everything was happy.

And then I learnt that I'd got a kids' telly job. It was called *Escape from Scorpion Island* in Brazil and was an adventure game show, like a kids' *I'm a Celebrity* . . . It was scheduled to go out every night for three weeks in September, that time of the year when they have just gone back to school. It meant that I had to miss the first three weeks of *TMi* but it was all CBBC so no upset.

Part of me was pleased, but the other part really didn't want to go. I was still a mass of insecurities. Dave and I had only been seeing each other for seven weeks and if I went away for a month – which was what it would be – then who knows what would happen. He was in a band and he was very handsome . . .

It was one of the most gruelling jobs I have ever done. We worked from six in the morning until midnight, filming three shows a day and it was absolutely knackering.

The kids were dropped on an island (not really, just a clearing near the coast) and had to make their way up a mountain when they'd be helicoptered off again. They were divided into two teams, Sting and Claw. They were presented with various challenges, one team pitted against another, and the winners gained 'advantages' which would help them at a later stage. There were fourteen kids and three production teams. What with the travel, helicopters and chaperones, not to mention insurance, the whole thing must have cost a fortune.

My co-presenter was a boy called Reggie Yates who had been an actor (*Grange Hill*) and a presenter on *Top of the Pops* with Fearne Cotton. Our hotel was fine, but I'd hardly get my head on the pillow before it was time to wake up again. Deep sleep? No chance. And it wasn't exactly social. At the end of the day, the production guys would say, 'Coming to the bar then?' and I was like 'I literally cannot, I am that tired.' While everyone else was doing one show in three, Reggie and I did all of them.

The first thing that hit the unit was flu – 'scorpion' flu – and I was taken to the nearest hospital. I remember falling asleep with a drip in my arm, waking up, and finding that the drip had gone in the wrong place and I had an arm the size of a melon. Although it looked like a third-world kind of hospital, they gave me a full-body scan and it was amazing. There, up on this screen, was my entire skeleton! They said that if I came back in a few days I could take it with me. But production wouldn't allow it. I said I'd pay to go and get it – I mean to have your entire skeleton like that would be just fantastic – but they still said no.

The mountain that the kids had to climb was a real

mountain. I didn't climb it, but I did have to go up in a helicopter. I'd never been in a helicopter before and when we got up there and were just hovering, lingering over this mountaintop, my brain simply couldn't cope. I have never liked flying. Part of me knows that I have to, but the other part would do anything not to get on that plane, and I go through this internal struggle every time I go to an airport. But the helicopter was far worse. So I passed out and had to be brought down. To cap it all I'd ruined their shot . . .

Reggie and I had one day off the whole time we were there. We were desperate to go to Rio. I mean, you go all that way, thousands of miles across the Atlantic to Brazil, and you don't go to Rio? It was an hour and a half by road and several of us had decided we wanted to go to a club and to party. But the one day Reggie and I had off it rained and rain there is like standing under a waterfall. Everyone else was sitting around looking despondent and reading books but I was determined. I wanted to go to Rio. I wanted to see *Christ the Redeemer*. So one of the crew, one of the cameramen, drove us. He was brilliant. Having said that, it was one of the scariest drives I have ever been on in my life, hairpin bends all the way. We went to Copacabana – Rio's famous beach – and it was still bucketing down. I looked at Reggie and said, 'You know what? Let's imagine this is Bacardi. That it's raining Bacardi and we'll pretend we're dancing in a Bacardi ad!'

When finally we did get to the club, I was so tired I fell

asleep at the table. Just folded my arms, put my head down and that was that. Oblivion. I only woke when it was time to leave and then, of course, we had to drive all the way back . . . This time we were on the outer edge of the road and it was terrifying. The rain was torrential and my head kept lolling but I knew I couldn't go to sleep. If I went to sleep we would crash. It was one of the scariest times of my life. I really did think we were going to die.

It was hard not being able to speak to Dave. There was no mobile reception; I just had email. When I went into my Hotmail account I'd scan my inbox praying that there'd be something from him, but there wasn't. But then one day he sent me a poem . . . and I cried. And that's what kept me going. This poem said exactly what you want to hear when you think you've been abandoned. 'Sorry I haven't written, sorry I haven't done this or done that, and you probably think that I don't like you any more . . .' Yaaaay!

Finally it was over and I have never been so keen to get on a plane in my life. I had butterflies in my stomach, in my legs, in my arms, in my ears, everywhere. And as we came in to Heathrow I could hardly bear the excitement.

I sent him a text to say that I'd landed and he came straight round.

'So what say we go to the Hawley?' he said. I was so, so happy, and so was he.

Of course we were in love, but neither of us wanted to admit it so we'd play those games where you know you want to say the L word but don't feel you can risk it.

Dave: I'm 75 per cent in love with you and 25 per cent don't love you.

Me: OK, well I'm 80 per cent in love with you and 20 per cent don't love you.

And then one day he said, 'It's 100 per cent.'

The following June (2008) I finally got to go to Glastonbury. Anna had always said that I'd love it and I just thought, What about being in all that mud? I'd never thought of myself as a festival person until I opened myself up to it. And that year it was really flooded and Dave and I were sleeping in this tent. It was in Strummerville, a camping area named after Joe Strummer, but a tent is a tent wherever it is and it was freezing and wet and there was mud everywhere. But I absolutely loved it and I haven't missed a Glastonbury since.

Dave never made me feel insecure. Yes, we had arguments, but over silly things, like when he shaved off his beard. But mostly we spent our time laughing and we got quite fat because all we did was cook and eat. I don't think either of us could be called a good cook, we just appreciated food. We'd make something then eat it. Foodie food. Comfort food. We were always eating. It would start with breakfast – perhaps chorizo and avocado, eggs, toast or we'd have a massive lunch. The one question always being asked was: 'What shall we do for dinner?' It was constant.

When I'd taken *TMi* with Sam and Mark, it wasn't so much going into kids' TV that bothered me, it was wondering how I'd get out of kids' TV. But I loved the job so much I didn't regret taking it at all. Then, as we were coming up to the end of the second series in April 2008, *Gladiators* came up. And because *Gladiators* was a family show, it was a really nice transition and, after all I'd been through, it seemed like magic. You finish one job and another one comes along!

Not only that but I'd actually been headhunted – the first time that this had ever happened. So I didn't have to do anything – no audition, no screen test – it was just say 'yes' and sign on the dotted line. Most exciting of all, Steve Jones, the commissioning editor of Sky 1, 2 and 3, said that I was 'undeniably the next big thing'!

The original show had been a big hit for ITV in the nineties – a key part of the Flack family's Saturday-night viewing and I'd always loved it. When Jo and I were growing up, Saturday night was all about watching telly together – something you really only get these days with *X Factor* and *Strictly*. As well as *Gladiators*, there'd be *Blind Date*, *The Generation Game*, *Stars in Their Eyes*, *Beadle's About!* – you could watch them all. It was also the one time in the week that Mum could relax, as we'd always get a takeaway, either kebabs from a place Dad knew in Thetford, or a Chinese from Watton.

Gladiators had lasted until the end of 1999, but Sky had bought and relaunched it the previous year: big show, big budget, new gladiators, new everything. The presenters had been Ian Wright and Kirsty Gallacher. Kirsty did one season and they got me in to do the second.

It was filmed in Shepperton on two vast sound stages. Thirty-two amateur athletes, chosen from the twenty thousand who applied were competing for a £50,000 prize against twelve gladiators – in effect professional athletes, Tarzan and Jane types. This wasn't like *The Games*, where celebrities competed in genuine sports events, the challenges were fantasy combative. Everything was really silly, from the challenges – like hitting each other over the head with giant cotton buds – to the gladiators' names – Destroyer, Oblivion and Tempest – and that was part of the fun, but to say it was hectic is putting it mildly.

Although it went out between January and March 2009, we filmed it in November, every day for three weeks. We stayed in a local hotel because we had five o'clock starts. It was certainly the most gruelling job I had ever done. The hours, the schedule, but worst of all it was shot out of sequence which made things very tricky in terms of memory: always having to remember who had already done what, things that the viewer didn't know about so neither could you. This was when I first realised that working in TV is not glamorous. When you watch the finished product you realise where all the hard work goes. That's when you get the satisfaction, when it's all put together. The best thing was getting to work with Ian Wright who was brilliant and really made me laugh. When I told my dad, he said, 'You can't work with an Arsenal player. We're Spurs supporters!'

*

Dave came out to Twickenham to stay with me a couple of nights before going off to LA to play drums on Rob Skipper's new album. Although Rob played guitar, he was best known for the fiddle and when the Holloways were dropped by their record company sometime that autumn, Rob had started his own band, called Rob Skipper & the Musical Differences, which might be a clue as to why they were dropped, or why they thought they were dropped.

The timing wasn't fantastic because eighteen months after we'd first met, Dave and I had just decided to move in together and had rented a flat above Woolworth's in Crouch End. In the end me and Jo had to do the moving because Dave was in LA and we very nearly came to blows because we couldn't put up the Ikea bed. It was a funny little flat which we called 'the flat within a flat' because the windows looked into an inner courtyard rather than onto the street or a garden. When people came to visit, they'd look out of our windows and say, 'What is this?'

In January 2009 Dave arranged to go for a week's skiing with his family. I didn't ski and so when Olivia Lee and Katie Langham said they were going to Sri Lanka for a bit of sun and would I like to go along, I said yes.

But I'd only been there a couple of days when I realised I couldn't do it. What with Dave being in LA and me doing *Gladiators*, we were in danger of losing touch. I decided I needed to go home so we could spend some proper time together.

While I was worrying about what to do, things in Sri Lanka were getting extremely uncomfortable. News was coming in of a bus being blown up in the local town by the Tamil Tigers – rebel freedom fighters or terrorists depending on your point of view. They were Hindu – originally from India – and wanted to break away from the rest of Sri Lanka which was Buddhist. The conflict was hardly new – fighting had been going on since 1983 – but the holiday had been so last-minute I hadn't realised how bad the situation was. Locally you sensed the danger was being underplayed because of tourism, which was still recovering from the tsunami of 2004, but as we watched the news on CNN I decided I wanted out, so I called Virgin and, for an extra charge of £50, I managed to change my flight though for some reason they only had one that left at 2.00 in the morning. Forget getting the bus. I'd get a taxi to the airport in Colombo.

The driver didn't speak a word of English and he'd brought his mate along which felt weird – although in retrospect it was probably for protection. It was pitch-dark and every so often you'd see pinpricks of lights and it would be another roadblock. Soldiers with guns would shout, 'Get out!' and I'd have to stand in the road while they went through my luggage, and looked at my passport, talking to themselves and peering into my face with their torches. Everyone was incredibly aggressive. Even when we were waved through – only to be stopped at the next roadblock – no one smiled. In the distance you'd hear the rattle of far-off gunfire. I was petrified. I just needed to get home.

But London wasn't the haven I'd been hoping for. Dave was pissed off that I'd gone to Sri Lanka and within a few days he disappeared back to LA.

It's hard conducting a relationship at long distance but as long as you're communicating in the right way, you can do it; unfortunately Dave and I seemed to spend our entire time on the phone arguing, really for no reason at all. Things were really tense, and that's when being apart matters because these tensions escalate and you can't kiss and make up.

The best distraction when things are going wrong in your emotional life is doing live TV. Because for that hour when you're live, you have to be switched on the whole time, and nothing else intrudes. You just can't let it. Unfortunately, in spite of being 'undeniably the next big thing', I had no work, live or otherwise. I'd been hoping for a recommission for *Gladiators* but it didn't come. It wasn't that I personally was dropped, just that the series wasn't recommissioned.

I didn't know how to be alone day after day and I was really struggling emotionally. And then Dave came back. It was now March 2009. Even though we'd been in the flat about six months it was still pretty bare – not much more than a bed and a table – but I'd done my best to make it look nice and welcoming and I'd lit candles. I can't remember now what time it was, but I went to meet him at the tube. Then something snapped and we had a row about him having had his phone switched off in LA. Suddenly he said, 'I just don't want to do this any more.'

I was like 'What?'

Then he packed a bag and left.

10

'You mustn't take it personally'

I was in shock. Over the previous few months I'd thought that maybe Dave and I should split up. It was one of those: 'Get out!', 'No, don't leave', 'Get out!', 'OK', 'No'. It wasn't until he actually left that I realised I didn't want him to go.

I waited until it was light and then phoned Josie. I just couldn't believe what had happened. I couldn't believe it was over. I thought, He'll come back, we've had these arguments before. He'll come back. If he only comes back, everything will be OK. We'll be fine.

But he didn't. In the flat within a flat I was insulated from everything, from the traffic, from the weather, from everything except my pain. I became numb. When I couldn't bear the loneliness any more I'd contact him and he'd send text messages saying *Just give me some more time*.

OK.

Days would pass and I'd begin to come to terms with it, thinking, Maybe we have broken up. Then he'd get in touch again, and it was clear to me that he couldn't deal with being apart any more than I could. So it was just this back and forth, and then gradually it started to sink in that it really was over.

The flat was still full of his stuff and one day I couldn't face looking at it any more, so I went and stayed with Jo who was now living in Queens Park. Once she'd had Willow, they'd needed to get somewhere bigger than Jason's bachelor flat. I was at Jo's when his text came in.

I've just moved all my stuff out.

He'd made his mind up, and when men make their minds up that's it. He'd opened a new music venue, a pub called The Flowerpot in Kentish Town. He'd get really big names to do little intimate gigs, like Damien Rice and Mumford & Sons who were just on the cusp of being huge. It was a cool thing to be able to say, 'I'm going to go and see some massive band in a small venue.' He knew all the right people, people who would do it for Dave Danger, because everyone loved him. Dave is someone who smiles at strangers, just like he smiled at me that night we met in Nambucca. So he felt it was a fresh start, and it was. For him.

As for the flat within a flat, how could I live there on my own? Eventually I phoned the estate agent and said, 'Look, I've broken up with my boyfriend, I don't know what to do, is there any way I can leave earlier?' She was really nice. She said she'd put it straight on the market but 'we won't be able to stop the rent until we get someone else to move in'.

Meanwhile another sideshow was starting to play out. The week after Dave packed his bag, friends took me to a club in Chelsea. I needed to be taken out of myself, they said. I needed distraction. I don't do clubs, I'm a pub girl but I went because I hadn't the strength to say no. And it dawned on me that this was my life now. I was going to have to start going out again.

It was organised by Natalie Pinkham and she'd said, 'Oh and Harry's coming along, so it should be fun.' I knew she was friends with Prince Harry, and I'd never met him, so I thought, Oh that's quite exciting, and for a moment I perked up. So I was just sitting there and he arrived with a few others in tow and we all spent the evening chatting and laughing.

The thing about Prince Harry is that he has no choice. He's not some egotistical rock star who wants loads of attention. That is his life. He didn't ask for it, he just has to deal with it. In fact I think he deals with it very well and he and his brother do great stuff for our country. On a personal level I really like him and he's a friend. I can only imagine how much he has to deal with in terms of press intrusion and I don't intend to make it worse by discussing him further here – it would be unfair. But I was photographed with him and we did have a friendship, and for someone from a non-place like Watton to meet a prince of our country is so unlikely it would be weird not to acknowledge it. However, once the story got out, that was it. We had to stop seeing each other – because that kind of destructive press attention wasn't what either of us needed.

I was so desperate for work that I was prepared to do anything. There were a couple of things in the pipeline, but I needed money in the bank, so in June I did a corporate gig for Mercedes with Lewis Hamilton. It was to publicise the Mercedes Driving Academy where driving skills were being taught to school-age children to help with road safety. The previous year Lewis had been crowned Formula 1 world champion driving for Mercedes, and so he was ambassador for this venture. He was taking one of the kids for a drive and I was in the car interviewing him about it.

I finished about seven o'clock on the Saturday evening and was on my way home when John Noel phoned.

'All right?'

'Yeah.'

'Job go OK?'

'Yeah.' I knew he wasn't calling up about the Mercedes job.

'Look, Caroline, there's a story going in tomorrow's paper about you and six boyfriends.'

'What do you mean?'

'Well the *News of the World* have got this list of boyfriends you've been out with and they're going to run a story tomorrow. They called me this afternoon and said it's a cheeky little piece that they'll run in the middle of the paper. So don't worry too much about it, they've just dug up a few of your exes.'

I happened to be staying with Katie Langham in Belsize Park so I said to her we should get a copy of the paper first thing in the morning, 'because apparently there's a story about me and some old boyfriends'. So we got up early and walked down to the nearest garage when there were only dog-walkers about. The Sunday newspapers were stacked up on the forecourt, and we could see the headline the moment we turned the corner: HARRY'S GIRL IN THREE-IN-A-TUB ROMP.

What?

It claimed that Jack Osbourne was an old boyfriend and that I had once 'romped' in a hot tub with him 'and another girl'. Romp? What does that actually mean? I had shared a hot tub with Jack once, but in a good way, and the tub was so small you couldn't have got more than three in it at a time let alone change position. And what's more I knew the name of the other girl involved, who they had thoughtfully omitted to identify, the only person who could possibly have been able to give them the details. As for being a 'cheeky little piece' in the middle of the paper, it was splashed over two full pages as well as taking up half the front page.

It was absolutely horrible. Cropped photos taken completely out of context, lurid headlines and claims that I had 'set my sights' on Prince Harry four years previously, and that I was only interested in dating celebrities. What? Me?

I was known for hanging out with indie musicians who barely had enough dosh to pay for a round and who lived in bedsits where trips to the launderette weren't that frequent. I have never gone out with people for status or money or because of who they are. It's just not who I am.

Nor had I ever been newsworthy before. The only time my photo appeared in the press was to promote a TV show. I was just a jobbing presenter. I wasn't Sienna Miller or part of the Primrose Hill crowd, although I did know people who were, because Primrose Hill was just up the road from Camden and I knew how their lives were made miserable by being allowed no privacy, no chance of living a normal life without being followed by these parasites.

At this point I had no experience of the media at all. But once I'd been photographed with Prince Harry (and five other people) in April, everything changed. I lost my identity. I was no longer Caroline Flack, TV presenter, I was Caroline Flack, Prince Harry's bit of rough.

When it comes to the Royals, the tabloids don't bother with mindless showbiz journalists. They use serious private investigators with deep pockets. Within hours of the news getting out they were camped outside my mum's house, my dad's house, my nan's house, my sister's house, my brother's house, though not Jody's house – London is just too big and they couldn't find it.

What was so thoughtless was that it's not just one person they're hurting. They made me out to be a sex-crazed monster and my brother had to read that about his little sister. Plus it was all, 'Prince Harry's seeing some common girl who's worked in a factory.' Why? Because they'd dug up that Jo and I had once worked in an abattoir packaging meat – the only holiday job you could get in Watton. (We also picked daffodils every Easter – £1 a crate – but they didn't bother to mention that.)

They got in touch with every Facebook friend. Every single one had been offered money for dirt. How do I know? Because these friends of mine told me. I got messages saying: *Look, I thought you ought to know . . . but of course we've not said anything.*

Except this one person.

About six months later, she finally phoned. She hadn't see me in ages, she said, so 'Why don't we have lunch?'

OK.

We met in Camden and the first thing I said was, 'Did you do it?' And my stomach lurched. There was always that one or two per cent part of me that thought maybe it wasn't her. That maybe she'd passed on the details to someone else without realising what she'd done. But then out it all came.

She had been 'set up', she said. 'They' had doorstepped her and had asked 'all these questions'. 'And at the time I was cross with you, so I said a few things and they were taken completely out of context.'

That Sunday morning on the forecourt of this garage in Belsize Park, Katie and I stood there deciding whether to buy all of the copies so that no one else could see them. But in the end we just bought one. Then walking back to

Katie's I called John Noel and read out the worst bits, my eyes smarting with humiliation.

'What?' he said. And then, after a slight pause, 'That ain't what I expected.' He'd put the lawyers onto it immediately, he said. And by the time the afternoon edition came out, the front page had been changed, but not much else. The next day the *Sun* (editor: Rebekah Brooks, former editor of the *News of the World*, same Murdoch stable) repeated the three-in-a-tub story but the headline now read PRINCE HARRY'S GIRL DUMPED.

In his letter threatening to sue for defamation of character and breach of privacy, the lawyer wrote that it was possibly the worst case he'd ever come across of a newspaper smearing somebody's reputation, and that it was all totally unfounded. When the *Sun* wouldn't back down, they began drafting the necessary documentation to proceed to litigation. In the end, however, it didn't come to that, and it was settled. They printed an apology, agreed never to repeat the story and agreed to publish a positive cover story on me in the *Sun*'s Saturday magazine *Fabulous*.

Even before all this happened, I wasn't in a good place. Dave and I had been together for eighteen months and it was a great chunk of my life. When a relationship ends friends always say, 'You mustn't take it personally. Just because it didn't work out doesn't mean you're a failure.' And yet you know that's not true. Whatever you thought were your positive qualities, whatever you did to make it work, however thoughtful, kind, funny, caring or good in bed you were, it wasn't enough. You failed. Otherwise you'd still be together. That is the logic of the break-up.

And now, after all the Prince Harry stuff, I was convinced that everyone would see me as trash. I knew that I wasn't. But there's that old adage 'mud sticks', and I could see it in people's eyes. But you can't go around saying, 'I know what you're thinking but, for your information, I'm not trash.' So the best thing was to go to ground.

At Jo's at least I felt safe. I put a shade over the Velux in the loft to keep out the light and I slept. At night I would open it and look at the stars. And I thought and I thought. But there was nothing anyone could do or say to make it better. Jo would come up with lentil soup and say, 'You've got to eat something.' But I lay curled up and couldn't be bothered to move. What was the point?

Willow would come up to see me, taking the steep stairs one step at a time. She was nearly four now, and her sweet little face would peer down at mine and she'd lie down beside me and whisper, 'You OK, Carrie?' She knew I was upset. She didn't even have to speak.

I lost two stone. It's called the heartbreak diet. And in fact I probably looked better than I had for years. Feel bad. Look good. My boobs completely disappeared and one day I bumped into Dave in the street and he said, 'You've lost all your best bits.'

'Yeah,' I said. 'My smile.'

Jason's Mum and Dad had a house not far from Cannes and Jo invited me to go with them on holiday – the idea being that it would cheer me up. I'd be in the sun and we both had great memories of the south of France. It should have been fun, but everyone was in a couple. Jo was there with Jason, Liz was there with Leigh and then there was me and the kids. Given the state I was in it was obviously no fun for anybody, so after a few days I flew home. Sometimes it's better if I'm on my own. In that way I'm a typical Scorpio, I bury my head in the sand.

I had never gone so long without a job. It was over six months since we'd filmed *Gladiators* and every conversation I had with John Noel began, 'What am I going to do next?' And one day he said, 'Well, BBC Three are doing something called *Dancing on Wheels* – Ade is one of the judges. I could look into that.'

Ade Adepitan was one of John's clients. I had played basketball and done an interview with him for my show reel, and I absolutely loved him.

'It wouldn't be a presenter's job,' John said. 'You'd be there as a celebrity.'

'You mean like *Strictly*?'

'Not exactly. You'll be dancing with a guy in a wheelchair.'

Until that phone call I had never heard of wheelchair dancing, but it turned out to have started in Sweden as a kind of recreational physiotherapy and has been going since 1968. *Dancing on Wheels* was designed to choose a couple to compete in the European Championships in Tel Aviv in October, although the series wouldn't be screened until February the following year.

The idea came from Brian Fortuna, who had been a ballroom professional on *Strictly* since 2006. Brian is American and his mother had a ballroom-dancing school and had run wheelchair courses for years, courses which Brian had helped her with. We were given five weeks' training before the shows began, after which – like *Strictly* – you learnt one new dance every week. But it was more like a fly-on-the-wall documentary than a straightforward competition. It was more about finding out about each other and, for me personally, it meant finding out about something I had never really considered before because I had never been around disabled people.

My partner was James O'Shea who when he was nineteen had been to a party, fallen on the railway line and got his legs cut off. Spending so much time with James was truly eye-opening. I learned how difficult day-to-day life is. One evening we went to the Lock Tavern for a drink. Inside was stuffy and hot, so I said, 'Let's go upstairs and sit on the terrace and get some air.' Up? Stairs? Forget it. Loads of places just don't cater for disability.

'I was an arsehole before I lost my legs,' he once told me, 'so this was the best thing that could have happened.' As a teenager he'd been heavily into sport – football, hockey, basketball, athletics – 1500 metres and hurdles. He said that if he hadn't had the accident he'd have become an investment banker or done bank robberies. Instead he took up dancing, performing all over the world. What happened had opened up a creative door for him. When he'd arrived at a beach in Thailand, people had said, 'You can't take a wheelchair on the sand!' He'd say, 'Just watch!' and abandoning the wheelchair he'd head straight for the sea walking on his hands with everyone staring at him in disbelief, and then he'd swim to wherever he wanted to go.

James is totally crazy. We laughed, we argued and we were quite fiery with each other, but in a brother-and-sister way. And he has an otherworldly, nearly psychic ability to understand you. He 'knew' me from the moment we were introduced. He knew all about my misery and used to bring me crystals and other healing stuff. My heartbreak therapy, I called it. But the best therapy was just being around someone so completely mental and so determined to get the most out of life.

Did it feel weird dancing with a guy in a wheelchair? No. Much more weird was other people's reactions. I thought it was an amazing thing to do and an extraordinary opportunity. I had a fairly simple job but James was brilliant, moving that wheelchair as if he were a kid with a skateboard, whipping around, racing turns and free-style glides. But he is very stubborn – he's had to be – and he didn't like being told what to do, he didn't like the choreography being imposed on us. He wanted to do much more of it himself.

At the beginning it had just been a TV show, but we were lucky enough to win, which meant competing in the final in Tel Aviv and there it stopped being just a job. I became really emotional because only then did I realise what a big thing this was in people's lives. There was a girl in a wheelchair and her partner was her dad. He had dedicated his whole life to making sure that she could be a ballroom dancer, and that got to me. There are a lot of arseholes in this world but there are also a few saints.

A postscript: a fellow competitor in *Dancing on Wheels* was Mark Foster, the Olympic gold medallist swimmer – he and his partner came second. And, after the show, Mark persuaded James to join the UK Paralympic swimming team. And in London 2012 he was in the final of the 100 metres breaststroke and came fourth, just missing out on a medal. But two months later he broke the British record in the European championships in Berlin.

We're still in touch and he sent me a photograph the other day with some prosthetic legs strapped on. He'd never wanted them before. Having no legs, he said, had never really stopped him doing anything. And it's true. He is totally fearless because the worst that could happen already happened. 'I live my life now,' he says, 'and that's enough.' He is just so, so cool.

When Jo had had enough of my wallowing, she suggested I get myself somewhere to live, and she helped me find this tiny little garden flat, a conversion, in Highgate. It was a basement really, with its own entrance, down some steps from the street, and we carried in the old Ikea bed and I put up some shelves and found a couch. I had never lived on my own before, and that first night when I closed the front door, it felt weird. Weird but good, as in 'Right, I can do this, this is my place and it's my space, these are my four walls and I can decide who comes here.'

But it was soon followed by 'But I feel really lonely.'

The landlady lived upstairs and she was always coming down and asking how I was getting on.

'I'm fine.' (Translation: Just let me live here in peace.)

'If you need anything or if there's anything I can do, just ask.'

'Thank you.' (Translation: Please leave me alone.)

It wasn't that she was horrible, she was just 'around' and – apart from James – I couldn't cope with anybody being nice to me. At Jo's I hadn't been able to really cry because of Willow. But now I could. Because no one would ever know. We filmed *Dancing on Wheels* Monday to Friday but once I was back in the flat I wouldn't go out. Only fear would make me forget the sadness, so I would watch the scariest films I could find. To make it even scarier I'd turn off the lights and leave my front door open. As long as I was scared, I wasn't sad.

A street lamp shone in the front, but my bedroom was at the back and that was always dark. The stairs up to the ground floor were still there, with the original door. So I'd hear tenants from the other flats coming and going – not that there was a lot of noise, just the creaking of stairs or conversations in the hall.

So I was lying in bed one morning and I overheard the landlady talking to the woman who lived in the flat above me.

'I think Caroline's downstairs,' the landlady said.

'I've been meaning to talk to you about that,' the other woman said. 'Because I keep hearing her crying.'

Her flat was directly above mine, and she was right. I would just cry and cry and cry, hour after hour, until I wondered where all those tears came from, and wondered if they would ever stop. I cried until my head ached and my eyes looked as if I had an allergy, red, swollen and watery. It was like there was a bottomless well that never dried up. There were always more. Even when I wasn't making a noise, they just seeped out of me; I would wake up and my pillow would be soaked.

To hear those two kind women talk was just the horriblest thing. It made me think, Oh God. So that's what I am. This sad mess that sits in this flat and cries. And that's when I decided it had to stop. 'I'm not going to be known as this crying and sad person.' From now on, if I wanted to cry I'd have to do it somewhere else.

I was now driving. One spring after I'd got a tax rebate, instead of blowing it all on a holiday I decided to buy a car and learn to drive at the same time. Living in London you don't really need a car – I'd go on buses or take the tube – but I thought it was something I just ought to do.

My instructor was a guy called Mohammed. We did two hours every other day so it was quite full on and luckily we got on really well and I learnt in three months. So the morning of the test Mohammed drove me to somewhere out near the M25.

'I'm really nervous,' I told him.

'You'll be all right. See you later.'

And when the examiner got in beside me and was

sorting out his marking sheet I told him, 'My mum always said I wasn't born to drive, I was born to be driven!' It made him laugh and the ice was broken.

'Look,' he said, 'I'm not from round here, so we'll just drive around these streets and you'll be fine.' So we just stayed in this residential area and did everything you had to. There were no major crossroads, no roundabouts, nothing difficult at all, so I was incredibly lucky and passed first time. I bought myself an old two-seater MG which turned out to be a terrible car, always overheating.

One evening I was on the North Circular, driving my MG and about to peel off for Highgate when my phone rang. It was Polly. She only ever called if it was something important, so I pulled over.

'You've got it!' she said.

And after my initial 'Yaaaaay!' I just sat there, tears pouring down my face.

I'm a Celebrity . . . Get Me Out of Here! is perhaps the most successful reality show in Britain. Two weeks before, I'd done a screen test for the spin-off show.

Financially, emotionally, I desperately needed this job, so I should have been nervous, but I hadn't been. My attitude was 'It can't get any worse' and I just went in and did it. It took the form of a full-scale mock-up of how the show would be done, complete with panel of celebrities, roving reporter and earpiece connecting me to the gallery.

I was a huge fan of the Jungle, and the spin-off was officially titled *I'm a Celebrity . . . Get Me Out of Here! NOW!* Since the first series in 2002 there had been a few slight changes but the basics remained the same. Ant and Dec had been there from the start but *NOW!* had had a number of different presenters. This year, however, there was to be a major innovation. Instead of happening in a studio in London, it would be done on site in Australia, in parallel with the main show.

In terms of my career, this was a massive step up. The chance to host a show on your own – especially if you're a woman – doesn't come along often – there are simply not that many opportunities. And after all the negative press around the Prince Harry exposé I was convinced no one would touch me.

But more than that, it was just such a brilliant gig, a job on my own, and a job where people could really see what I could do. It was a job that was going to lead to the rest of my career – though I didn't know that at the time. At the time the most important thing was that it would take me thousands of miles away from Camden.

And after telling my mum, then Jo and then Dad, I told Dave. I would bump into him now and again because we were in the same circle. But it was never a good idea. It seems like a good idea at the time, but you always go back to square one. The sadness just would not go away.

So I called him, and I shouldn't have.

'Well done.'

'I'm going to be away for a month.'

'Right.'

'So you won't see me for a month, more like six weeks.'

'Have fun.'

11

The Jungle

The previous year's *I'm a Celeb* had been won by Joe Swash. He'd been a great favourite with viewers, so they decided to bring him back as my 'roving reporter'. Joe was one of those local kids who'd gone to the Anna Scher school in Islington. He'd been recommended by a friend of his mum's who just happened to be Linda Robson who just happened to have been to Anna Scher herself... And, like half the Anna Scher kids, he'd ended up in *EastEnders* – playing Mickey Miller. Joe is a genuinely funny guy, a bit of a Frank Spencer type who doesn't realise that what he's saying is so funny.

Anyway, we were travelling out together and had been given seats next to each other in Emirates Business Class. It was one of those where you lie fully stretched out and it was as if we were sharing a double bed, and we'd never even met...

From his first 'Aw'wight, Cawaline? My name's Joe' he never drew breath. It was a non-stop twenty-four-hour flight and he talked to me for the entire journey. It turns out he's a worse flyer than I am, so any sort of turbulence or bump and he'd pop up like a meerkat from his 'bed', grab my arm and go 'Erghghrrh!'

Even worse, he farted the entire journey.

'What's that smell?' I said, the first time it happened.

'I'm a bit of a nervous flyer.'

'Oh my God, you're disgusting!'

There was no getting-to-know-each-other time, it was immediate, he was like my little brother.

So about an hour before we landed, he said, 'Just going to the toilet, Flack.'

Fine.

He was in there about forty minutes and I was beginning to worry when finally he emerged. Joe Swash is an East End version of Rupert Grint with bright ginger hair, and pale, pale skin and loads of freckles. But the Joe Swash who came back to his seat looked different, and not in a subtle way. I peered at him as he sat down and then I realised what it was: he'd sprayed himself with fake tan. In the toilet.

'What did you do that for?'

'I need t'look brahn, don' I?'

'But you're ginger! It looks weird . . .'

Talking with Joe was like playing table football – one of us would throw in the ball and then we'd whack it backward and forward until it flew off the table. Goals were a rarity. We argued from the moment we were on the flight to the moment we got off. But as a way to survive the tedium/terror of a long-haul flight I can recommend it.

We were put in a hotel in Kingscliff near Brisbane on the Gold Coast, where *I'm a Celeb* is done. We'd thought everyone would be staying there, but for the first two weeks it was just me and Joe.

So that first night we have dinner, and then go to bed.

Knock, knock, knock.

'Flack, Flack!'

I open the door.

'What.'

'Can I stay in your room?'

'No!'

'I just want to stay on your couch.'

'What's wrong with your own room?'

'Nuffin'. I just don't like stayin' on my own.'

'Stay on my couch then.'

I'd had a few strange propositions in my time but . . . I thought, there's no way I'm giving him any sort of come-on, but in fact he was completely genuine. He just didn't want to be on his own. He wasn't that young – only three years younger than me – but it was almost as if he needed someone to look after him the whole time. And I didn't mind, because he used to annoy the hell out of me and it kept me occupied and it kept my mind off Dave. We'd be by the pool on our own, working our way through the menu of cocktails, and we'd argue about anything. Arguing was our way of communicating.

Swash: 'Anyone can learn to sing.'
Flack: 'No they can't.'
Swash: 'If I earn my fee I can sing.'
Flack: 'No you couldn't. You can either hold a tune or you can't.'
Swash: 'No, anybody can.'
Flack: 'What, anybody can sing like Beyoncé?'
Swash: 'Yeah.'

And I promise you that this argument went on for hours. We started at two in the afternoon and we were still arguing the next day at five o'clock in the evening. And people would go: 'Are you still at it?' Here's another one I remember:

Swash: 'I could be Simon Cowell if I wanted to.'
Flack: 'No you couldn't.'
Swash: 'Yeah I could.'
Flack: 'No, he's got talent. He's obviously got the knack for what he does.'
Swash: 'No, I could do that.'

Once one argument came to an end, we'd start another one, because neither of us would ever give way. He'd have an opinion and that opinion could never be changed and he'd probably say the same about me. Joe Swash and I had nothing whatsoever in common and yet we found this really lovely, trusting friendship. I knew everything about him and he knew everything about me. It was like being on a desert island. We were stuck with each other. So what do you do? You become bosom buddies.

As the Jungle was a UK show and went out live, we were working nights and my internal clock went completely haywire and we spent the entire six weeks feeling jet-lagged. Sometimes we'd be awake at four in the morning and Joe and I would go trundling down to the beach for a walk, just like an old married couple, always arguing and having no sex.

On the other hand I had never felt so comfortable on a job in my life. My producer was Sarah Harris who had been my researcher on *The Games*. I couldn't believe how far she'd come in five years. Yes, I knew she'd been a good researcher, but suddenly here she was producing the whole show! Sarah is a brilliant producer. When you hear that steady voice in your ear, you know she's got everything under control, and you're free to do your job. I felt completely safe in her hands.

I'd first used an earpiece on *TMi* and it's fair to say it takes a bit of getting used to. There are some presenters who like to hear everything that's going on in the gallery. I don't – I find it too distracting – so Sarah knows to switch it off. The gallery have their job to do and I have mine.

She also knows that I'm generally happier left on my own. If I've got a three-minute interview, for example, there are some producers who constantly cut in, 'Two minutes to go' . . . 'One and a half minutes to go', which I find really off-putting as it stops me listening to what's being said and listening well, to me, is what makes a good interview. I never have a set list of questions. I have a first question and a last question and if you listen to what the other person is saying the result is far more natural. Sarah knew this and she knew that all I needed was a 'wrap it up now' that gave me twenty seconds to either stretch it out or cut it short.

All the production team had flown over from England, but the crew were entirely Australian and they were really chilled. Twenty minutes to going live on air an English crew are on high alert: 'Twenty minutes to go. We need you to be down on set!' With the Australian crew it was, 'Yeah, twenty minutes, guys, you've got ages.' And at five minutes, I'd be saying, 'Shouldn't we be going down?' And Kyle, the Australian floor manager would say, 'Yeah.' Then at two minutes, it was: Bloody Hell! 'Kyle! you've got twenty seconds!' 'OK, let's go!'

Our 'studio' was a treehouse in the forest not far from the camp. It was fairly rustic with a bench and a low table for the panel to sit at, as well as whichever celebrity had just been eliminated. It was reached by a canopy-high walkway and the crew were our 'audience' providing that bit of laughter for us to bounce off, and laugh they did. They were brilliant and it helped everyone up their game.

It was a four-part show and one night we got to our third ad break and Sarah's voice in my earpiece said, 'Everyone OK?'

So I said, 'Yeah.' But for the next half-minute I thought,

Why did she say that? This wasn't usual. Then, thinking back, I realised that the crew were strangely silent. Nobody had been talking that much, and now Sarah. What could it be? Most likely something I'd done ... I mean, there was only me and the panel, and it was my job to keep them under control. So I'd either leaked something about what was happening in the jungle, or I'd asked a dodgy question. It's standard procedure not to tell you during the show because it would only put you off. But I thought I'd check anyway.

'Is everything all right, Sarah?' I asked.

'Fine.'

Something was different. 'Whatever it is, they'll tell me off afterwards,' I said to myself. 'Just push it aside.'

So now we were into the final part. And I just didn't get it. The crew weren't reacting. No laughter, not even at Joe, even when he was being his most Frank Spencerish.

So the moment the show ended, I said, 'Right. Let's have it. That was the most awkward—'

'Walk away,' Kyle said before I could finish.

'What?'

'Walk away.'

'Why?'

'Walk away.'

I walked away.

It might have looked like a mock-up of a jungle but this was a real tropical rainforest, and there had been a snake up in the gantry coiled round one of the lights directly above my head for the entire show. Everyone knew I was terrified of spiders, so no one wanted to tell me as they knew I'd freak out. And they were quite right. I would have done, live TV or no live TV.

However high profile it was, and much as I had enjoyed it, *I'm a Celeb* was still only six weeks' work a year, and it just wasn't enough. I needed something longer. Then we heard that Holly Willoughby was leaving *The X Factor* spin-off show *The Xtra Factor*. She'd only done one season but she'd just taken over *This Morning* from Fern Britton, as well as hosting *Dancing on Ice* and she couldn't do all three. John Noel was desperate for me to do it. He'd put me up for it the previous year, when Holly got it. But this year he was determined I would at least get to meet Simon Cowell.

Simon was based in LA so John asked if he would see me and it was, 'Yeah, OK.' Once that was agreed, Polly set up other meetings. One was with the William Morris Agency so that if I ever went out to the States for work, I'd have representation already set up. Another was with a TV channel called E! – for the same kind of reasons. But the main reason was Simon Cowell.

I decided I wanted to see him on my own. I prefer not having anyone with me – I just feel more comfortable one-to-one. So I ordered a taxi and went to the address. It was somewhere in Beverly Hills and as I stood outside the house I thought, Hmm. This doesn't strike me as the kind of place Simon Cowell would live in. Not that I had ever met him, but even so . . . It was quite rustic and, while not falling apart, it wasn't what I would call pristine. Definitely the shabbier end of chic.

So I knocked on the door, and a gracious-looking lady opened it.

'I'm here to see Simon,' I said.

'Hi. Come on in,' she said and showed me into a living room.

So I went in, sat down and looked around. It was full of antique furniture, oil paintings and the odd Chinese bowl and figurine. I was surprised. Somehow I had never imagined that Simon would have this kind of taste. After a few minutes, I got up and walked around looking at the pictures more closely, and saw there were photographs of George Bush on the wall. And I thought, How strange . . .

After about twenty minutes the lady who'd opened the front door came back in.

'I'm sorry, but who are you here to see again?' she said.

'Simon Cowell.'

'Oh,' she said. 'He lives next door.'

Unbelievable. God knows who lived there, but I made my excuses and fled.

At least it broke the ice with Simon because it was the first thing I told him and he went, 'Yeah. They hate me next door.'

So, after the initial how-do-you-dos we were off.

'If it was up to you,' he said, 'what would you do with the show? What kind of things would you like to be there?'

Talk about making it easy. If I'd felt nervous before (and I had) now I was motoring. Ideas came pouring out. *The*

Xtra Factor is for fans, I said, and not even that, it's for super fans, because not every *X Factor* viewer turns over to watch *Xtra Factor*. The main show can give you the fruit, *The Xtra Factor* should give you the juice, and it's the presenter's job to squeeze out every last drop. I'd heard what a good listener Simon was, but it was more than that. He makes you feel that everything you say is the best idea he's ever heard, so you walk away feeling incredible. I told him that it had to be presented by a super fan.

'You've got to love that show. And I love that show.' And I did. This wasn't some tactic designed to ingratiate myself. I really do love that show. I could do it as my special subject on *Celebrity Mastermind*.

When I left, he kissed me on both cheeks, smiled deep into my eyes and said, 'I really think this is going to work.'

Yaaaaay!

'You know what?' I said to Polly when I called her on the way back to the hotel. 'It's in the bag.'

No it wasn't.

Two days later we heard it had gone to Konnie Huq, a very clever (as in Cambridge University) former *Blue Peter* presenter (1997–2008). So perhaps it was all sewn up before I even got to LA.

The result was that I went back into the Jungle for a second series, and I'm so pleased I did, because the second series was brilliant. Not so much to do with the celebrities – you don't really get to meet them until they are booted out and then all they want to do is go

216

home – but the panellists who dissect what the celebrities have been up to and then help welcome whoever has been expelled that night.

When presenting *I'm a Celeb NOW!* you are in the position of a viewer. I knew nothing more than people at home would know. We'd all go in at midnight, watch what had been happening in the camp, and then write the script for that night's show.

For the hour we were on, it really was like being a host at my own party. My job was to make the panellists – the guests – feel comfortable, to keep the conversation going, to bring everybody in if I could and not let one person hog the limelight, and generally to keep up the party spirit. It was a really simple but brilliant format. And it was genuinely funny; we laughed the whole way through. Because, unlike most shows which involve a panel, they didn't just turn up for a few hours – in and out, barely drawing breath – they'd be there for an entire week, so you'd be hanging out at the hotel every day and inevitably you'd bond and it all added to the free-and-easy, wise-cracking atmosphere on the set.

Everything of course depended on the panellists. Jack Osbourne came on a couple of times just before he got married to Lisa – and it was great to see him. At the start I'd felt very protective of him, but there was no need; he's very clever and very funny. Then there was Melanie Blatt from All Saints, a proper non-invented girl group from the nineties, and who has worked since as a presenter and is wonderfully forthright. I knew her from having presented at the Brits earlier that year and we'd become friends. As for my old mucker/mentor Leigh Francis, he was his usual outrageous self who had to be muzzled rather than encouraged.

But the best week of all, from my point of view, was when Gemma Cairney and Dawn Porter (now O'Porter) came out, neither of whom I really knew. Gemma is a Radio 1 DJ. I first met her when I guest-presented *Big Brother's Big Mouth* in 2008. Dawn is unclassifiable. You can't put her in a box. She writes, she does crazy things on television, she is simply one of the funniest women I have ever met. The great thing about her is she is completely fearless and doesn't care. She goes, 'Oh Fuck it. You've made a mistake? So what? I've done worse.' She can't even read out a menu without making it side-splittingly funny. And Dawn, Gemma and me, we just gelled. We all knew *of* each other – and had vaguely seen each other out and about – but we didn't actually *know* each other.

As this was my second year in the Jungle, I knew my job backwards, and as well as being a host on camera and working my arse off, I'd become the host in real life. So I'd be like 'Welcome to the show! This is what we do in the day. We just sit by the pool and drink cocktails!' We'd go to bed, we'd get up at midnight, we'd do the job, and we'd be back at the hotel by ten o'clock in the morning. It was a crazy, brilliant week. When we got bored with just sitting around, we'd go out on bike rides and we just had the most fun. People say you don't really make friends later on in life, but I completely disagree. It's not that you meet someone and go, 'Oh!' But one day you wake up and find that you're staying in touch all the time.

My one great luxury is holidays. If I had a family it would be different, but I don't. So I'd say to Josie, 'Come on, we're off. I'll pay, let's go.'

And Josie was the best person in the world to go on holiday with. She might take a bit of persuading but I was good at persuading, and if I timed it right, she'd be prepared to leave her boyfriend and her cats just so I wouldn't have to go on my own.

Over the years we have been on some funny holidays – usually in the winter when we'd go somewhere not too far away, which meant either Egypt or Dubai. One year, when she couldn't come with me, I went to Dubai with another friend called Laura. We stayed in the Honeymoon Suite in a brand-new hotel called the Banyan Tree. And although I generally think Dubai's a bit weird, this was one of the most beautiful resorts I have ever stayed in. You each had your own little hut on the beach but each hut also had its own infinity pool and it was just stunning. We had little golf carts to go back and forth to the main part of the hotel, but otherwise we were on our own and we spent a week just sunbathing.

In Egypt there was much more to do. Josie and I would go on all the excursions, then at night we'd get into our pyjamas and watch box sets in bed. We'd get back to the room about six o'clock – once the sun had gone down – and then we'd get room service to bring us up spaghetti bolognese and watch back-to-back *Sex in the City* like real proper girls. That was our dream holiday.

For New Year 2011 I flew over to New York to see my friend Camilla Romestrand and then went on to Los Angeles where Dawn Porter was living because her boyfriend Chris O'Dowd was filming *Bridesmaids*, and Gemma Cairney joined us.

It was Gemma's first time in LA and she turned out to be the funniest tourist you have ever seen. She has the loudest voice on the planet, and a laugh that's nearly as bad as mine.

'Oh my God, look at that!'

'Oh my God, there's the Hollywood sign!'

'Oh my God, it's the Viper Club!'

'Oh my God, it's Grauman's Chinese Theatre!'

'Oh my God, I just saw Demi Moore on the Freeway!'

Going shopping with friends is often a disaster as you end up getting something you wouldn't have even looked at on your own. In this case it wasn't a pair of shoes they were egging me on to buy, it was a tattoo. The streets of West Hollywood are full of unexpected corners with quirky little shops. And one afternoon Gemma and Dawn and I walked past the window of a tattoo parlour.

Dawn: 'What about it?'

Gemma: 'I've always wanted a tattoo . . .'

Me: 'Let's do it!'

And in we went. As Dawn had the camera, I went first and had a unicorn done. A winking unicorn . . . Fifteen minutes of torture and dubious taste filmed for posterity. But then, when it came to their turn, suddenly it was . . .

Hmmm . . .

Well . . .

I'll get rid of it one day. I just need to summon up the courage – apparently it's even more painful taking it off than having it done in the first place.

Funny thing about tattoos. I'd had two linking hearts done on my wrist when I'd finished the first series of *I'm a Celeb*. I'd decided to stay on for a couple of weeks and met up with my good friend Jessica Bendine. Jess is a celebrity booker and works on *Never Mind the Buzzcocks* and we'd met through *TMi*. She spends her life reading spiritual self-improvement books even though she needs no improvement, spiritual or otherwise. She'd agreed to fly out and join me at the end of the Jungle and we'd come across an English guy in Sydney who'd done all David Beckham's tattoos. The hearts represented me and Jo, and Jo said she'd get matching ones done. Guess what: she still hasn't got around to it.

When I'd come back to London after the first *I'm a Celeb*, I thought I was over Dave. And then I saw him . . . Never pick at a scab, my nan used to say, and she was right. You cut yourself, it starts to heal, it itches and so you pick at it and pinpricks of blood seep out and the next thing you know it's bleeding again.

All my friends were Dave's friends. All Dave's friends were my friends. Mine, ours, yours . . . you, me, us – a never-ending circle I couldn't escape. At least not in Camden. They say that to get over a man you have to get under a man. But I wasn't interested in getting under anyone. For nearly two years I was emotionally dead.

But there was something about that trip to LA that freed me up, a miracle that even six weeks in Australia hadn't achieved. I felt removed and different. I started feeling that Dave Danger (actually his surname is Healy) wasn't my whole life, that there might be a future without him. In LA there was no one around to say, 'So how are you feeling now?' Dawn and Gemma were more 'Dave? Who's this Dave?'

'Just a guy I met who I can't seem to get over.'

'Well, it happens. Things like that do happen, and you do cope with it eventually.'

And then they'd move on to talking about something else – about some Hollywood landmark that Gemma had just spotted, or a dress Dawn had seen in a vintage shop that might just be Valentino – because they weren't that interested. So you move on too. But it was so strange, because for so long I'd felt it was Dave who defined me.

One day Dawn was busy and I took Gemma to Venice Beach – I'd first been there with Jack Osbourne the time he did his White Knight act. Venice Beach is a kind of Camden in the sun, complete with canal, and we passed by this psychic and he sweet-talked us in through the door.

There was something about him that glued you to the spot.

'You like a bit of both, don't you?' he said to Gemma before we'd even sat down.

'What do you mean?'

'You like men and you like women.'

'Oh, I don't know about that . . .'

'Well, you gonna in the future.'

Then he turned to me.

'You've got the gig.'

'What?'

'You goin' for a new job?'

'Well, as it happens, yeah.'

'Well, girl, it's yours. You're gonna get it.'

It was that trying-for-*The-Xtra-Factor* time of the year again. Konnie Huq had left after just one season. And John can be a Rottweiler when he wants to be, and he wasn't giving up – 'I'm telling you, Caroline, it's got your name written all over it.'

This time I did a screen test along with a million others. And nothing. So the weeks passed and the weeks passed.

X Factor gossip was by now standard tabloid fodder. By early 2011 rumour was rife: after nine seasons, Simon Cowell was stepping down as a judge. He was going over to the States to launch American *X Factor*. It wasn't limited to the tabloids, even serious newspapers wondered if the show would survive the absence of 'Mr Nasty'. Because however misanthropic he was, they wrote, he was the only one who told the truth, which meant he was the only one the singers believed. He was also the one who'd be signing them up for his record label if they won – and even if they didn't.

At that year's LAFTA comedy awards at the end of January I was asked if I was set to replace Konnie Huq. I said that I was already doing the Jungle which I absolutely loved and that the two shows clashed. All true.

And still I heard nothing, and still nothing was announced. Months passed. Literally. They left it and left it and left it and left it.

So, it's late May 2011. Five months after I'd done the screen test and the day before the arena auditions are due to start.

'I obviously can't have got it, Polly, or we'd have heard. But I'd just like to know.'

'Caroline, I'm pushing, I'm pushing but I cannot get an answer, but they're saying that you're still the favourite. There's nothing more I can do.'

'This is ridiculous. I mean, auditions start tomorrow!'

At two o'clock I'm sitting on my couch, staring out of the window, contemplating life with a mouse as my sole companion when my phone rings. Polly again.

'The job's yours if you want it. There's just one thing . . .' she hesitated. 'It's not on your own. It's with Olly Murs.'

'Olly Murs?' I said. 'But he's not a presenter, he's a singer.' He had come second in X Factor two years before.

'Well, that's the deal they're offering. Are you in or out?'

'I'll think about it.'

I put the phone down for five minutes, then called her back.

'I've thought about it. I'm in. I'll do it with Olly.' I had never met Olly Murs, I had no idea what he was like apart from hearing him on *X Factor* when admittedly I had been a fan. 'So what now?'

'You need to be on a train in three hours. You start tomorrow.'

12

Bub-feelings

Unknown voice on the phone: 'You're booked on the 6.24 from Euston to Birmingham where a car will meet you and take you to the Hotel du Vin. The driver knows what you look like. The stylist will find you on the train and give you what you're wearing tomorrow. OK?'

OK.

'Safe journey.'

First I need to phone my mum and then I need to phone Jo. Then I need to pack. Oh my God, I've got to pack!

I've got a date. I had a date. I've got to cancel the date.

Polly on the phone: 'Just to let you know we couldn't book Rachel, she's in Corsica, so you'll be styled by their in-house person just for now. She'll meet you on the train. I'm calling *I'm a Celeb* to let them know that you won't be doing the next series.'

'I need to speak to Sarah first.'

'Well do it quickly.'

Oh God . . . She'd been so good to me . . .

Euston. By now the news is out. And my phone doesn't stop ringing. Everyone in the world is calling me.

OMG . . . OMG . . .

'Hi. Caroline?'

I look round. A young woman is heaving two suitcases onto the seat. 'There's nowhere to try things on so we'll just have to find a toilet. OK with you? I'll go and see what there is.' She goes off to recce and I sit staring after her.

Less than four hours ago I was in my flat, thinking about my mouse, convinced that the *Xtra Factor* gig had gone for another year, probably disappeared for ever, and now WOW! I've landed the job that I've wanted ever since I started in TV.

The stylist comes back and we go through the suitcases, then into the toilet to try them on. I go in, she stands outside and tells everyone her friend isn't feeling great . . . We go for a blue top and black culottes plus she gives me some back-up dresses in case I don't like the outfit once I can actually see what I look like. The mirror in the toilet is too high and too small, even standing on the seat.

Hotel du Vin, Birmingham. I'm handed tomorrow's call sheet: I look down the list: Presenter: Caroline Flack, 6.30 a.m. And then someone says, 'This way please.'

The door opens and four faces turn to look at me.

Dermot, Tulisa, Gary Barlow and Kelly Rowland from Destiny's Child and one of them hands me a glass of champagne.

'Welcome to the team!'

I knew Olly Murs, of course I did. What *X Factor* junkie wouldn't? I think I even had a little crush on him. He was an *X Factor* success story, coming second in series six in 2009 and signed up by Simon anyway. But it had been a close-run thing, and he'd nearly been eliminated, and would have been if it hadn't been for Dannii Minogue deciding to send Jedward home rather than him. His first single had gone to No. 1. And now he was a pop star . . .

'He'll have an entourage,' Josie had warned when I'd called her. 'A massive entourage. They all do.'

The next morning a car drove me to the LG Arena and I went straight into hair and make-up. And there he was.

'Hello, I'm Olly.'

'Hello, I'm Caroline.'

They put us in a dressing room for fifteen minutes and then the door opened and someone said, 'Right, time for your first link.' And we both looked at each other . . . But we got on instantly and it's never faltered since.

When we walked into that arena, and saw the audience and felt the atmosphere and the buzz and the production, it was mind-blowing. Of all the things I'd worked on, I'd never seen anything that big. And this was just for the auditions! Whenever the judges walked in, they'd play *The X Factor* music *De-De-De-De* and the crowds would go

'Yeeeeaaah!' And every time Olly showed his face, it was 'Ollyeeee!!!' The noise was ear-splitting.

People talk about chemistry when it comes to romance, but it's not limited to sex, and whatever you want to call it, it was there between Olly and me. On the one hand Olly is totally 'I'm Olly and I'm from Essex' but he can suddenly come out with something really profound and it's like 'Where did that come from?' I'd been around musicians and singers before, but Olly was different. Everything was new and he was so keen to learn.

'Listen, Caz, I don't know what I'm doing, so you tell me.' But Simon knew what he was doing. Olly had been there. He knew it from the inside. He was a pop star. I didn't know anything about being a pop star. But our USP was that we were so easy in each other's company – we would take the mickey out of each other rather than other people. Sometimes you have to work with people you don't instinctively get on with, but you make it work, because you're a professional and that's your job, however, it is much, much more difficult. But with Olly and me it was instant. We got on really well from the off.

That first day was 1 June 2011 and we really did hit the ground running. Although the show wouldn't air until mid-August, the *Xtra Factor* team were there from the start of auditions: first Birmingham, then Glasgow, then Manchester, Cardiff, London and finally Liverpool. *X Factor* was a crazy world to step into. And you do get a little sucked into it, absorbed in it. It's impossible not to, because from eight in the morning till midnight, that's all you're doing.

And then I started hearing from Dave.

I remember feeling surprised. Because with everything that had been going on in my life, I'd begun feeling normal again. I'd been to America. I'd got this fantastic new job. There was a sense of 'I feel good again, I'm feeling really good about everything.' I was back to being myself. Just. Only just.

But now here he was, up to his old tricks. He'd be in touch and then he wouldn't reply. This was constant.

'I'd like to see you.'

'How are you?'

Fine, fine, fine, fine, fine.

And then came Glastonbury, which conveniently fell into the gap between Manchester and Cardiff. Months before I'd arranged to go with Dawn Porter, Chris O'Dowd and the rest of the gang. We were staying as we always did in the backstage hospitality area where there are showers and civilised things like that.

Beyoncé was a really big moment. Here she was, a legend, probably the biggest R & B star in the world, giving the ultimate glitzy, high-octane performance in a field in Somerset. And we all decided that, rather than standing at a viewing point, we were going right to the front. Sunday night is always the nicest time to be at Glastonbury. The sun was just going down behind the Pyramid stage and it was one of those amazing moments when everything comes together. So we got there really early and elbowed our way right in. But I'm so small I couldn't see. So Chris, who is a massive person, put me on his shoulders and Beyoncé was incredible. It was magical. She sang 'Halo' – backed with film of Glastonbury in the mud – and two years later when Dawn and Chris got married, that's what they played at the wedding.

The whole thing was great, and Dave came and watched it with us and he and I actually walked back together afterwards. As usual he was camping in Strummerville, just as we'd done three years before. He didn't want to come and sleep with me where I was, and I didn't want to go and sleep in a tent. So fine.

'But can I see you tomorrow?' he said.

'Really?'

'Yeah. It'll be nice. Perhaps I can come back and stay at yours?'

'You've drunk too much. You won't remember,' I said.

'I will. OK, see you tomorrow.' Then as he started to walk away, he turned. 'It was nice to see you, Carrie.'

'Yeah, nice to see you too.'

I'd had a brilliant weekend and as I drove back I thought about what Dave had said: 'See you tomorrow.' Before it had always been, 'Oh, it's not the right time.' But did he really say that? Is he gonna come back? After two years, is he really gonna come back?

And you look for clues, you always look for clues, trying to crack the code. A month before Glastonbury we'd bumped into each other and he'd said the usual thing about how he still hadn't met anyone yet. But then he'd said something else.

'I'm not in love with you any more. I'm in love with the idea of you.'

What can you say to that? 'Thanks . . .'

So that evening, at eight o'clock, there was a phone call.

'I'm in Camden. Can I come round?'

'OK.'

I could never say no, because I felt that I loved him so much. But part of me was saying, 'Here we go again.'

So I let him come round and he stayed over.

And then the next day he kept calling. And I thought, That's not like him.

That night I was out to dinner with John Noel and Polly, and he called again. 'What are you doing tonight?'

'Just having dinner. What are you doing?'

'We're having a pub quiz down at the Flowerpot. I'd like you to come.'

'Won't it be too late?'

'Come when you can.'

Suddenly it was him asking me, rather than me asking him and it felt lovely. It felt like these two horrible years of misery had been worth it. So we started seeing each other again. Boyfriend and girlfriend. And it felt good.

I had done all the things you're not supposed to do when you break up with someone and you want them back. You don't talk to them, you don't text them, you don't cry. You don't turn up at their house knocking on their front window with tears in your eyes. You don't tell them you still love them. If any girl ever says, 'I've done something mental', I say, 'Well, I did even worse and he still came back so don't worry about it.'

As the *Xtra Factor* team wasn't needed that year during boot camp, we had three weeks off. The last two months had been pretty full on and I felt like getting away.

'I was thinking of going on holiday,' I said to Dave, once I'd made up my mind. 'Do you feel like coming with me?' This was quite a big thing to ask and I was nervous.

'I'd love to.'

'Where would you like to go?'

'I'll go anywhere with you . . .'

Oh!

So we went to Mallorca and stayed in a really nice hotel up in the hills above Palma. And we started talking about 'us' and why we'd broken up. In all this time we had never done that. And then something suddenly clicked in me, and I thought, You've never apologised for any of it, have you? Did I really expect an apology? I don't know. But something perhaps, some acknowledgement of how much misery he'd caused. And so I stood there, looked at him and just thought, I'm over this.

And now I felt guilty. Guilty that it was over and that I was still with him. I knew I had to tell him. Because something had switched and it felt really weird so I phoned Josie.

'What! Two years you've been waiting for this, Carrie!'

'I know. But I don't think I can do it any more.'

Because even though he was a nice man, a lovely

man – and still is – he was an arse. Back then forward, leaving, calling, not calling ... I'd had two years of pain and uncertainty. And I just thought, I don't think I can go through that again. And I don't have to. I was over it. I realised I had completely got over it. One way and another this man had taken over my head for over four years and turned me into a gibbering wreck for two of them. And I knew it would only happen again.

So we flew back home. I didn't break up with him there and then, because I didn't know how to do it. And at the back of my mind there was always that thought: Oh, those feelings must come back surely. They'll come back and we'll be fine.

But the feelings I had weren't nice warm, loved-up feelings. They were Bub-feelings.

I called Jo: 'I think I've got Bubs.'

'You can't have! There is no way on heaven or earth that you can have Bub-feelings about Dave. You are besotted!'

'Jo, I'm not kidding. I've got Bub-feelings.'

'What timing!'

'I know!'

And that was it. After all that crying and loss of sleep, the loss of weight, loss of this, the loss of that, it was over. And I said to myself 'I will never feel like that again.' I was determined never to feel like that again.

Dave Danger is the definition of heartbreak for me, that one big defining break-up, and while I know there'll be ups and downs, I know that I will never feel like that again.

*

Nothing you've seen on television prepares you for the sheer noise levels of *The X Factor* live shows. First they have a warm-up guy who builds up the tension so the audience is on the edge of its seat waiting for something to happen. Olly and I would stand at the side and you could feel it. Then Dermot comes on, and everyone screams for Dermot.

'Welcome to *The X Factor*!' ROAR ROAR ROAR!

'Do you wanna meet your judges?' ROAR ROAR ROAR!

Then *The X Factor* tune starts and the judges walk out and the audience goes completely mental.

That first time I remember shouting at Olly, 'Oh my God, this is nuts!'

But things are only just beginning. When the first contestant comes out, ROAR ROAR ROAR!

Olly and I would recognise some of the singers as we'd have already interviewed them, for our show. Thousands of people turn up for the original auditions, and these are seen by teams of producers and researchers who whittle them down to something more manageable. Some days I think we'd interview nearly a hundred. On *Xtra Factor* we tended to be given the 'characters' to focus on. Because just like all the other spin-off shows *Xtra Factor* has a large element of comedy.

One thing I've always hated on reality TV is how people get the mickey taken. I've never done that. Have fun with them, yes, but don't look down your nose. Let them tell their story and if it's funny, laugh – or say out loud, 'You wally!' But no rolling of eyeballs with that I'm-better-than-you-are sideways look at the camera. Luckily Olly felt exactly the same; we're not the kind of people who enjoy humiliating anyone. And neither of us were part of that 'ironic' style of TV where it was cool to be aloof.

We didn't want *Xtra Factor* to be like that, we wanted it to be this little friendly show. So we just laughed a lot. We made it funny. When people made us laugh, we'd laugh out loud, not behind their backs. We did meet a lot of off-the-wall characters but we weren't there to mock them. We were their shoulder to cry on. We're the friend they're going to tell what happened and how it felt when they come off stage.

From all the many contestants we'd talked to, we'd only use four clips for each show, but every single singer had to be interviewed because you never knew beforehand who would turn out to be telly gold. Just think of Susan Boyle on *Britain's Got Talent*. Without the pre-performance interview it would have been a very different story. We had to get to every contestant who came through the door. The researchers fill out basic information on a standard sheet.

NAME: this
AGE: this
WANTS TO BE: this

It was our job to get the rest. I couldn't wear heels as my feet would hurt too much, so I had to stand on a box so that the difference in height between Olly and me would stay the same. It was either keep your shoes on, or back on that box, girl! So:

Me: 'Hello, what's your name?'
Boy: 'Bob.'
Me: 'How old are you, Bob?'
Boy: 'Nineteen.'
Me: 'How long have you wanted to be a singer?'
Boy: 'About five years.'
Me: 'And who told you you were good?'
Boy: 'My mum.'
Me: 'And what does she think about you coming to *X Factor*?'
Boy: 'She thinks I'm an idiot.'
Me: 'Oh No! Is she watching . . .?'

It's easier to ask questions when you don't know the answers. When I first started on TV I had no idea what questions to ask. I needed to write them down, and then learn them by heart. But by this point I knew how to do it.

Me: 'What's your name?'
Woman: 'Tracy.'
Me: 'How old are you, Tracy?'
Woman: 'Fifty-five.'
Me: 'How come it's taken you so long to want to be a singer?'
Woman: 'I've always worked in a factory.'
Me: 'What factory . . .?'

You needed just enough information to give the viewers a taster. And because you did so many, you got to know what to ask. Somehow in the short time you've got you have to get the best out of them. Olly turned out to be a complete natural. I have never known anyone take to anything so quickly.

'Olly, it's taken me ten years to learn this job and you just did it in a day!'

In fact he's one of those annoying people who is naturally good at everything. And when you consider that he was also releasing an album at the same time, he was probably getting up four hours before me and then finishing four hours later, because he had so much to do. And he never moaned, not once. I moaned all the time although it was only really the one moan that I just kept repeating: 'My feet hurt!' to which the standard reply was, 'Shut up!'

In terms of sharing the job, I took more of the structure, the what's-your-name stuff, then Olly would ask a question and if it looked like it had a follow-up, I'd leave it to him. Otherwise I'd chip in. It was a very good balance and felt like a true partnership. And Olly having been on *X Factor* himself opened the door to a whole other area of discussion.

'So, Olly,' I might say, 'you came second. Have you got any advice for Tom/Dick/Harriet?'

Although the questions always started the same – name and age – from then on you had to try and make them different because you never knew what four interviews would be used in the show, it all depended on the performance and the judges. It may not sound difficult, but coming up with forty different ways of asking basically the same thing was mentally exhausting. And each time you had to sound fresh. Stale is unfair on the contestant and the viewer and doesn't make for good television.

Whatever days off we had between cities, I'd go back to London and do the boring things, like being there when the plumber came to fix a leak. At that time I was renting a little one-bedroom flat in a street just off Camden Square. It was one of those classic Regency terraces, all white stucco and window boxes, and although it had only one bedroom, I loved it. It was a new conversion with masses of light coming in through huge windows.

Now that I had a proper job that lasted more than a few weeks, I'd looked at buying somewhere, but the estate agent said I'd lived at too many addresses to get a mortgage. And how come they're so expensive, I'd asked?

'Usually people buy in twos.'

So I got rid of the MG and bought myself a little white Mini.

I had a really nice comfortable life in London as a single woman. I was happy, I was content. I had good friends. I was just a walk away from Camden. For company I had a little mouse who would not go away. I hate mice, so when he'd popped out one day and scurried along the skirting board before he disappeared, I called the mouse man.

'Look, I'm going to be honest with you,' he said. 'You haven't got mice. I think you've got a mouse.'

'So what do I do?'

'I'll put a trap down.'

'Not one that kills it!'

He said, 'Fine, I'll put down a humane trap that'll just catch it.'

But the mouse wouldn't be caught. He was so brave. He would come out and I'd see him scurrying up and down, but he wouldn't go in the trap. I'd leave a trail of cereal thinking he'd eat it bit by bit and follow it into the trap. Nothing. So I went into a hardware store nearby and explained the situation. I wanted to get rid of him but I didn't want to kill him, I said. So the guy showed me these plug-in things that you put into electric sockets that release a sound that mice hate. I bought his entire stock of seven. Apparently mice hate mint so he sold me these little sachets that you distribute around the place. I put them everywhere till the whole place smelt like a half-finished roll of Polos. Next day I walked in the kitchen and the mouse was sitting right next to a plug, in between that and the mint.

Fine, right, OK. I'm going to have to go nuclear. So I buy a big old-fashioned trap with a bottom that their feet stick to. And it worked. I didn't use any kind of bait, no cheese, no cereal, no chocolate. Nothing. He just walked in. So I took him down to Camden Square and set him free. As I opened the little door, I told him, 'That's it. Don't come back!'

Two days later, back. Same mouse, no question. So then I told him that he could live there. 'You stay out of my

way, I'll stay out of your way, and we'll live here together.'
He was probably my first proper pet. He was like Stuart
Little, my own Stuart Little who'd sit there, all bright-
eyed, cleaning his silky whiskers with tiny pink paws. But
it wasn't long after that that I left and he didn't come with
me.

Although I loved that flat, I felt I needed something
bigger. I have this problem with clothes and I thought if I
had two bedrooms, I'd turn one into a big wardrobe. I
found this great place in Muswell Hill on two levels. The
bedrooms were downstairs and the top floor was a big
open-plan lounge with a huge skylight, and it was
definitely the nicest flat I'd ever lived in.

After the first live show a group of us went to have
drinks at a hotel. My producer had brought with him a
contestant from the previous year. His name was Harry
Styles. I knew who he was. I already knew that he had a
crush on me – he'd made it pretty obvious. He'd said it in
magazines and he'd said it to friends. It was flattering and
I found it amusing. He was a kind of cheeky man/boy
with a captivating smile who got what he wanted.

By the time One Direction guested on X Factor in
November, Harry Styles and I had been seeing each other
for a few weeks. I'd broken up with Dave and I was like
'I'm ready for something completely different. Oh look,
this is going to be fun!'

In the entertainment industry nobody asks what age
you are any more than they ask how many A levels
you've got. They're both totally irrelevant. I've never felt

I was much older than Harry anyway. I still feel eighteen and probably act that way half the time – all those years in kids' telly probably didn't help. What I hadn't realised was that working on X *Factor* puts you under such public scrutiny . . . Although it was just a bit of fun we decided it was best to keep it to ourselves, as we were both working for Simon. We were both single, we got on well and we had a laugh. He met Jody and the kids (and yes, Jody fancied him too, as did eight-year-old Willow who went to school and told everyone Harry Styles had stayed over).

It was only when it became public knowledge that things turned sour.

At the beginning it was all very playful. He joked about being attracted to older women. There was twelve years between us – exactly same as there had been between me and Stuart up in Cambridge. No one seemed to be bothered then about the age difference. And from what little I know, it's a standard teenage boy thing. Someone in his position would never be romantically interested in a thirteen-year-old girl for example (and apart from anything else it would be illegal). Unfortunately thirteen-year-olds were his fan base . . .

One Direction were five boys Simon had put together the year before from solo performers who hadn't made it through. They'd ended up coming third but Simon had signed them anyway. It was good timing. The *High School Musical* phenomenon had come and gone and left a void which needed to be filled. And because of Twitter suddenly kids could communicate with other kids around the world. And the word spread.

A lot was made in the press about how young One Direction were, but there's a huge difference between age and immaturity. It wasn't like all they'd seen of the big wide world was a paper round. They'd been thrown into the jaws of X Factor and had more than survived. They'd each failed individually but had been given a second chance, and they had taken it. That takes real character and maturity. They had money. They had a book out that had gone straight to No. 1. And everywhere they went they were greeted by screaming teenage fans. They were amazingly mature – they had to be.

Their debut – 'What Makes You Beautiful' – had gone to No. 1 in the UK charts and was the most pre-ordered single in Sony's history. They had just signed a deal with Columbia Records in America. They had a tour coming up in the States in February 2012. It was all theirs for the taking.

Dictionary definition of 'X Factor': 'a quality you cannot describe that makes someone very special'. And Harry had it in many different ways. It's not just that he can sing – it's much more than that. He charmed everyone he met, from eight till eighty. As for him and me hooking up, it made us laugh. I remembered Mark Balaam, standing there outside Watton High School by his Ford Escort. He too had been seventeen but he was deemed too old . . .

Even when Harry and me were spotted kissing, no one except the gossip pages had taken much notice, and even then it was, 'Oh, we all thought Caroline Flack and Olly

Murs was the story, but all the time it was Caroline Flack and Harry Styles!'

So what was I supposed to do? Plod along in life making safe decisions?

It began to go wrong when Harry was papped coming out of my house in Muswell Hill one morning. The next day Jan Moir, a columnist for the *Daily Mail*, went to town.

'Caroline,' she wrote, 'is a classic me-first cougar', a 'predatory older woman'. In any other environment, she said, I'd have been 'suspected of sexual harassment or using my rank for sexual gratification'.

I was thirty-one.

I looked like 'a bargain-basement Miss January, a Rank starlet circa 1962' while Harry 'looks like he should be wearing green velvet and scampering next to Santa in a Christmas grotto, feeding carrots to the reindeer'. Harry was 'still a child. And a boy child at that; little critters who tend to be much more immature than girls of the same age.' Our 'liaison was not only inappropriate ... it was creepy'. 'Clearly she revels in the warped kudos of being the woman who bagged the hot guy that millions of teen fans are screaming about.'

And once that was out, it was open season. After that anyone could say anything. In the street people started shouting at me 'Paedophile' and 'Pervert'. And then the fans got the message. A One Direction fanzine had me as a voodoo doll, with arrows (pins) pointing to various bits of my anatomy. 'Crows feet, caused by old age'; 'Hair: dirty-blonde dye job, but probably just happy the bad dye job covers up the grey hairs.' 'Caroline was born in 1979, which in China is known as the year of the goat. Big surprise, she looks like one.' Finger: 'Zero engagement rings. Because nobody wants to be with her.'

No one really knew what to do and it was hard to control. I took Harry to see John Noel when we were deciding how to play it. And John said, 'Well, if you like each other, if you're fond of each other, then fook 'em. Just get on with it.' So that's what we did. But none of us expected it to turn so vicious and truly nasty. So perhaps we did the wrong thing, who knows. But it wasn't a nice time. There was a moment when we just thought, Shit, this has gone really dark.

From then on there was no escape. My front door at Muswell Hill opened straight onto the pavement and there were always a dozen men with cameras waiting outside. One morning I got to my car only to find my tyres had been slashed. There were all these men standing around and instead of helping, they just took pictures of me looking at the car. I shouted at them and told them to go away. But if I'd said what I really felt – 'You scum of the earth, fucking arsehole bastards' – they'd have said I'd had a rant and printed it.

Nothing like this had ever happened to me before. With Prince Harry they'd used private investigators in their quest for dirt, not showbiz reporters. The private investigators hadn't bothered me, just everyone around me. Two tabloid journalists stood up for me – Bryony Gordon and Dan Wootton – but that was no compensation.

For the first time I understood why celebrities wear sunglasses. Until then I barely owned any and I only wore make-up when I went out, not if I was just going to the shops. They turned me into a person who now has to put on make-up and sunglasses every time I leave the house and that's not who I am.

Perhaps the worst was Twitter. However vile they are, newspapers have to be careful because of libel and privacy. But Twitter is different. Nobody censors that. There were a few pathetic ones: I particularly remember *Fuck you. I can't believe you're going out with my boyfriend. I hope you get eaten by an angry elephant.* But the worst was *Die bitch, die. Watch where you go – we'll be following. You won't live. Come near and I'll shoot you.*

13

Fanta and *Limón*

The only problem with unconventional relationships is other people. Neither of us could really understand it. No one was forcing anyone to do anything. The truth is, it wasn't a big deal until the press made it a big deal. And how people do love a scandal . . .

'Who's done something wrong?'

'She has!'

'Who?'

'Cougar Caroline!'

And it went on and on until eventually it stopped and the bullies hiding behind their computers found someone else to pick on.

But there was no way we could go on. Because you start behaving differently when you feel you're being watched. And we were. It wasn't only Harry and me. They photographed Jo driving me in her car and started being nasty about her. Have a go at Cougar Caroline if you must but leave my sister out of it.

As for One Direction, they were now the next big thing. Five different guys who would never have met each other if it hadn't been for *X Factor* – Niall from Ireland, Zayn from West Yorkshire, Harry from Cheshire, Liam from West Midlands and Louis from South Yorkshire. Five different guys, five different voices, something for everyone, and the songs were really catchy. And, yes, they are adorable. Unfortunately I was caught up in the madness. I was the enemy. So as they were getting bigger, I was getting more and more abuse. And it wasn't just from the fans, it was from everyone, particularly journalists, grown women and men who should have known better.

Without anyone noticing it had switched from 'Harry Styles is so young', to 'Caroline Flack is so old'. I'd become a laughing stock. Mostly it would be jokes, which I could cope with, but I would get 'Cougar!' or 'MILF' shouted at me in the street. (MILF stands for Mother I'd Like to Fuck.) I got offered a million pounds to be the face of Cougarlife. com, which is a website for 'cougars' (dictionary definition: older women interested in younger men). I wasn't even old enough to be on the website. You had to be thirty-six and I had just turned thirty-two. I was like 'No, I'm not doing it!'

Until this point I'd been comfortable in my own skin. I was comfortable with my age, with my life, with the way I looked. I had never really had any doubts or insecurities about myself. Then I actually started questioning who I really was. Am I fat? Am I old? Am I wrinkly? Am I ugly?

And that was awful. People say you have to expect that kind of scrutiny because you work in television. Really? Why? Who says so?

With the tabloid press having set up camp in Muswell Hill, I couldn't stay in the flat. I remember my neighbours coming up and knocking on my door asking if I was all right. And they would say, 'We're so sorry. It's horrible.'

And I would say, 'No, I'm the one who's sorry. I'm sorry that there's all these men lurking outside the house and you've got kids.'

So I did what I always did, and I went to Jo's, to the loft of new beginnings. It was a good place to hide. No one knew where Jo lived and, although they did their best to follow me, we worked out ways around it. I'd take a black cab to a hotel and then get into another cab because taxis can go along bus lanes where the paps couldn't follow. One night I remember driving up to a small hotel in Hampstead, opening the door then closing it, then driving off while the car that was following stayed watching the hotel, thinking I was inside.

I did a U-turn once because I'd gone the wrong way, and then thought, Funny … when another car behind did exactly the same thing. I remember calling John Noel in desperation and just saying, 'I'm being followed. What shall I do?' Although you don't want to spend your whole life being paranoid, I couldn't risk them finding out where Jo lived.

'Just come to the agency, park up and come in the building.'

One night I shall always remember. I took a black cab to a friend's house and this guy on a motorbike was weaving in and out, and the driver said, 'Someone following you, luv?'

'Might be.'

'Right. I'll deal with it. Hold tight.'

But even with his foot right down and handbrake turns, we still couldn't lose him. When we got to where I was going, I said, 'Just stop here and I'll run in.' Next moment this photographer had his camera hard up against the window meaning I couldn't get out.

'Don't you move, luv,' the cab driver said. 'Leave it to me.' He was an older man but solidly built, a bit like a boxer. And he got out, and bodily pushed this man in leathers away from the door.

'I'll have you done for assault, mate,' this pap snarled, a man half the driver's age.

'Think I care?' my driver retorted. 'What you're doing is wicked.' And then he punched him in the face. 'And now you can fuck off.'

I have no idea if the cab driver knew who I was. He was just doing what he thought was right. I don't know his name, but whoever you are, I'd like to say thank you.

I began to notice changes in people's behaviour, even people I thought were my friends. They didn't turn against me, but they didn't get in touch. Afterwards it was a different story.

'God I feel like you went through a really bad time, I really wanted to get in touch with you.'

So why didn't you . . .

'You've really been through the mill, haven't you?' Or 'I really felt for you during that moment.'

Great, thanks.

But equally my real friends were amazing, and having friends around at that point was really important. Olly was a real rock. Harry was a friend of his so he could have easily have just backed away, but he didn't, he was ace.

I had a text message from Melanie Blatt saying *Is anyone looking after you?* She lives in Ibiza with her parents and her little girl, so I just flew out and disappeared for a few days and saw what it was like to live there out of season. It was such a thoughtful thing to do.

There were others I didn't really know – let me mention Rufus Hound, a comedian. He really stuck up for me. So Rufus, thank you. That made such a difference.

But my greatest thanks are reserved for Dawn Porter. I don't know what I would have done without her at that point, both in person and for writing a really supportive blog. She said everything I wanted to say, but if I'd said it, it would have sounded defensive and I had nothing to apologise for. The last thing I want is to sound 'Poor me, Poor me' because nothing really happened. The pressure was emotional and psychological.

'Are you going to be doing *Xtra Factor* again for us this year?' asked Simon Cowell. It was at the after-party at the Brits later the same month.

'I guess so,' I said. Unless, I thought, you've decided to

bring down the guillotine. I still didn't know him. He'd only shown up once during UK *X Factor*. Everyone was being normal, and then suddenly the room went weird – a bit like the snake up in the gantry in the Jungle – 'What's happened? The room's changed!' Oh, Simon's walked in.

He looked at me and said, 'You're not the girl I thought you were going to be you know?'

'What do you think I was going to be?'

'I don't know, I had no idea what you were going to be like. Tell me: were you two really in love?'

'No, but it was a bit of fun and we weren't hurting anybody.'

'It really astounded me.'

'Life can sometimes take you by surprise, Simon.'

'Well, I'd like to apologise for the way you were treated.'

At the worst point of the whole business, I went off radar, switched off my phone and stopped doing Twitter. But after a couple of weeks I went back on. I couldn't let these people rule my life and there were enough followers who were being really supportive.

Around the same time Dawn forwarded me an email she'd been sent, adding simply, 'Caroline: please explain!' She had her own website with a contact email on it and this guy had asked her to pass it on.

> Hi Dawn,
> I thought it's better emailing you as it's very difficult to describe on Twitter. This weekend and today

particularly I felt such an idiot for being kind. This is something I've never felt before, not like this anyway. I am black and blue from both beating myself up over it and some of the not so favourable comment from various people I've seen on Twitter throughout the day. I've always maintained right from day one that going public has to be the way Caroline wants it to be, and not to creep out one way or another beyond her control.

And I've also known all along that there are multiple reasons as to why she has not been able to contact me directly, and is perpetually telling me that she loves me, which I know she does. And at the same time has been trying to put me off. I think we all know by now that that's never going to happen. Every night for the last two months, I've been thinking about just coming and getting her. I've looked at local caravan sites to come and stay for a few days whilst I find her, and even thought about sending her a load of motorcycle gear so I can come and pick her up on my bike. I've always resisted the temptation, which is the hardest thing I've ever had to do. Simply because I know that deep down she needs to be comfortable with what happens. Quite apart from that, there are one or two situations, you know which ones, which can potentially severely damage her if they came to light, way beyond her control. So there is far more to this than just the fact that she is a celebrity and therefore under constant scrutiny. If it were that easy, I would have come and found her months ago. That would not be easy as all I know is that she lives in Camden, and although it came out on the radio yesterday that she's now staying with her sister, I've no idea where. I had a fleeting glance of the front of her house which I saw on a YouTube video, which was about her being ill last week. I know what her local pub is and that's about it. I've even thought about getting a ticket for the X Factor audience just so I can go and find her there. Caroline, on the other hand, has my company details, home address, numerous telephone numbers, and a couple of email addresses. I am desperate to deliver Mr Kipling in those.

But in order for that to happen I need to know where, when and whether there will be someone there willing to sign for them. Please let me know what I need to do. Whether it's just come and get her, where and when, or for her to contact me.

Love Peter.

So then I looked him up on Twitter and I realised that he messaged me every day and I had never noticed them because there were just far too many, and it was hard to notice his besottedness among the death threats. Because he said 'deliver Mr Kipling', we called him Kips. Everyone was like 'Have you heard from Kips recently?' And yes I probably had, because the emails kept coming and Dawn kept sending them on. They were crazy and creepy but we just laughed them off, although we made sure everyone knew, including Security at *X Factor*, because I was back in the show and by the end of May the madness had kicked off again.

Auditions started in Liverpool, then moved on to London and on 5 June we were in Manchester. I was in the middle of an *Xtra Factor* interview when Tim Dean, my producer, came in.

'Caroline, you need to come to your dressing room straight away.' So I got escorted to my dressing room by Security, and there was a balloon, some chocolates and a card just saying 'I Love You'.

'This is the guy, isn't it?' I said.

'Yes. He got in the building but he's gone now. We just wanted to tell you that he had been here.'

He hadn't reached as far as my dressing room, as I'd first thought when I'd seen the things – they'd been delivered in the usual way. But he had got as far as reception where he kept asking to be let through, saying, 'I'm Caroline Flack's boyfriend,' and Security twigged. He'd driven up from Wales where he lived with his parents and was in his forties, they said. They had no reason to arrest him, so they simply removed him.

It turned out that he suffered from erotomania which is a form of schizophrenia where you believe someone is trying to contact you. Everything you say is directed at them. Even from the way I stood in a photograph: if I crossed my feet, he would think I was giving him a signal.

A couple of weeks later, in between auditions at

Newcastle and Cardiff, I was at the Hackney Big Weekend with Radio 1 because Gemma Cairney was DJ-ing when Polly called me.

'What's up?' I said.

'He's there looking for you.'

'Who?'

'Kips.'

'Where?'

'Hackney, at the festival.'

I left. The police found him and arrested him for harassment and took away his computer. And then there was silence until we heard he'd sent an email to Adam Crozier, head of ITV.

Dear Mr Crozier,

I'm writing to give you a fair warning of a serious situation which has been ongoing for some time. I further give you the opportunity to deal with it internally without the need to pursue criminal actions and go public with the whole story. I'm not going to go into too many details but let's say for over a year I've been in a relationship with Miss Caroline Flack, one of the presenters of the Xtra Factor. However, her ex [meaning Harry Styles, who he usually called The Weasel] and a number of the production team of the programme have been doing everything they can to as they term it stab me in the back. Read into that stalking and harassment. It's got so bad that in the June of this year, this chap Mark Bassett [who's my friend and a producer] on the Xtra Factor team, along with another member of the team, both infiltrated my laptop and mobile phone [this was the police – so he thought they were members of the team who'd come to arrest him], hacked my company website and various other electronic element [sic] of my personal life. As I used to write Caroline a lovely sexy poem on Twitter each night, they thought they would try and stab me in the back by hacking into the SD card on my phone and adding some very nasty pornographic videos. Following which they had me arrested at the beginning of June for so-called stalking. [Until then I didn't realise how dark this was actually. I didn't know he had pornographic videos.] This is a complete non-sense and utter rubbish. During my six weeks bail terms he had a harassment information warning notice put in place, such that Caroline and I are not allowed to talk to each other. I assume his feeling is if she doesn't want him, she's not having me either. Bearing in mind that Mark and those other members of the Xtra Factor team have already been repri-manded by their employer Louis Walsh once last year for harassing me, yet they still choose to continue this disgusting behaviour regardless. Since then, he in particular along with the rest of the team have been desperately trying to break the terms of that notice so he can have me re-arrested. I have approached the police and I have a solicitor lined up, both of which are closely monitoring the situation. [I feel quite sorry for him now.] I would just like to give you the heads up and warn everyone that if this doesn't release nicely and tries anything else on, I will simply have him and the other members of the Xtra Factor production team arrested and spread it across every front page news media in the land. A bit like the Jimmy Savile situation. I therefore urge you to look into this situation and deal with it internally within ITV before they deteriorate any further. I am particularly well connected in the television media and film industry, and happen to run the only commercial UAV flying school in the UK. The BBC did a piece on UAVs just before Christmas. I thought you might like to see it [link to website] I look forward to you dealing with this as a matter of urgency.

Best wishes Peter

I particularly enjoyed the bit about Louis Walsh being 'their employer' ... Kips was re-arrested and then we never heard anything again.

Everyone imagines that Judges' Houses on *X Factor* must be the most fun, but in fact it was the least fun, because all the production teams – one per mentor – would be split up to go to the different places, but Dermot and I would have to fly to all four. That year we went from Dubai to Las Vegas to the Caribbean and then Kettering in the Midlands in the space of about two weeks. We'd get off the plane and head straight into make-up. I remember arriving in St Lucia and we were so jet-lagged. The hotel was called Jade Mountain and it was simply amazing. I walked into my room and I cried. Happy tears. Happy that we'd got there and it was so beautiful but tears of emotion because I was just so tired. Each room felt like it was carved out of the mountain. There was no glass or walls, just an infinity pool that opened out to this amazing view of the sea and the peaks of the Pitons. The bed was swathed in netting and I didn't understand why until I woke in the morning to find it covered with brightly coloured birds. I felt like Snow White in the 1937 Disney film.

St Lucia was such a relief after Las Vegas, which I had hated as a place, although I did have a white wedding . . . It was a skit we did for *Xtra Factor*, in the famous Little White Chapel where Britney Spears got married – a marriage that lasted all of fifty-five hours – as well as Bruce Willis and Demi Moore and Peaches Geldof and her first husband. On this occasion I was marrying Louis Walsh.

We were all knackered. It was midnight by the time we started filming as we'd had to wait till the main show was over to use the cameras. The 'ceremony' was conducted by an Elvis Presley lookalike. When he got to the point of saying 'If anyone knows any reason why these two people should not be joined together' Sharon burst in, shouting 'Stop' and then trying to grapple and yank me away.

As the music would be added later, it had to be done in

total silence. So as I walked up the aisle to imaginary music, in a white silk bridal gown, it was just like being back at school when I got chucked out for giggling. I could see Gemma in her yellow dress sitting in the pews, pretending to be one of the congregation, her shoulders shaking with laughter and meanwhile I was wetting myself even though I had my legs crossed. And yes, once Louis and I had exchanged our vows, we kissed. On the lips. Me and Louis Walsh. Exclusive!

Although Olly and I were still officially team *Xtra Factor*, much of the time he wasn't there. Irony of ironies, he was opening for One Direction on their American tour ... I hadn't realised quite how much I'd missed Olly until he was back for the live shows. Suddenly it was really fun again. Also by then things were more settled generally. Kelly Rowland had left late in the day and it had taken all summer to find her replacement. Geri Halliwell came as a guest judge, so did Rita Ora. But it was Nicole Scherzinger of the Pussycat Dolls who finally got the gig – talented, beautiful, classy and not afraid to speak her mind – she had everything.

At this stage I'd be watching all the singers on a monitor in my dressing room, then noting down the judges' comments, and working out what questions to ask. What does everyone sitting at home on their couch want to know? What will they be talking about afterwards? While you can't skirt round the issues, you do it in the nicest possible way and there's nothing to be gained by putting them on the spot. I remember one meeting where a producer said, 'Apparently there's someone who's being a complete diva and we want to call them out on *Xtra Factor*.'

'I'm not a tabloid journalist,' I said, 'and this isn't a personality contest, it's a singing contest. And I'm not doing it.'

Most *X Factor* contestants come from a really ordinary background and they've never seen anything like this before. And people say, 'Oh they've changed!' Well of course they're going to change. They've never been thrown into the spotlight before, they've never had all this attention, people are doing things for them, they're on a show that says they're going to be a star. If suddenly they go a bit diva-ish, and get a little overexcited, so what? They're not horrible people, they're kids. And I hate it when production staff start complaining: 'Oh so-and-so's being really difficult now he's become famous.'

The fact is, if you do suddenly become 'famous', if you do begin to be recognised in the street, then life is very different. And this is not some cable channel they've crept into, this is *X Factor*, the biggest show in TV, and everything about their family and their life is suddenly all over the papers. Of course they don't know how to deal with that immediately. Everyone has different ways of coping and perhaps it might not always be the best way, or the way you'd do it if you were thirty, or even twenty-five. But I have a lot of understanding of what they're going through.

I am usually rubbish at knowing who's good and who's

not – let alone picking the winner – but that year I remember two standout auditions. One was James Arthur. I knew then he could be a contender to win, and he was, and he did. I had never seen raw talent like that on *X Factor* before. He was in a class of his own. Ella Henderson was another one that year who I thought was amazing. To bring such emotion and depth to what she was singing at such a young age was amazing. And those lyrics . . . When I was sixteen I would have written a song about mixing drinks from my parents' cabinet and here she was writing a song about loss and grief which was beautiful. And it touched me even more because she was writing about her grandad. She had lost him at a really young age, just like me and Jo.

People can slag off *X Factor* all they like, saying, 'It's exposing vulnerable people, it's changing the music industry,' but when you see and hear kids with so much talent – it's entirely justified in my view. They don't teach music in schools any more, except in private schools. Just like playing fields and sport, music isn't seen as important. People like Ella Henderson or James Arthur would never find another way into a career as a singer. Then, suddenly, they get this opportunity to go on a TV show and make something of their lives. And let me tell you, it beats stacking bloody shelves in Tesco's or packing meat in an abattoir.

The great thing about *Xtra Factor* was that everyone could let their hair down, judges, contestants, guests, like former contestants who'd come in – everybody. The atmosphere was always genuinely relaxed, a kind of 'school's over' feeling, and Olly and me really fed on it and our 'double act' seemed to get better and better, and more and more fun as the weeks went on. But all too soon it was over – there were only five live shows. And I already knew what I'd secretly dreaded – that Olly wouldn't be doing season ten. I totally understood – he was a singer and he had his career to think about, but even so . . .

Back in the summer of 2011, my first year with *X Factor*, during the boot camp break, I'd popped out to Ibiza with Gemma Cairney and Beccie Abbot who were working on a Radio 1 show, *A Night in Ibiza*. We were just sitting down and chatting backstage – an outdoor area with about forty people – when I saw a guy sitting at another table and I thought, Oooh. He's rather nice. I liked the way he was dressed – cream trousers, white T-shirt, really classic. It wasn't studied, just natural as if he hadn't thought too much about it. I had no idea who he was but I kept catching his eye and I could see he was never going to come over to me so in the end I walked over to him and said, 'Haven't we met before?'

'No, I don't think so.'

'Oh well, I'm Caroline.'

'Let me get you a drink. Have you ever tried a Fanta *Limón*?' (This wasn't just Fanta and lemon, there was vodka in it as well.)

'I don't like lemon.'

'No, you should try this. It's really nice.'

'Well, I won't like it because I don't like lemon.'

'Just try.'

'OK.'

So he got me one and I tried it.

'No, I don't like it, because I don't like lemon.'

And then we just started to chat. His name was Jack Street, which I thought was the coolest name I'd ever heard and as a joke I said, 'Hmmm Caroline Street, that sounds pretty good.' It was so over the top but it didn't seem to matter.

He was there looking after a band called Disclosure, who were basically two brothers, who were twenty and seventeen when they started. Babies, but geniuses. They'd obviously spent a lot of time as young kids just making music. (Yes, one of them had done A level music and they'd both learnt piano and guitar.) They'd uploaded some tracks online and Jack had found them. Basically they were making electronic dance music for a new generation, but using live vocals, and were on the cusp at that point, Radio 1 having just started playing them.

Then as we sat there, Jack got a phone call from his best friend, another Jack, announcing that he was engaged. So we were all, 'Oooh congratulations!' And there we were clinking glasses and the rest of it, and I was thinking, But I don't know who this guy is, or anything about him! The only thing I did know was that we were both from Norfolk.

'So are you coming out later to this other club?' he asked.

'No, I'm not very good at staying up.'

'Oh, come on.'

But it was already about two in the morning, and I said, 'No, I need to go home.' Because in spite of what people like to think, the all-nighter thing isn't me. But even before I got back to my hotel he sent me a text saying, *It was so nice to meet you, let's meet up while we're here in Ibiza.*

And I put, *I'd love to, from Caroline Street.*

The next day he messaged me again and said, *Would you like to come to a party tomorrow night?*

I'd love to. So we went and when I saw him I just thought, God you are so handsome. And from then on that was it. We just spent the rest of the holiday together.

When I got back to London he kept saying, 'Do you want to meet up?' but the truth was, 'Not really . . .' As far as I was concerned it had been a holiday romance and it was great, but for some reason I felt completely different when I got back to London. He'd suggested we watch a film on TV – *The Descendants* with George Clooney. And it was so, so sad and it was then that I decided I didn't want to do this. I wasn't in relationship mode. Also he was only twenty-six and it was like 'You're fun but I don't think I could ever fall in love with you.' There was nothing about him, I thought, that could be relationship material.

*

The last *X Factor* audition the following summer was at Wembley and finished on 18 July. We'd then had a break until boot camp at the beginning of August. The moment I was free I headed to Suffolk, to Latitude, a really gorgeous festival, near Southwold. Latitude is like a proper grown-up festival, really civilised with readings and poetry as well as music.

Dawn had just published her first novel called *Paper Aeroplanes* and was doing an onstage talk, so she suggested I join her. I could sleep in her Winnebago, she said. Then Jo decided to come along too and she brought a huge teepee to sleep in, so it was going to be a really fun girls' weekend. As well Jo, there was Josie, Dermot's wife Dee, Gemma Cairney and a friend of Gemma's called Camilla and another girl called Laura.

I loved Latitude from the moment I arrived. It's the kind of place with funny stalls – in a way it feels like a big village fete – and there are kids playing everywhere and at night you can see couples wandering around with a baby asleep in a wheelbarrow. It's small so you don't have to walk miles to see different stages as you do at Glastonbury, which means you end up seeing many more bands. We were all just wandering around, getting the feel of things, and when I went to get a burger I came back wearing an Afro wig. They thought it was so hilarious they all bought one too – we looked exactly like the Jackson Five.

The main festival area is surrounded by woods and in the evening there's a DJ and you dance till three in the morning under the trees, just lit by fairy lights and it's really beautiful. By the time we got to bed I was so tired I completely forgot to take off the wig. What a mistake. The next morning when I saw my hair, I knew I couldn't possibly go out looking like that, so I crammed the wig back on. It was mid-July and incredibly hot and I was walking around in this massive Afro wig when suddenly I bumped into Jack.

'Hi,' I said.

'Hi,' he said. Then, after a split-second's double take because of the wig, he turned towards the couple he was walking with and said, 'This is Carrie. Carrie meet my mum and dad.'

Oh My God . . .

Over the last couple of months things between Jack and me had started to get a bit more datey, and he'd stayed over a couple of times at my flat, but I still wasn't entirely sure if it was a good idea. His parents lived in Norwich, which wasn't that far away, and the three of them had just come for the day. Jack had been planning on going back with them, but I said, 'Why don't you stay?'

'I really ought to go back.'

'Oh come on, stay. It was such fun last night.'

So he stayed. And it was such fun. Dermot was DJ-ing. It was his fourth year at Latitude since he'd first come with Radio 2, where he has a weekly show which focuses on new music and live sessions. So Dermot was there doing an indie disco, and everyone was dancing. He started about ten and just went on until the dawn chorus proved too much competition. I was so tired that I fell asleep on

Jack's arm. I slept for three hours, Jack said, and he didn't move the entire time. When I finally woke up I saw that I had dribbled all over his arm. 'Why didn't you move me?' I asked.

'You looked so peaceful, I didn't want to disturb you.' That's when I fell in love with him. I thought, He sat there all night while I had an Afro wig on dribbling onto his arm and he's still here.

Jo was giving him a lift back to London early the next morning and we found somewhere to bed down in her teepee. And after leaving them, I walked back to Dawn's Winnebago where I still had my things. There was nobody up. I didn't see a soul and it was so early the grass was still wet with dew. And there I was still wearing this ridiculous Afro wig, and I just thought, Uh oh . . . here we go. Falling in love again.

Dawn drove me home in the Winnebago. And when she dropped me off, she said, 'By the way, Caroline, you stink.' I realised that I hadn't had a shower since I'd arrived, having gone straight from *The X Factor* to Suffolk.

14

Strictly

Xtra Factor in 2013 without Olly just wasn't the same. Nor, in fairness to Matt who had taken over from him, should it have been. I think that if you change people, you need to change the format, if only slightly, because Matt Richardson and Olly Murs have such different personalities. It's not like changing one of the judging panel which happens all the time on X Factor – obviously there the format isn't going to change, even if the dynamic does – but a spin-off show like Xtra Factor can go pretty much where it likes, and often did, which was what was so good about it. It's a bit like Doctor Who in that respect. Each Doctor has a completely different personality and there's no attempt to mimic the one who went before, in fact it's quite the opposite. It's seen as an opportunity to do something completely different, not a setback. But I think that in some way they expected Matt to do what

Olly had done, which was quite difficult if not impossible. You can't just expect someone to step into someone else's shoes without changing something.

Personally I love Matt, and he is without a doubt the funniest person I know. But the show wasn't doing that well. When *X Factor* was at its height with 14 million people watching, 4 million would turn over to *Xtra Factor*. But by 2013 only 9 million were watching the main show and hardly anyone was switching over to find out the extra stuff about contestants. So a shake-up was probably inevitable. However, until they had someone else in place, they kept me hanging on.

With most productions you have a rough idea where you are at the end of the season, but nothing to do with *X Factor* was that simple and I began to get a sense of foreboding. Auditions normally start in late May so there would be echoes coming back, mumblings of dates and stuff. I heard nothing. Then sometime in late March 2014 a couple of the producers asked me to meet them for breakfast at the Riding House Café north of Oxford Street and basically said: 'We're going to be making some changes in *Xtra Factor* this year. We don't know whether we want you back or not, but we might. But in the meantime we're going to screen test other people.'

After three years it was a truly horrible thing to hear. It was a bit like if you'd been fostered and suddenly your foster parents said they weren't sure about you any more, and they might try and look for someone they liked better.

My intuition had told me this wasn't going to be a

comeback meeting, so before I went I told myself that no matter what happened I was going to take it graciously, I was going to listen to what they had to say, and even if I felt like stamping my feet and storming out, it wasn't going to happen. So I sat there with both these producers, who I obviously knew well because I'd been working with them, and when they broke the news, I took a deep breath and said, 'OK, fine.'

'Look,' I said, 'I love this job. I live and breathe this job. And so I'm not going to step down because I think that would be weird because I still want it. As far as I am concerned working on *Xtra Factor* is the best job in the world. But please let me know as soon as possible which way it's swaying and if you do decide to go with somebody else, then I'll step down.'

And as I walked to where I'd parked my car in Great Portland Street, I felt my eyes stinging. But I felt that I'd done it the right way. I had told the truth and I had kept my dignity. The meeting we'd just had was part of the job, both for me and them. There was no point making enemies. Bitter words are corrosive and can do lasting damage. Later that afternoon they sent Polly an email telling her what a lovely meeting they'd had, so it had been the right thing to do.

Then barely two weeks later, I was back at the same cafe for another meeting, this time with the BBC, and this time my intuition was not sending up distress flares because the subject under discussion was *Strictly Come Dancing*. I had always wanted to do *Strictly*. In fact in one of the *Xtra*

Factors I'd said so on air and done a little paso doble-type twirl. I'd even had a meeting with Danny Cohen, who had recently been made director of television at the BBC, and told him I was interested.

So in the spring of 2014, when things were beginning to look unpromising at *Xtra Factor*, Polly had been in touch with the *Strictly* office. It was still a good six months before the show went on air, so she'd asked whether they'd started casting, and if they had – or when they did – that Caroline Flack would be interested.

They didn't pussyfoot around. After a couple of minutes of how-are-you?-good-and-you? they asked the key question: 'Are you not doing *Xtra Factor* this year?' I was perfectly honest. I told them I didn't know.

'But I would like to see if this could be an option.'

'They' were two women, Louise Rainbow and Vinnie Freeman. Louise had just been appointed executive producer for that year's *Strictly* and Vinnie was in charge of booking all the talent. And they sat there and proceeded to sell me the show, telling me how much fun it was, as well as the nuts-and-bolts of how it worked and how much work I would have to put in.

It's a very female-orientated production. Tess Daly and Claudia Winkleman present it and a good many of the backstage team are women so it all felt very comfortable. But it was a risk. It wasn't an obvious rung on my career ladder. I'd be there as a performer not a presenter. Could I perform? To say I'd be out of my comfort zone was putting it mildly.

This time there were no tears in my eyes as I walked back to my car. My eyes were sparkling with excitement. It wasn't an instant 'Can I have it?' It was more 'Let me think about it.' As for what I would do if *Xtra Factor* came back the next day with 'Caroline, please we need you!' I didn't know. And I don't know now. But fate soon made that particular dilemma irrelevant.

It was the day before I went to Ibiza, this time with my friend Lou Teasdale and her sister Sam. At the same time Jack was heading off to the States for a month-long tour. I was in the kitchen when Polly's name flashed up on my screen.

'I'm really sorry,' she said. 'It's *Xtra Factor* I'm afraid. They're not going to go with you this year.'

'Thanks.'

'Is that all you're going to say?'

'OK. Who're they going with?'

'Sarah-Jane Crawford.'

'OK. I'll step down. Call them will you? Tell them I'm stepping down.'

As the phone clicked off, Jack came in and found me in tears.

'What's happened?'

'I don't want to talk about it. I don't want to talk about it, I don't want to talk about it.'

I literally could not talk about it. He knew I'd been waiting for news and he just gave me a hug and said, 'I'm so sorry.'

It had been so much part of my life for three years, so

much fun, so much everything. 'Where else am I going to find something so enjoyable? Who else would ever pay me to lark around?' It had been my life. And now what? I had never lost a job before. And it was so public. It was like 'If I'm dumped from that, am I going to be unemployable?'

I knew that somehow I had to think positively. I had to stop myself going into a negative tailspin. But I had no experience of how to do it. Luckily I had my bag to pack, Jack to say goodbye to ... But it was so, so hard. That show had been my anchor for three years and now I felt completely adrift.

When I got back from Ibiza the first thing I did was call Polly. 'Look, I've been having a good think while I've been away and I've decided I'd like to give *Strictly* a go.' So she phoned the BBC and told them that I was definitely interested. But casting something as complex as *Strictly* involves all kinds of variables: numbers of men, numbers of women, age, balance, natural talent versus likeability and quirkiness. There needs to be someone for everyone to root for. I knew from what Louise and Vinnie had said that the process was far from straightforward and by the time I made a decision they might not have a place for me.

When *X Factor* time came round the papers were full of Sarah-Jane Crawford. I knew her and I was pleased for her but I also knew the job and how difficult it was, particularly on your own. And, comparatively speaking, Sarah-Jane was a novice. She was a radio DJ but had no TV experience at all.

Once the auditions were underway I had a call from Simon Cowell's office, asking would I be available to take a call from him at 4.00 that afternoon? Yes, I was available. (That's how it works. He doesn't just phone and hope you answer.) It was a joint call with Peter Fincham who runs ITV, and they said they wanted to explain in person why things had had to change. It was really nice to get a phone call and not just be told through my agent. At the end I said, 'Do you know what? Thanks for the opportunity over the last three years.' And I meant it, I truly meant it.

Peter Fincham stayed on the line after Simon had gone and said, 'So what are you doing next week, Caroline?'

'Well, not working by the looks of things . . .'

'Are you a fan of football?'

'Why?'

'I'm taking some people to Brazil for a bit of a jolly. It's the World Cup. Would you like to come?'

The first thing I did was phone Jack, because he is the biggest football fan of all time and he was still in America – and I hated him not being around and it was happening more and more. Disclosure, the band he looked after, were now huge and Sam Smith, who'd come to notice singing on one of their records, and now another of his clients, had won the Critics Choice Award at the Brits that spring.

'Guess where I'm going next week,' I said.

'Where?'

'Brazil for the World Cup!!'

'What! But you don't even really like football.'

'I know!' But I did go and I watched the England v Uruguay match in São Paulo and though England lost it was brilliant.

Back in London, I had lunch with Natalie Pinkham. She'd just found out she was pregnant, so we went to a vegan restaurant near where she lives and on a table was a copy of *Marie Claire* with Abbey Clancy on the cover. Abbey had won *Strictly* the year before and it reminded me to check with Polly to see what was happening. I was just walking along Kensington High Street, vaguely looking into shop windows when my phone rang. Polly.

'Caroline. They're offering you *Strictly*, do you want it?'

This time I didn't say, 'I'll think about it.' That copy of *Marie Claire* had been a sign.

'Do you know what, Polly? I will.'

Yaaaaay!

I walked back to my car with my feet not touching the ground, smiling at everyone I passed and literally laughing out loud. In fact guffawing! 'You're gonna be on *Strictly*!' It was so weird. I've never done anything like that in my life before. And everyone I told said it was the most excited they'd seen me about any job ever. It was almost like I'd never had a job before. 'Oh my God! *STRICTLY!*'

Strictly Come Dancing started on BBC1 in 2004, the same year as *The X Factor*. It was basically a modernised *Come Dancing*, the ballroom dancing programme that began in 1949 and ran for forty-nine years until 1998 and which both Nanny Flo and Nanny Ivy used to watch religiously – they'd both grown up ballroom dancing before the war. It was what you did for entertainment. It was how you met boys. (The 'Strictly' comes from a very successful 1992 film by Baz Luhrmann called *Strictly Ballroom* set in the competitive world of professional ballroom dancing in Australia.)

The format hasn't really changed since the beginning and even three of the original judges are still there. There are fifteen celebrities and fifteen professional dancers to partner them. There's no 'star' treatment. Nobody does *Strictly* for the money, they do it because it has the reputation of being the happiest show on television where everyone has the time of their lives.

Jack, however, was not convinced. When he got back from LA I took him down the road for dinner and said, 'I've got some news.'

'What?'

'I'm doing *Strictly*!'

He gasped. 'Really?'

I'd mentioned the possibility before but he hadn't taken it seriously.

'Are you sure this is what you want to do?'

'Definitely.'

'Well, if you want to, then do it. But I'm still not sure it's the right thing.'

But then he'd never seen me dance apart from at a rave.

I was lucky because I had several months to get myself fit. John Noel has a weekly fitness class for his staff run by a guy called Rory, so the moment we knew what lay ahead, Rory began to knock me into shape. My problem is that I eat all the time and I can't do diets. And Rory kept telling me, 'You know only 25 per cent is down to exercise, the other 75 per cent is diet!' Things became a bit more urgent when I found out who else would be doing the show. As I told him, 'Everyone's so thin and lovely and beautiful!'

Nothing in the world would make me miss Glastonbury and that year was no different, except in one crucial respect: no more camping! Because Disclosure were performing on the Other Stage and Jack had his own Winnebago. The big surprise for me was Dolly Parton who was really good. There were more people watching her than had watched the Rolling Stones the year before!

That August I was back again in Ibiza, this time with Jack, and I bumped into Nick Grimshaw. When I told him I was doing *Strictly* he looked astounded and then excited.

'Oh my God!' he said. 'So is Scott!' Scott Mills is another Radio 1 DJ. I was so pleased to think that I'd have someone there that I knew.

Over the years I had done a couple of things for Comic Relief. In the spring of 2007, when I was working at *TMi*, I'd hosted the CBBC coverage of *Comic Relief Does Fame Academy*. In 2011 I did *Let's Dance for Comic Relief* with Joe Swash, a few months after we'd finished the second series of the Jungle *NOW!*.

Then in the summer of 2014 I was asked by Sport Relief if I would go out to Rwanda and report on how the money they'd raised was helping to rebuild the country twenty years after the genocide. They also asked who I'd like to work with, and I'd suggested Dermot's wife Dee who had been my producer way back on the *Pepsi Chart Show*. Quite coincidentally she'd already been approached by them. So we decided it was meant to be.

I had been to Africa before, but to West Africa, to the Gambia, for a week with Josie after I'd learnt that I was going back for the second *Xtra Factor*, and that I hadn't lost my job as I'd feared. Although we were basically on holiday we had visited some schools and taken a supply of pencils with us because they were like gold dust. But poor though the Gambian people were – and they were very poor – it was nothing compared to Rwanda.

During a three-month period, between April and July 1994 – when Jo and I were fourteen – over 800,000 people were slaughtered in the Rwandan Genocide leaving millions of children with no one to look after them but older brothers and sisters. Of course it had been on the news at the time and I remember being vaguely aware of it. But because it was so horrific, we tended to be shielded from the details, both at home and at school.

Sport Relief had funded two specific projects in Rwanda and it was humbling to see what amazing work is being done. Although hundreds of thousands of children had lost their parents, they still owned the family land and the first project we visited is helping to teach these young people the skills they need to run their farms, learning to grow anything from tomatoes to pineapples and watermelon and then how to sell the produce at market so they can make a living for themselves and their families.

The second was a women and children's refuge that, from my perspective, was emotionally really hard. One young woman we met was exactly my age. She had watched her parents and then her brothers and sisters cut down by men with machetes, so she started her own orphanage. She introduced me to a little girl of six who had been raped by her father and contracted gonorrhoea and syphilis as a result. As for the emotional damage, it cannot even be imagined. It was utterly heart-wrenching.

As I watched these little people skittering around, doing what kids do, hiding behind the skirts of the helpers, tentatively giving me their hands, I thought of Willow and Delilah and Zuzu and imagined what their lives would have been like if they'd been beaten and raped and I could only be grateful that they were in a safe place. But thanks to the tenacity of the people I met, helped by charities on the ground, who are in turn funded by organisations like Sport Relief, it's not all doom and gloom. There was a lot of positivity there, with everyone intent on getting the country back to what it was.

Overall it was a sobering experience and when I got back to London I wanted to talk to Jack about it. But what I had to say was harrowing – how even now they are still discovering pits filled with bodies – while he was in a different place, literally and metaphorically, in LA, living the Californian dream.

*

Strictly is done at Elstree Studios in Hertfordshire on the sound stage where they shot *Star Wars*, but from the outside it's anything but glamorous and looks like an aircraft hangar. It was the beginning of September and that first day was exactly like the first day at a new school. The contestants all mill around and vaguely chat, and then a curtain is pulled back to reveal the professional dancers. It's a bit like a speed-dating session. Meanwhile it's all being filmed.

Of course I had watched *Strictly* in the past, but I only recognised people like Brendan Cole and Anton du Beke, who'd had been doing it for years. I had never seen Pasha Kovalev before, but for some reason I was drawn to him straight away. I just went up and said, 'Hello, I'm Caroline,' and he went, 'I'm Pasha.'

While all this getting-to-know-you was going on, a producer was trying out different partners together. First they put me with Anton. He had me laughing within seconds and I thought, Actually this could be quite funny … Then I was tried out with another couple of guys but never with Pasha. They kept putting Pasha with Pixie Lott and I realised I felt really jealous, because by then I'd made up my mind: Pasha was who I wanted. Whenever I passed Vinnie, I'd say in a loud stage whisper, 'Pasha!' Like every five minutes!

Following that first introductory session we spent a couple of days learning the routine for the opening number and staying the night at a hotel down the road, which we would do every Friday until Christmas. Some people had never performed on a stage in their lives and I suspect it did all look rather village hall, which only made it more impressive when you saw what people eventually achieved.

The opening number is a group dance – there was no particular theme as far as I remember – but while you're learning it, the professionals are watching like hawks, all whispering with one another, deciding who they want to partner. They want to win as much as you do, perhaps even more. Not only would they get to come back for the next series, but it's how they sell tickets for their own tours. And of course while they're watching you, you're busy eyeing up the competition, and desperately trying to learn these silly dance moves at the same time.

'So, what did you do today?' Jack asked when I got home.

'I spent the whole time chatting with Tim Wonnacott,' I said.

'Who's Tim Wonnacott?'

'He presents *Bargain Hunt*. He's an antiques expert. He has a moustache, a bow tie and glasses and he's lovely.'

'This is weird.'

The next day I said to Vinnie, 'What time do I have to meet Pasha next week then?'

No reply.

'Vinnie, did you hear me? What time do I have to meet Pasha next week?'

'Caroline. Stop it!'

Next came a full dress rehearsal for our opening routine,

in costume, with Tess and Claudia doing it as if it was the real thing. For the first time we were paired off with one of the professional dancers, though they said that he or she wouldn't be our final partner. So when they put me with Pasha I felt utterly deflated, as if my balloon had just had a huge great hole gouged out of it. Dancing with him now meant we wouldn't be dancing together in the real thing. All my pathetic nudges and hints to Vinnie had come to nothing, and had probably done me harm. He and I looked at each other.

'I'm gutted,' I said.

'Me too.'

But what do you do? The show must go on. I tried to make the best of it. The one that got away ... At least it felt reassuring to be strutting and prancing and not feeling like the worst one there – nearly always the case at college.

In the great tradition of TV entertainment shows, the official pairing off was all very theatrical, with great long pauses and rolling of drums – well, I can't remember if there were drums, but it felt like there were. We were assigned our partners one by one. When it was my turn a whole posse of male dancers lined up on the dance floor. I remember that Pasha gave me a little wave when his name was read out – the only one to make any sign – and my heart did a little flutter. And then Claudia said:

'Caroline, you have got' – U.N.B.E.A.R.A.B.L.E. P.A.U.S.E. – 'Pasha!!'

I literally squealed with delight! I was so, so happy and

Pasha was too. He did a little dance, his feet twinkling away as he came towards me, took me in his arms, then bent me right back till my hair was touching the ground! Only later did I discover just how lucky I was. Pasha had come second in two of the three *Strictly*s he'd been in and the previous year he'd gone out in an early round.

We now had three weeks to rehearse our first dance, which he'd decided would be the cha-cha-cha. I very soon realised that my experience with *Dancing on Wheels* was going to be no help at all. The only time in my entire life I'd had a go at proper ballroom dancing was one night on holiday in Egypt with Josie when, for a laugh, we had entered a competition in the hotel where she danced the man's part, and I was the girl and our main problem was that her massive boobs and mine kept bumping. In spite of that we came second.

Everything from here on in was down to Pasha. He decided the order in which we'd do the dances. He did all the choreography and he decided on the music. We rehearsed in a dance studio in Kentish Town – it was halfway between where Pasha lived in Notting Hill and Stepney where I had just bought my first flat. Most of the celebrities got their dancers to travel to where they lived – but I wanted Pasha and me to keep a feeling of equality. We were in this together.

For the next three months we would spend about eight hours a day rehearsing, and a camera crew would turn up now and then. But eight hours a day with someone you don't know was definitely weird. It wasn't all dancing – I wouldn't have had the stamina – it was as much about getting to know each other.

Thankfully we both like to lie in – the one thing we had in common. So I would get there for eleven and Pasha would trundle in about half-past, though one of us would regularly be late as we would get stuck in traffic. Production offered to send me a car, but I preferred to drive. I'm really happy in my car and always get lots done, phone calls, listening to songs on the radio. Thinking. I catch up on life in my car. And on a practical note it means you can go on to somewhere else afterwards.

Pasha had used this studio before and it was right near Kentish Town High Street. We soon developed our little routine. He would always bring me a coffee from the Costa he passed on the way and we'd take a lunch break at the same little Spanish deli and sit there and chat chat chat chat chat. Every Thursday the woman would say, 'Good luck this week!'

If I'm honest, I liked going to rehearsals more than I enjoyed doing the actual show. Everything about it: from getting a coffee, walking into the studio – it was like a proper job.

'Morning!'

'Morning.'

Chat chat chat chat chat.

I absolutely loved it.

We rehearsed from Monday till Thursday. Friday and Saturday we were at Elstree and Sundays we had off. I would have trained on Sunday if I could – and in fact we did towards the end – but Sunday was when Pasha worked out the choreography for the next week's dance. He was very clever. He actually started us with the hardest dances because, he said, 'I know you're going to be good at salsa, so we'll do that in the semi-final.' At which I said, 'But we're not going to get to the semi-final!'

'Yes, we will.'

He was right. The salsa was our best dance, and we did get to the semi-final, and it was the perfect time to do it, just when the competition was getting harder and our rivals (we hoped) were struggling.

If it works – which it obviously did with Pasha and me and I know it did for others as well – you develop a really lovely relationship with your partner. It's not like falling in love exactly, but you do fall in some sort of fashion, because you're so in awe of them, and the whole thing about ballroom dancing is that it's so intense and so intimate. I mean most of the time you are inches away from each other, and a lot of the time even closer than that.

It wasn't all hearts and flowers. Pasha was a hard taskmaster and he really pushed me and it could sometimes get heated.

'Caroline, that's not right!'

'I am trying!'

But he never talked back, he would just go, 'OK.'

'Pasha! Say something!'

'Now you're choosing to have an argument with me!'

'No, I'm not!'

'OK.'

'But we need to change that move, Pasha!'

'No, you can do it. I know you. I know you can do it.'

'I can't!'

Silence.

'Grrrrrr!'

'You're just too fiery for me!'

'You're just too chilled for me!'

But although he could be very tough and uncompromising, suddenly he'd say, 'Right, Caroline, you're too tired, you need to go home.'

If things got too fractious I could always pop in and see Scott who happened to be in the studio next door rehearsing with his partner Joanne Clifton, though they were only around for eight weeks – as they were eliminated on week six. Until then we would regularly watch each other's routines before going to Elstree.

Usually you'd only ever see other couples on Friday at the dress rehearsal. We'd watch whoever it was and I'd say, 'Wow – they're amazing!'

And Pasha would say, 'They're good,' but then add, 'but you're good.'

At which I'd always say, 'Not as good as them.'

Until I met Pasha I had never been friends with a Russian. In fact I had barely met any Russians. He and I are exactly the same age – he's six weeks younger – but his life couldn't have been more different. He grew up in Siberia when it was still the Soviet Union. By the time he was a teenager he was studying to be a ballroom dancer. Then, when he was an amateur champion, he got a Green Card and moved to America with his girlfriend when he turned professional. But trying to get him to tell me stories about his life when he was growing up was really difficult. 'The only thing that happened,' he used to say, 'is that I was always really cold.' So he always wears a polo neck, even in the summer. Just in case.

What he really enjoyed talking about was politics. Politics? I never talk politics – but in the end we did, and we have such different views. Actually we both changed. I totally saw his point and he totally saw mine. I have to say that Pasha is one of the most interesting people I have ever met.

About halfway through that first three weeks of non-stop, killer training, I did an evening DJ-ing at a fashion party with Josie. My hair needed a trim, I decided, and as a hairdresser friend of Gemma Wheatcroft's called Hannah Wynne was there, she said she'd do it. I was looking in the mirror, as you do, and for no real reason that I can remember said, 'I might have it short. What do you think?'

'I'll do it, if you're sure.'

'Go on then.'

So off it came. On a whim. It took about ten minutes. There's a guy going around saying that he created my bob. He didn't. It was a girl called Hannah Wynne.

Looking back, I think I might have been subconsciously making a statement, not so much to the world, but to myself. I'd always played around with my hair, especially in terms of colour, but perhaps I'd somehow hidden behind it up until now. Now I was changing. Life was changing.

Without a doubt my favourite among the celebrities was Judy Murray. She is just so, so funny and can take the mickey out of herself like nobody else. When she had been slated by the judges, I'd send her a text saying *Well done Judy. You were really good when you did that lift.* And she'd go *Don't lie. I looked constipated.* Or I'd say *You were brilliant when you did such-n-such,* and she'd go *Don't lie. I looked like I had a stroke.* I think we were the only two who used to go out on our own, like naughty girls on the lash. I even took her to a couple of gigs. Jack was doing a Sam Smith tour in the UK and when he was playing Hammersmith Apollo in early November he said, 'You should bring a couple of your friends.'

'I'll bring Judy Murray.'

'What!'

'I'm gonna bring Judy Murray!' And in fact her son Jamie and his wife came along as well. So the four of us went and we had a brilliant time.

The other person I got on really well with was Pixie Lott. Although we did mix in the same circles occasionally, we had never actually met before *Strictly*. She is the sweetest, most positive little ray of sunshine I have ever met in my entire life. And in the first couple of weeks I thought, She can't be for real, this is an act. But the more I got to know her, the more real she became. If I could freeze her, I'd put her on top of my Christmas tree. Pixie lives in Pixieland. I'd quite like to live there too, because nothing in Pixieland is complicated.

How different from the world Frankie Bridge and I live in. Frankie (of the Saturdays) was the first person I spoke to before the curtain was pulled back the day we arrived and I immediately felt I had another ally as well as Scott. I felt I'd known her for ages as we had mutual friends though we'd never actually met. She is the only person I know who worries as much as I do. Every Friday we'd arrive at Elstree and there'd be Frankie and me going, 'What if this happens? What if that happens?' And then Pixie would breeze in and go, 'Morning girls!' How is she so happy?

Towards the end all of us girls were on WhatsApp and we'd text each other constantly.

Monday, *Yeah! Learning a new routine, all happy.*

Tuesday, *OK, time to take it a bit more seriously.*

Wednesday, *Shit, we've only got one day to go. Panic!*

So Frankie would get Monday breakdowns. I had Wednesday breakdowns. Pixie never had a breakdown. Pixie was always in Pixieland.

One slight worry I'd had before I went in was the costumes. I know everyone expects them to be OTT and not something you'd wear to your nan's eightieth, but even so . . . I was happy with my legs to be out there, but cleavage: a big NO. And the first week when I saw the cut-out things that Frankie and Pixie were wearing I got quite panicky and said to Vicky Gill who made our costumes, 'Please, please don't put me in one of those . . .' But gradually as I toned up and became more confident I would wear something a bit more revealing.

I soon discovered that if you went to wardrobe and were nice to them rather than confrontational they listened and they'd work with you, saying, 'OK, we can make it a different shape.' Whereas if you stamped your feet and said, 'I'm not wearing that!' they would totally switch off. Vicky was always open to positive suggestions.

'Vick?'

'Caroline.'

'I'd quite like some tassels here. Any chance?'

'Yeah.'

My all-time favourite was the midnight-blue high-to-the-throat, bare-shouldered, big-skirted dress, slit up the front, that I wore for the paso doble. The worst was undoubtedly the salsa outfit, all pink spangles and in-your-face cleavage that I absolutely hated. But because I loved the salsa, I wasn't that fussed. We got the first four 10s of the series – in the semi-finals – so I'm not about to complain because it was so utterly brilliant and amazing.

Working on *Strictly* is very schizophrenic. On one level you have to block out three months of your life because you might just win. But at the same time you can't look that far ahead. Pasha and I agreed at the start that we'd just take it week by week. Every week I was convinced we were going to go out. And Mr Calm would come straight back with, 'We're not going out this week.'

Although I was exercising more than I have ever done in my life, I didn't really lose any weight, mainly because instead of one burger I was eating two burgers, but I was definitely toning up.

Unlike *X Factor*, on *Strictly* the judges stay at a distance, which makes things a whole lot easier. You'd see them around and go hello, hello, hello, but otherwise they kept themselves to themselves. There was no fraternising, no cronying up. Also you'd see them as experts rather than judges. It's never about how you're dressed, it's never about personality, it's solely about technique and as a result it was never hurtful and the technical criticism always helped, because actually everything they said was bang on the button. It might have been live TV but I was really listening to what they had to say, nodding and thinking, Yeah, I know. That's exactly what I did.

'Caroline, your shoulder's up.' I know you're exactly right.

'Caroline, you don't look comfortable on that bit.' Spot on.

Also, unlike other shows, it's not about them. You don't know about their love life, you don't know who they're married to, you don't know what they're doing, they don't get papped. They're just these brilliant experts and they're the best in the world at what they do – Len Goodman and Bruno Tonioli fly back and forth across the Atlantic as judges on the American version of *Strictly*, *Dancing with the Stars*. How they cope with that schedule I do not know.

The real surprise for me was Craig Revel Horwood. He's the judge who's the most feared, the judge who people like to compare to Simon Cowell, but it turns out he's just a pussycat. Craig is one of the best judges on any programme on TV and was definitely my favourite, not only because he's totally honest, but because he is just so nice off camera. But when he's judging he never takes his hard-man role too far, he's just pantomiming. His real obsession is musical theatre, and while Len and Bruno jet off to the States for *DWTS*, he's jetting off across the world choreographing and directing musicals.

No one gets thrown off during the first week and Thank God, because when our music started – the Jacksons' 'Can You Feel It' – I was so, so nervous. Pasha and I weren't just doing our first dance in public, we were the first dancers on the floor, we were opening the show! Usually you don't know your position until the dress rehearsal but I'd seen a script lying around, so I knew. That night we got our lowest score of the whole series – a 6 from Craig – but I hardly noticed because I was feeling ecstatic. I just had such a great time out there. Until we ran up those stairs, I hadn't been sure that I was really enjoying it. But from then on I was hooked.

Pasha had told me the cha-cha-cha was 'fun, fast and playful' and above all that I mustn't forget to smile, and I smiled so much I felt my face was breaking. In fact we did the same dance again in the final and that time got full marks – four 10s – though we actually made more mistakes. But I think everyone was marked low on their first outing on the principle that you've got to have room to improve.

That first night was especially emotional. Mum and

Jody were in the audience while Dad, I knew, was in the Green Room. When the VT is being shown – the rehearsal footage and so on that's been shot the previous week – and you're just standing there waiting to dance, everyone in the audience is looking at you. Jo was in the front row and I didn't dare catch her eye because I knew if I did I'd start laughing. So I tried my hardest, but it was impossible. We looked at each other and laughed just as Claudia said, 'And now, dancing the cha-cha-cha we have Caroline Flack and Pasha Kovalev.'

Can you feel it . . .

Jack had said he wasn't coming but in the end he did – he'd been in the Green Room and I found him later talking with Dad. *Strictly* have a strict dress code – so he was wearing proper leather shoes with jeans! And it was so great to see Mum and Dad getting along together, basically just for me for the first time since they got divorced.

I always felt more comfortable in the fast dances, and in week seven, when we did the waltz, we'd found ourselves in the bottom two. I wasn't surprised as I found traditional ballroom dances really difficult and I feel I blagged my way through.

Our marks hadn't been any different from the week before, but every week, as dancers get eliminated, it gets harder and you have to keep upping your game. We ended up in the dance-off against Alison Hammond of *This Morning* and her partner Aljaž Škorjanec. It was the second week Alison had been in the dance-off so she wasn't that surprised, she said, when they didn't get through. But in a way it was good for me. Pasha has this line, 'It's not how you fall, it's how you get up again.'

Falling was a constant preoccupation with me. Falls happened when lifts went wrong, and doing lifts with heels was a nightmare. And I'd go, 'I can't do lifts.'

'You can do lifts.'

'I can't do it.'

And then he'd lift me and I'd scream.

The week we did the Charleston I got a text message from Josie, saying *I think something's happened to Rob*. People were writing things on social media, like *what shocking news* and *I've lost my best friend*. And then Dave called. Dave's former bandmate, the fiddle player for the Holloways, Rob Skipper, had died of an accidental overdose of heroin on 3 October in Brighton. Tragedy is a much overused word, but this was. Rob was one of the most talented men I've ever met; he was beautiful – all curly hair and gorgeousness and he was only twenty-eight. He was always getting into all sorts of trouble but he had a smile that meant he got away with everything. Because he was Skipper, naughty little Skipper. He left behind his beautiful wife, George, and their lovely daughter, Elizabeth. I don't think any of us will ever come to terms with his death.

I texted Pasha and asked if he'd mind if I went to the funeral. He said, 'I think you should go.'

Jack drove me to a nearby cafe where Dave was waiting

and he and I went together. Rob Skipper was buried in Brompton Cemetery close to Chelsea and Westminster Hospital where Jo had had Willow.

The hardest dance of all was the Argentine tango. It wasn't like the others. It was a different style of dancing altogether and something Pasha couldn't choreograph, so some Argentinians came in to teach us. A further complication was that the man who taught us didn't speak English. In the end Pasha changed it to make it more dramatic for the show.

Poor Pasha. That week he had flu and was so poorly. But he staggered in and stuck it out like the true professional he is, though I would try not to touch him too much for fear of catching his germs – one of us had to stay healthy. But this was the Argentine tango which means you're in as close proximity as it's possible to get before the nine o'clock watershed.

And after all that, when we came to the performance, I completely forgot what I had to do, so we made it up as we went along. When the music ended and we walked towards the judges to hear their verdict I was close to tears. 'Sorry, sorry,' I whispered. And Pasha whispered back, 'Don't say anything,' so I didn't. It was the quarter-finals and I knew that I'd lost it for us. All that work, week after week, and I'd thrown it. And then we got these amazing marks. Everyone gave us 10 except Craig who gave us 9. I had forgotten that my microphone was still turned on, and afterwards everyone picked up on what they thought they'd heard, and said: 'What was all that about?' I just shrugged as if I had no idea what they were referring to. Nobody ever knew that we just made it all up. So we spent all week learning these complicated steps that we didn't even get to do.

But Pasha understood. He knew the reason. My private life was in shreds.

15

'Roxie (the Name on Everyone's Lips)'

When did Jack and me begin to go wrong? It happened so gradually that it's impossible to pinpoint.

We had such a lovely relationship. It was easy. We were easy. It was just us. Although I was in my early thirties I'd never had that closeness before. I could tell him anything. I felt comfortable telling him all my innermost thoughts. I hadn't had that since me and Jo used to tell each other secrets under the bed sheets before we fell asleep.

As it started to fall apart, so did I. His voice started changing. His smile changed. All the sparkle had gone. When the person you care about more than anything in the world stops caring about you the way they used to, it makes you doubt yourself. And I did just that, over and over again.

In the eighteen months since we'd been properly

together, Jack Street had become the most successful music manager in the world. And as he was going up, I became less important. At first I didn't mind. Why would I? That level of success in such a competitive world is amazing at any age but Jack wasn't even thirty. But it had got to the point where I wondered where I fitted in, if I fitted in at all.

In the age of Twitter and Facebook the world becomes very small and there's nothing people like more than a good gossip. I heard that Jack had been seen out with a singer in LA. And before you could say snap it was all over the papers. He was young, he was powerful, so – in hindsight – it was probably inevitable. Then one evening he called and told me he'd had an offer accepted on a house in London. I didn't get it – we'd been talking about buying a house together.

'What do you think this means, Pasha?' I asked him the next morning.

'It means he's leaving you.'

'No, it doesn't.'

'Yes, it does.'

'No, it doesn't.'

But it did.

It was a rerun of Dave. Jack came back from LA and said it was over. One way and another Los Angeles has played a big part in my love life. Even though I knew he was probably right I was angry at the timing. He had seen me come back from losing *Xtra Factor*. Now I was finally finding my feet – I felt that he could at least have waited three weeks . . .

And I wept. I'd be in the middle of a dance and I'd start crying. All Pasha could do was put his hand on my shoulder. He's the most unemotional person I have ever met in my life and he couldn't work me out. When we did our individual interviews before the final, they asked me what I thought I had got from Pasha and I blubbed, said all sorts of things which boiled down to: 'He looked after me.' When Pasha was interviewed he said, 'I came into this *Strictly* being my usual self, non-emotional, hardened to everything. Caroline is the first person in my life to make me emotional, and I feel emotional.'

That week – the semi-final – we had two dances to do, the salsa and the foxtrot and we got four 10s. And the first thing I thought was: Maybe Jack will see it . . .

For the final, you reprise two dances that you've done and then there's the show dance, which can be anything you like. I'd always had this idea that we'd do a Michael Jackson number – something really fast and upbeat. But Pasha said no. 'You're not in the mood to do Michael Jackson. You're emotional, you're sad, you're depressed, you're going through a really emotional time and you need to use your emotions.'

So then we sat down and went through a whole load of songs. Originally it was going to be Robbie Williams's 'She's the One'. But I said I wanted it to be a woman's song. And Pasha said, 'That's fine. We'll just use a woman singer.' So we searched for 'She's the One' with a woman singer on my iPad, but 'Angels' came on instead and Pasha said, 'This is the one. This is the song we should use.'

'But why?'

'Because this is you singing about saving yourself. You don't need anyone else to save you. You're singing. The angel is you, you're saving yourself.' And he was so right. And then we found a gospel version, and Pasha said he had a vision immediately for the choreography. I said, 'If it's going to be a slow dance, can I do it barefoot?' I just knew that's what I wanted to do. I wanted to do something in no heels.

He decided on a 'contemporary rumba kind of a dance'. He wanted me up in the air, being thrown about and doing another death drop where you fall to the floor and get caught at the last minute. I was so nervous because when we'd done a death drop before – in the American Smooth – I'd tripped on my dress, losing a crucial mark (from Craig) in the process.

The choreography he did for 'Angels' involved lift after lift after lift. It started with a lift and it ended with a lift. But in the end, compared with other things we'd done, it was easy, because it was like a contemporary dance, which is what I love. And it was so, so emotional . . . Most of the time I was dancing with tears in my eyes. When the music stopped, we didn't pose, we just hugged and hugged and hugged.

We'd started the final with the cha-cha-cha, the dance that had started the whole competition. The last was a reprise of the Charleston which I could have done in my sleep and it was just fun. I felt we could enjoy ourselves – somehow the pressure was now off. But even when we'd finished and we had a perfect score of three sets of four 10s, I still didn't think we would win. Because it's not the judges' votes that count, it's the public's, and I was convinced they would go for Frankie. She and her partner had done a whole Astaire/ Rogers routine for their show dance, which I'd seen at the dress rehearsal the day before and they were brilliant. Frankie and I were the only girls left now and that night the two of us had sat in her hotel room and talked about how we were going to start a *Strictly* rehab to try and get over it . . .

When I started to cry again Pasha said, 'It doesn't matter now, it doesn't matter, because you're going to win.'

I dried my tears and said, 'I'm crying because I'm happy.' And then we had to go out onto the dance floor and wait for the votes to come in. I could see my mum, Liz and Jo in the audience – three blonde heads standing out from everyone else. And then suddenly it was Tess saying, 'The votes have been counted and verified and I can now announce that the *Strictly Come Dancing* Champions, 2014, are . . . Caroline and Pasha,' and I sank to my knees and then Pasha lifted me up in the air for our final lift.

After it was all over, Pasha told me that he'd singled me out on that first day.

'I was only watching you.'

'You're just saying that, Pasha.'

'No, I wanted you!'

'No, I wanted you!'

'No, I wanted you!'

I was so lucky. I lucked out. I lucked out completely. Pasha was a brilliant teacher and he gave me such confidence. And so much of it was about confidence. Once you're in front of those cameras your memory just goes and nerves take over. But you learn. Every day I learnt something new.

I said it on camera in the interview I did before the final: 'I had started *Strictly* at a completely different part of my life, and now everything's changed.' And it had. Though perhaps not entirely. At the moment I heard our names and sank to the floor, I thought about Jack and wondered if he was watching.

I woke the next morning, to a feeling of emptiness. After the after-party I'd gone to see Josie because it was her birthday and had just caught the tail end. I'd been so tired I'd fallen asleep on her sofa. Then I'd come home and slept in my own bed, my own lonely bed. But now, waking up to a grey dismal dawn, I was faced with the truth. *Strictly* was over, Jack and I were over. It was Christmas. The year was over. I felt as if someone had put cling film over my bed and I was lying there covered in cling film.

I was just numb. It was just two days before Christmas and yet the thought of Christmas filled me with dread. I called Josie and cried on the phone. She came round and told me to get up, get dressed and go to Jo's.

'I can't. Because I just can't be around happy people.'

'Well, you can't stay here on your own, it's just ridiculous. I mean, Carrie, you've got nothing to be sad about. You've just won *Strictly*!'

On paper I should have been ecstatic, but I didn't feel that way. And so I phoned Jack. It was the first time I'd caved in. I began to cry as soon as he answered.

'Well done for *Strictly*,' he said.

'What are you doing?'

'I'm off to work. Well, have a nice Christmas.'

So getting on with your life then, are you? How come I'm

not getting on with my life? I didn't say it, but that's what I felt. I didn't call him again and I did go to Jo's for Christmas. And somehow she waved her wand and it was the nicest Christmas ever. Mum, Jo, Paul and of course Willow and Delilah and Zuzu, everyone crammed in together, a real proper family.

Once the girls had opened their presents on Christmas morning, I said, 'Right, coats on, scarves on. We're going for a walk in the park!' So while Jo was cooking Christmas dinner, that's what we did and Zuzu insisted on wearing her new rabbit slippers. It was exactly as I expected: everyone was happy, kids skipping, running, brand-new bikes wobbling along the paths, bobble hats everywhere, dads grinning, mums laughing. But instead of making me feel miserable, it was infectious. It was all: 'Merry Christmas!', 'Merry Christmas!' And people were coming up to me and saying: 'Congratulations on *Strictly*!' It was the first time I'd spoken to anyone since the night it had all happened and I thought, Oh this is fun. 'Happy Christmas!'

It was the most perfect winter's day, freezing cold but sunny with a blue, blue sky. And I felt like smiling at everyone, just as James Stewart does in *It's a Wonderful Life* in Colour when he realises that he's got another chance.

That evening, when the girls had gone to bed, we played stupid party games, like charades and one of Jason's sisters had brought a funny game that involved song lyrics which you then had to sing. Mum, naturally, was the star turn.

My brother Paul is one of those people that you can't be sad around. He just wants to have a good time all the time. He's very funny, and does nothing but laugh. So what I'd dreaded most turned out to be the most fun. You'd think I would have learnt after all these years, from the lion ornament coming to life onwards: the fear of something happening is always worse than the reality.

Of course *Strictly* wasn't strictly over. We still had the tour to do, but I already knew that I wouldn't be dancing with Pasha. I'd signed up for it not long after the show started, simply because I was loving it so much and I hadn't realised quite how different it would be without him, and it wasn't the same, and doing the same show night after night was soon really boring. Judy wasn't there, neither was Pixie nor Frankie so I had none of my mates to talk to. But the audiences were wonderful – kids, grandads and grandmas – and you have to do your best for them. Even so I was so glad when it was finished. And then I went to LA to see Josie. She lived in Brentwood just west of Beverly Hills and the first morning after I arrived we went for a hike in the Canyons. We didn't drink or party, we were just catching up and it couldn't have been more perfect.

But then I had to come back: I had a meeting with Simon Cowell.

All the way through *Strictly*, Simon would regularly get in touch to say, 'Well done, I think this is a really good thing for you.' And when I won, he sent me a *Congrats, Simon*. Then during the tour he sent me a message saying *Would you like to meet up?*

Hmmm.

I had no expectations. I just thought, I'll see what he's

got to say for himself. He has fingers in so many pies that a bit of me thought there might be a job offer in the wings.

This time I made no mistake about the address. It was a large house in Holland Park, less than five minutes' walk from the first bachelor pad where Jo lived with Jason and where I'd slept in his garage surrounded by bin bags containing my whole life. Simon's London house was obviously different to the LA house, but equally as tidy with lots of Diptyque candles everywhere. We had a couple of glasses of wine and chatted lots about *Strictly* – everyone, even Simon Cowell, is fascinated by *Strictly* – and about *X Factor* and how that had gone. He talked about Eric, his little boy, and about his dogs Squiddly and Diddly. Simon is so easy to talk to and that's what's so disarming about him. He's very charming and makes you feel the centre of attention.

'Well,' he said as he showed me to the front door. 'It would be nice to catch up soon and hopefully we can do something together.' And that was more or less it. All quite ambiguous. As I left I thought, Well, there you go. That's Simon for you. Even so I felt quite strong, thinking: You got rid of me but now you've asked me back in, so it's a bit more on my terms.

I'd got a naughty pleasure in telling him just how good *Strictly* was. I didn't actually say, 'What a lucky break and how lucky that you sacked me!' but it was sort of implied – I just said, 'It all happens for a reason, Si.' And he was fine. He's got a good sense of humour about most things.

*

About a month later, Dermot stepped down from the job. And within two hours I had a phone call from John Noel saying, 'Simon wants you to present the show with Olly.'

The first thing I did was to call Olly. And then I called Dermot, because I wanted to know the real story. I didn't want any weirdness between us. But we kept missing each other. It was like phone tennis: he'd phone, I'd phone, he wouldn't pick up. I always left the same message: 'Dermot, call me!' Then finally he called back and sang one of my *Strictly* songs – 'Istanbul', the song we did the Charleston to.

A few weeks earlier Dermot had done a twenty-four-hour dance marathon for Comic Relief, and I taught him our routine – Pasha's part – and then I went along and we did it together. So as soon as I'd heard that, I knew he was fine about everything. But it was about two days before we actually got to speak.

As John Noel is Dermot's agent as well as mine, Dermot knew I'd been offered the job.

'You've got to take it, Flacky,' he said. 'Don't think twice.'

Dermot O'Leary is such a nice man. He's the one person in the industry who no one has a bad word for. You meet taxi drivers and they say, 'I had that Dermot O'Leary in my cab the other day. Great man.' And they're right.

I was in awe of Dermot long before I met him and, once we started working together, he has been my mentor. I watched him, I watched the way he worked, I watched how he did things and saw how he still got nervous, and I'd think, Well, if he still gets nervous, it's all right to be nervous.

Dermot had said, 'Don't think twice,' but I did. Of course hosting *X Factor* was something I wanted to do. But was it the right thing? Wasn't it a step backwards? Of course not, the other voice said. It's the main show. But I've already said goodbye to *X Factor*. Isn't there a saying, 'Never step in the same river twice?' Yes, but it's not just you, is it? It's you and Olly . . .

I talked to Jo, I talked to my mum. And I talked to Jack. I don't have a business brain, Jo doesn't have a business brain, Mum doesn't have a business brain but Jack does. I think with my heart, he thinks with his head.

'Why do you wanna go back to that sinking ship?'

'It's still the biggest job in telly, Jack. When am I ever going to get offered a job like that again?'

But then I remembered he'd been just as negative about *Strictly*. But my heart had won that time and I'd been right.

In the end it was Olly that swayed it. Dermot was the best, and a hard act to follow. But it wouldn't just be me stepping into Dermot's shoes. It would be me and Olly.

I said Yes.

At the final of *Strictly*, after the show dance, after I'd wiped the tears from my eyes, we walked over to hear the judges comments and Bruno had said, 'I can see you in the West

End.' And Darcey Bussell said, 'I'd have you in my company any day.'

When I was at Bodywork, musical theatre was always the dream, and even before – that's why I'd gone there in the first place. And when we were rehearsing, Pasha was always saying, 'You could be in a musical' . . . 'You should do musicals' . . . 'You should definitely be in a musical.'

But musical theatre isn't just about dancing.

Shortly after New Year, when I was on tour with *Strictly*, John Noel was contacted by a big casting director called David Grindrod, who works closely with Andrew Lloyd Webber.

'We'd like to put Caroline in the West End,' he said. 'We know she can dance, but can she sing?' So once I got back from the tour, John and I had a where-do-we-go-from-here strategy meeting. Because *Strictly* is so high profile, I was now in the most extraordinary position, he said, and wanted me to go into the West End.

'This has opened you up to a whole new career, something that could last even longer than you thought before. It's time to use it, it's time to show what you really can do.'

He was obviously right in that the whole ditzy-girl-presenter thing couldn't go on for ever. A few more years, and then what? But a career in musical theatre . . . As long as you're fit, you could go on doing that for a very long time.

They wanted to see me for Roxie in *Chicago*, David Grindrod had said. I had loved *Chicago* ever since I saw it on a group trip from college, and it's one of the most successful musicals of all time. The character of Roxie Hart is based on the real-life story of a woman who stood trial for murder in 1924.

So John found me a vocal coach and I recorded 'Roxie (the Name on Everyone's Lips)' about how she wanted to be famous. I watched Renée Zellweger in the film so I could try to get the accent and ended up really liking her because she's just a girl who ends up killing her lover because he's a dick. So, taking a page out of Pasha's book I thought, Well I can use my current situation for this.

The audition was nerve-racking. I knew I had to walk in there oozing confidence but I was just so nervous. The last time I had sung was for the Spanish champagne commercial and even then it was dubbed ... Thank goodness they'd given me half an hour with the pianist beforehand. We went through it once and he said, 'You're not doing it right. You've got to take it down. The monologue before the song represents your inner thoughts. You're not trying to sing to everybody.' And so I tried it again, and he looked pleased. 'Much better,' he said. 'It's completely different now.'

There were three of them: the director, the producer and someone else.

After I'd sung it, the producer said, 'Can you go back and do that note?'

'What note?'

'The big note.'

'This one?' I said, and hit it.

'OK. That's no problem. So now can you do the monologue as if you're telling an audience and not just me?'

So I did it again, the way he'd asked.

A week later they called and said I'd got the part. Now it was just a question of when . . .

16

Boot camp

July 2015

'Three, two, one, ACTION!'

> Olly: Welcome to the *X Factor*. We have searched the
> nation to find the best talent there is.
> Me: And with the arena auditions complete it's time
> for our acts to face their next challenge.

Scene: an overcast morning in late July. We're standing by
a pond outside the Grove Hotel ('London's country
estate') in Hertfordshire and I'm freezing. It's boot-camp
time on the juggernaut otherwise known as the *X Factor*.
Somewhere out there a fleet of coaches are taking the
scenic route, going mile after mile around the M25 as
camera crews shoot 'reality' footage of this year's

hopefuls, while Olly and me and the production team enjoy the actual reality of an English summer – runny eyes, runny noses and goosebumps.

Hard to believe it was only three weeks since I was in Mallorca with *Love Island*. There we had twelve young people looking for love and lust. Here we have two hundred young people looking for fame and fortune. By the end of the week they'll be whittled down by a third, perhaps more.

To think I got bored of non-stop sunshine and couldn't wait to feel cool again . . . But the news on *Love Island* is good. The final episode had bigger viewing figures online than *Coronation Street*. Audiences took time to build, and while it may not have been every mum and dad's cup of bedtime cocoa, it pulled in younger viewers and it looks likely that there'll be a second series. Apparently the moment the 'islanders' left the villa they couldn't keep their hands off each other, even the ones that didn't see any action in the house, even the ones who said they didn't really like each other; every one of them was desperate to get out to get it on.

But Mallorca seems like another life away. Now here I am back in the land of *X Factor* with guys in khaki cargo pants, pockets bulging with everything from lip balm to headsets; girls with clipboards or canvas pouches sprouting powder puffs and mascara; an army of young TV professionals wearing black X-marked T-shirts.

It's weird, Olly says, finding himself at boot camp again. We didn't really cover it on *Xtra Factor* or if we did we weren't in the thick of it as we are now.

'You know, Caz, it really takes me back being here. All the tension and stress, and the noise. I remember how tired I was. All the time, just exhausted.' And he obviously remembers the food. This time he's ordered his own in. I'm happy just to have burgers.

Last night was mayhem – somewhere between first-day at school and Stansted on a bank holiday. I felt sorry for people staying here as ordinary guests. There wasn't a room where there wasn't somebody singing. Every corridor was filled with groups – there are so many this year – huddles of kids everywhere you looked, arguing about their song choices – there's a playlist of twenty – trying out their harmonies, wandering the garden with ghetto blasters that they get issued with, queuing for the choreography room, queuing for the vocal room, queuing to register, queuing for something to eat. Some have arrived in 'character', with hair that looks like it might need its own passport, while some look like they might just be nipping down to Tesco's. In what used to be the kitchen garden when the Grove Hotel was a grand private mansion, there's a huge canvas-topped stage where they'll soon be giving it their all. If only the rain would stop . . .

We've already had ten days of arena auditions and seen forty singers each day. The judges made their decisions immediately. Three yeses out of four and you were in. And not one of them believes they won't get through. Not one of them believes they won't be at the live shows, with their families and supporters waiting in the wings.

Here I am at my fourth *X Factor* and I have to say I think

it's going to be the best yet. The talent is stronger than ever, which means it's going to be tough to get through. I'm already looking forward to seeing everybody on stage because I know just how good they are. Dermot used to say that too many acts went through to boot camp because the judges got swept along by the response of the audience, and this year more have come through than they'd counted on. But what do you do when the talent is there?

This is definitely the year of the vocals. There have been years when the voice hasn't been the deciding factor, when it was a bit 'You look like a pop star, perhaps we can just mould you into one.' But 2015 won't be about looking the part. Those days are over – just think Ed Sheeran and Sam Smith. This year it's about finding the most talented singers the UK has to offer.

Back in my bedroom at the Grove, bags and boxes everywhere. Gemma is busy putting things away so I lie on the bed out of the way, clasping my knees, trying to keep warm, waiting for the kids to come back from their road trip, while vaguely watching TV where former *X Factor* contestant Rylan Clark is cooking on *This Morning*.

'Good news about *Strictly*,' Gemma says. 'When's the rehearsal?'

'Two weeks on Wednesday,' I say. 'So put it in your diary.'

It's not only good news it's great news. I've been released to do the valedictory dance with Pasha and I can't wait. More good news is that the business about the woman who claimed I was having 'casual sex' with her husband has disappeared into nowhere land. But it's harder than you think to prove you didn't do something. Luckily I was in LA when she said I was in Reading at a fetish club . . .

Knock knock.

'Hi, Caroline, got some pages for you. Links we need to do once the rain stops.'

Enter my producer Aloysius, known as Sam to his friends and Delicious to those he's even closer to. 'Not sure about the velvet curtains in the corridor,' he says. 'A bit *Fifty Shades of Grey* and have you seen Olly's room and all those ostrich feathers on top of his bed!'

Hahaha!

And now here's Phoebe, *X Factor* researcher. They're all spinning.

'I thought I'd come up and talk it through with you guys and fill you in with everything that's going on. We were trying to get the numbers down to a reasonable amount, but we like them, we really like them. It's a good place to be. What we love, and what we cannot get enough of is all the edge of the action. We want it to be led by you guys. We're looking for more ad-libbing. We need to be totally on it. Drama and fun, and a touch of pandemonium. And you guys are the tool for everything.'

It's the first time I've been on *X Factor* when Simon has been a judge and he's utterly terrifying. There's a different dynamic. It's a bit like having your head teacher there or your dad – you're just a bit more wary of what you say.

Everyone is, whether they realise it or not. But it's getting easier. For me it's just a question of working out his humour. A lot of the time you think he's being serious but he's not. He's not the caricature Simon Cowell we think we know. With Simon everything's a joke.

On Sunday I got held up coming in and he said, 'Morning, Caroline. Were you on time today?'

Convinced he was having a go, I went over and said, 'Sorry I was late.'

'I invented the word late. You don't need to apologise.'

I still have to get the measure of him, not get offended and learn to punch back.

And, as Gemma always says, 'Just don't take it personally.'

The good news is that he's a really big Olly fan, so getting him to open up isn't difficult. If he wants to extend the interview he'll just say, 'Let's go over here and talk more.' Talk more? Simon? What's happened?

What's happened is that they've changed the role of host. It's not like it was with Dermot. Olly and I are in it all the time. It's like they've taken the show we used to do – *Xtra Factor* – and put it on the main show. So we're busy, busy, busy. And what a relief that we're not doing Judges' Houses. The press were full of how gutted we were when the news got out. Gutted? If only they knew . . . It was jet-lag central.

There's a whole different feeling within the production this year. I feel it. Olly feels it. Before we never really felt part of the gang. I always felt that the show needed to become warmer, and now it has, and I think that's what I've brought from working on *Strictly* and realising how warm that was and what a difference it made.

But the best thing is that Olly and I are reunited.

Knock, knock.

Who's there?

Room service.

Room service who?

I chortle, but nobody else laughs.

It's tea and cakes.

'Enjoy,' the girl says.

I fully intend to.

My new life starts here.

Acknowledgements

I would like to thank Iain MacGregor at Simon & Schuster for sticking with my vision for this book. Thanks are also due to Jo Whitford and Martin Bryant for their sensitivity. Also everyone at Liz Matthews as well as Dan Medhurst for his lovely portrait.

This book wouldn't have happened without my tame (ish) Rottweiler John Noel and his team, especially Jadeen Singh who kept me at it. John Noel has looked after me since I first had the mad idea of going into television and I owe him more than I can ever repay. Particular thanks to Polly Hill: over the years you became my friend as well as my agent and I miss you. Alex Mullen, Andrew Antonio and Andrew Sharland who in their different ways have done their best to keep me out of mischief.

No words can express what I owe to my wonderful Mum and Dad, Christine and Ian Flack, whose love of music and musicals kick-started my career. Most of all I want to thank them for their unwavering love and their support and fortitude over these last few difficult years. I have also plundered their memories which include the fascinating story of how fate brought them together, as well as the ups and downs of my grandparents' arduous but enthralling lives.

My co-Flacks have had to put up a lot from me over the years whereas I've had nothing but laughs and pleasure from you and my wonderful nieces and nephews. Liz and Paul, thank you for being there. You have been the best role models a sister could wish for.

As for Jody, my twin, she's my good angel, giving me everything from unconditional love to a roof over my head, from beans on toast at two in the morning, to a shoulder to cry on and an endless supply of tissues, not to mention being cameraman, producer and editor of my first show reel. Over the last few months her memories of our childhood have been invaluable in triggering my own and for a brief while we became once again George and Alfred.

For all its shortness in terms of years, my life has been long in friendships for which I count myself extremely lucky. Things would have been much less interesting and much more difficult without them, especially when the going got tough. So thanks to my friends old and new without whom life would have no flavour: Josie, Anna and Angus, Katie, Olly, Dawn and Chris, Gemma, Lou, Sam, The Gug, Sam and Mark, Matt, Leigh and Jill, Hannah Denty, Jess, Liz, Charlotte, Hannah, Bryony, Beccie, Jade, Lliana, Danny, Jason, Camilla, Natalie, D-Day, Tom

ACKNOWLEDGEMENTS

McKay, Dave, Ophelia, Pabs, Tracey, Jack O, Nicola, SJ, Pete, Dee and Dermot, Olivia, Sarah Tyekiff, Jane, Gem Gems, Melanie, Nikki, Debbie, Diggy, Tim, Olivia, Andy and anybody I stupidly may have forgotten right this second . . .

And a big thank you to those people who continued to have faith in me, even when I'd lost it myself: Patrick and Theresa Kerr and Chris Bond, not forgetting the most amazing teacher of all, Pasha Kovalev.

Finally I would like to thank Pepsy Dening for making sense of my helter-skelter life.

In life sometimes it feels as if your worst bits all help you find your best bits. So even if it hurt at the time, it got me to the place I'm in now, so in a weird kind of way I'd also like to thank Jack.